God's Final \

God's Final Victory
A Comparative Philosophical Case for Universalism

by
John Kronen and Eric Reitan

B L O O M S B U R Y
NEW YORK • LONDON • NEW DELHI • SYDNEY

Bloomsbury Academic
An imprint of Bloomsbury Publishing Plc

175 Fifth Avenue   50 Bedford Square
New York   London
NY 10010   WC1B 3DP
USA   UK

www.bloomsbury.com

First published by Continuum International Publishing Group 2011
Paperback edition first published 2013

Library of Congress Cataloging-in-Publication Data
Kronen, John, 1961–
God's Final Victory: A Comparative Philosophical Case
for Universalism/by John Kronen and Eric Reitan.
p. cm.
Includes bibliographical references and index.
ISBN-13: 978-1-4411-3065-5 (hardback: alk. paper)
ISBN-10: 1-4411-3065-9 (hardback: alk. paper) 1. Universalism.
2. Salvation–Christianity. 3. Hell–Christianity. I. Reitan, Eric. II. Title.
BX9946.K76 2011
234–dc23 2011022486

ISBN: HB: 978-1-4411-3065-5
PB: 978-1-6235-6849-8

Typeset by Amnet International, Dublin, Ireland

To our parents:
Anne, Esther and Palmer Kronen; and Reidun and Paul Reitan,
who first taught us about God's love by their love for us.

'If I were to paint God I would so portray him that in the very depths of his divine nature there would be nothing else than a fire and passion which is called love for people. Correspondingly, love is precisely that thing which is neither human nor angelic but divine, yea, God himself.'
–Martin Luther

CONTENTS

Acknowledgements

The ideas and arguments for this book have been evolving for many years, and have benefited from the suggestions and criticisms of countless people. Special thanks go to Thomas Talbott, Robin Parry, Thomas Sullivan and Sandra Menssen; to our colleagues at the University of St. Thomas, St. Paul and Oklahoma State University; and to our partners, David Bonk and Tanya Reitan, for their love and support.

Chapter 2 is reprinted, with revisions, by permission of the Publishers from 'Species of Hell', in *The Problem of Hell*, ed. Joel Buenting (Farnham etc.: Ashgate, 2010), pp. 199–218. Copyright © 2010.

Section III of Chapter 5 and portions of Section X of Chapter 7 are revisions of material that originally appeared in 'Eternal damnation and blessed ignorance: Is the damnation of some incompatible with the salvation of any?', by Eric Reitan, *Religious Studies*, vol. 38, no. 4 (December 2002), pp. 429–450.

Copyright © 2002 Cambridge University Press. Reprinted with permission.

Sections VIII–X of Chapter 6 are revisions of material that originally appeared in 'Talbott's universalism, divine justice, and the Atonement', by John Kronen and Eric Reitan, *Religious Studies*, vol. 40, no. 3 (September 2004), pp. 249–268.

Copyright © 2004 Cambridge University Press. Reprinted with permission.

Sections VI–VIII of Chapter 7 are revisions of material that originally appeared in 'Human Freedom and the Impossibility of Eternal Damnation', in *Universal Salvation? The Current Debate*, eds. Robin Parry and Chris Partridge (Carlisle, Cumbria: Paternoster, 2003), pp. 125–142. Reprinted with permission of the publisher. Copyright © 2003.

Sections I–IV of Chapter 8 are revisions of material that originally appeared in 'A guarantee of universal salvation?' by Eric Reitan, *Faith and Philosophy*, vol. 24, no. 4 (December 2007), pp. 413–432. Reprinted with permission of the publisher. Copyright © 2007.

Section VI of Chapter 8 is a revision of material that originally appeared in 'Universalism and autonomy: Towards a comparative defence of universalism', by Eric Reitan, *Faith and Philosophy*, vol. 18, no. 3 (April 2001), pp. 222–240. Reprinted with permission of the publisher. Copyright © 2001.

Chapter 1

Introduction

1.1 Towards a Comparative Defence of Christian Universalism

Many theists believe that some sins call not only for divine displeasure or judgment, but for *retribution* – that is, punishment imposed by God as a just and proportionate penalty for sin. This belief coexists alongside the observation that, in this life, well-being does not always accord with virtue. Some of the worst sinners lead lives that, if not exactly happy, are characterized by wealth, comfort, physical health and access to a range of pleasures – a fact which has led many to embrace the view that God visits post-mortem sufferings on the wicked in proportion to their guilt.

At its most extreme – an extreme historically embraced by most Christians – this notion has been developed into the doctrine that the wicked suffer *eternal* torment. To many theists this doctrine is not merely consonant with their tradition's Scriptures, but is intuitively appealing. Consider, for example, Peter Berger's words:

> Deeds that cry out to heaven also cry out for hell. This is the point that was brought out very clearly in the debate over Eichmann's execution. Without going into the question of either the legality or the wisdom of the execution, it is safe to say that there was a very general feeling that 'hanging is not enough' in this case. But what would have been 'enough'? If Eichmann, instead of being hanged, had been tortured to death in the most lengthy and cruel manner imaginable, would this have been 'enough'? A negative answer seems inevitable. No human punishment is 'enough' in the case of deeds as monstrous as these. These are deeds that demand not only condemnation, but *damnation* in the full religious meaning of the word – that is, the doer not only puts himself outside the community of men; he also separates himself in a final way from a moral order that transcends the human community, and thus invokes a retribution that is more than human.[1]

Our aim in this book is to critique not only the intuitions underlying Berger's views, but any soteriology which holds that some rational creatures will be forever separated from God. Our aim, in other words, is to systematically challenge the doctrine of eternal hell (hereafter DH) in any form. At the same time we defend DH's chief rival, the doctrine of universal salvation (hereafter DU), which holds that ultimately all rational creatures will enjoy eternal blessedness in communion with God. More precisely, our aim is to show that, granted certain core Christian principles, *no* form of DH is as plausible as *some* form of DU. We call this a 'comparative' defence of DU.

Of course, there are alternatives to DH and DU – most notably annihilation-ism (DA), according to which the unregenerate will eventually cease to exist, and what we will call the doctrine of soteriological agnosticism (DSA), accord-ing to which, *for all we know* based on Scripture and reason, DH, DU, or perhaps even DA, might be true.[2] But we think our argument for favouring DU over DH offers a template for a similar case favouring DU over DA and DSA – a point which should become clear once the former case is made. As such, we explicitly address DA and DSA only in the concluding chapter.

In making our comparative case, we seek to rely on doctrines that are histori-cally endorsed by most Christian theologians precisely because these doctrines emerged through the vital engagement of the Church with the gospel message as revealed in the Scriptures. As such, our argument aims to be conservative in its foundations (if not in its conclusions) and dialectical in its approach.

When we say our argument is conservative, we mean 'conservative' in a sense that should not be conflated with 'fundamentalist'. In our usage, 'conservative' does not imply unswerving allegiance to a particular conception of orthodoxy regardless of the strength of opposing arguments, but rather a commitment – insofar as it is reasonable in the light of relevant arguments and evidence – to conserve doctrines that mainstream Christian tradition has long held to be cen-trally important (e.g. the doctrine of the Trinity, the Incarnation, the Atone-ment, etc.). In this sense of 'conservative Christian', not only are C. P. Krauth and C. Hodge conservative, so too are I. A. Dorner and even F. D. Schleier-macher – while such thinkers as Hegel and Emerson are not.[3]

When we say our argument is dialectical, we intend this in the Aristotelian sense. That is, our argument aims to convince its target audience by adopting many of their own starting points. In other words, our critique of DH is not external to the tradition within which DH has been historically embraced, but is internal to it, relying on premises acceptable to most conservative Christians. This does not mean that we accept *all* the premises invoked by what might be called 'extreme' conservatives in support of DH (for example, we reject certain views about the nature of the Bible sometimes presupposed by 'hellists' – that is, supporters of DH). However, when we do reject such starting points and the arguments they motivate, our critique will, again, be internal, based on proposi-tions that most conservative Christians, moderate or extreme, would accept.

Because we use traditional Christian starting points, some may think this is more properly a work of theology than philosophy. Clearly, it *is* theological. Nevertheless, we regard our project as ultimately philosophical because, in evalu-ating DH and DU in the light of central Christian teachings, our primary objective is to show that a Christian belief system that includes DU is more rationally coher-ent than one that includes DH – and the task of examining the rational coherence of alternative worldviews strikes us as being the essence of philosophy.

Perhaps our book is best classified as a work of Christian philosophical theol-ogy. However, it is not therefore irrelevant to non-Christian theists since we intend also to show that, even apart from distinctively Christian arguments, a powerful comparative case for DU can be made on the basis of premises that are widely shared among theistic faith traditions.

This last fact might cause concern to some Christians – perhaps sharing C. F. W. Walther's view that one cannot be a universalist without denying the necessity, if not the fact, of Christ's Atonement.[4] However, such worry is unwarranted. One may be convinced that a good God wants to save all, is capable of doing so, and hence *will* do so, without so much as considering the specific steps that God might take, or need to take, in order to do so – and hence without considering whether the means He used (or had to use) are those that Christians affirm. As such, an argument for universalism that makes no reference to the Incarnation or Atonement does not thereby rule out the belief that universal salvation is achieved (indeed, can *only* be achieved) through the Incarnation of Christ and His atoning work.

Of course, not everyone embraces Christ in this life, even in the implicit sense of placing their trust in an "anonymous" Christ. Hence, universalists cannot hold (as many conservative Christians do) that sinners need to perform the subjective act of placing their trust in Christ before death in order to be saved. However, this does not mean that universalists have to deny the role of Christ's Atonement in salvation.

There are two reasons for this. First, universalists might hold that we are saved by what God does for us through the Atonement, regardless of what we subjectively do in response. Secondly, universalists can treat subjective faith in Christ as necessary for salvation so long as they hold that there is no time limit for attaining faith, such that it could emerge for the first time *after death*. This possibility is central to some key arguments developed in this book.

Admittedly, the idea that one can be converted after death is contrary to what was taught by most Christians until around the eighteenth century.[5] However, the discovery of the New World and the vast empires of India and China produced a gradual shift in the Church's thinking. Beginning, arguably, with certain seventeenth century Jesuits, Christian intellectuals began to hold that those who had no way of knowing Christ during their lives could be saved as long as they did not reject the 'common' grace that God gives to all fallen humans.[6] Many contemporary Christian thinkers who embrace DH also hold that all will be given an adequate revelation of Christ, at least *at* death, if not before it.[7]

Walther's worry, however, that universalists must deny the necessity of Christ's saving work is related to another concern, expressed by Jerry Walls. Walls worries, in effect, that if the doctrine of hell is set aside, then Christianity is trivialized. He claims that supposing hell to be 'the alternative to salvation' lends 'a sense of urgency and moral seriousness to the quest for salvation' and also highlights 'the majesty and glory of God's work to save his fallen children.'[8]

It is, however, entirely compatible with DU to hold that, apart from God's saving work, our fate would be horrific. That is, universalists can agree with

Walls that the alternative to salvation is hell – that eternal anguish is what we *would* endure but for God's saving work – even if they think no one actually endures this alternative. Furthermore, many universalists hold that there are those who *do* endure this alternative, although not eternally: while all are ultimately saved, some of the most recalcitrant sinners actively resist God's saving grace for an extended time, enduring a finite 'hell' – that is, an immediate experience of what it means to exist in the 'outer darkness' apart from God – the experience of which ultimately breaks down their recalcitrance.[9]

In this view of things, none of the 'urgency and moral seriousness' attached to the quest for salvation must be set aside, let alone any sense of 'the majesty and glory' of God's saving work. A rescue boat that comes to the scene of a shipwreck is no less praiseworthy because it succeeds in saving *all* the passengers rather than only some. It is what they are saved *from* that determines the relative importance or triviality of the saving work. [10]

1.2 Overview of Argument and Methods

With these preliminary points in mind, we proceed to a general outline of our argument for DU, in terms of structure and method. In barest outlines, our argument proceeds as follows: in Chapters 2 and 3 we offer an overview of species of both DH and DU, thereby setting the stage for our comparative defence of DU. Then, in Chapter 4, we give reasons to reject the common assumption that the witness of Scripture univocally favours DH over DU. In Chapter 5 we begin our project in earnest by offering a prima facie case for favouring DU over DH, given a Christian understanding of divine love. We then identify two broad strategies that might be employed to overcome this prima facie case – the first appealing to retributive justice, the second appealing to the importance of respecting the autonomy of the damned. In Chapter 6 we turn to the first of these strategies, looking at the set of broadly retributive versions of DH. Despite being the dominant versions of DH in the history of Christian theology, we argue that, given core Christian doctrines, these versions are simply untenable; and that efforts to rehabilitate them in light of the challenges will fail.

We then turn our attention to what we take to be the strongest versions of DH: those that invoke respect for autonomy as God's motive for permitting some to suffer eternal separation from God. Defenders of these versions typically argue that, whatever the difficulties with DH, DU suffers graver difficulties because there can be no guarantee of universal salvation without compromising creaturely autonomy – something that a morally perfect God would never do.

In responding to this challenge, we confront a deep division among Christian theologians relating to whether God can legitimately confer upon creatures what the tradition had dubbed 'efficacious grace' – grace that is sufficient *by itself* to save sinners, because it transforms their characters so that they fully repent of all past sins and embrace God without reservation. Although we tend to favour the view that God *can* legitimately confer such grace, we do not want to rest our argument for DU on the assumption that this is true, largely because so many contemporary defenders of DH base their case on premises that appear to be at odds with it.

Hence, we offer instead a disjunctive argument: if we assume that God *can* legitimately extend efficacious grace, there is a version of DU that is clearly preferable to any version of DH – namely, the version which holds that God is able to ensure the salvation of any rational creature by supplying efficacious grace whenever necessary (whenever creatures ultimately fail to come to God of their own accord). This is the argument we develop in Chapter 7. If, on the other hand, we assume that God *cannot* legitimately extend efficacious grace, a different version of DU is then preferable to any version of DH – namely, the version that holds that God saves all by indefinitely sustaining the unregenerate in conditions suited to inspiring free repentance (a crucial part of our argument will be to show that doing this *does* provide a guarantee of universal salvation – contrary to what many suppose). Chapter 8 is devoted to making this case.

Thus, while we are not left with a single version of DU that stands out as the most defensible doctrine for Christians, we are left with the conclusion that Christians should favour some version of DU over any version of DH. In Chapter 9, we draw these final threads of argument together and relate them to a few remaining concerns – such as whether the doctrine of annihilation (DA) or the doctrine of soteriological agnosticism (DSA) offers a stronger alternative to DU than does DH (we argue that they do not), and whether there are convincing pragmatic arguments for maintaining some version of DH or, at the very least, DSA (we argue, on the contrary, that pragmatic concerns actually dictate in favour of DU).

This brief overview of our project gives rise to two issues that we think should be addressed in this introductory chapter. First, why do we attempt to answer the question in a manner that is essentially philosophical rather than primarily scriptural (that is, primarily through biblical exegesis and interpretation)? Second, why is a *comparative* defence of DU in the light of central doctrines required, rather than, for instance, a direct deduction of DU from those doctrines?

The first concern would presumably be premised on the observation that when we confront the fate of human beings after death, we are dealing with a matter for which human reason simply lacks the resources to reach any conclusions; it would be better, therefore, to rely on the Word of God as revealed in Scripture.

There are really two claims here: that human reason is *not* up to the task, and that Scripture *is*. The latter is an issue we will take up with some care in Chapter 4. For now, it is enough to note that we do not find the scriptural case for DH decisive, in part because the texts offered in support of DH are ambiguous, and in part because the 'hell texts' are counterbalanced with 'universalism texts' whose plain sense supports DU. In fact, we make use of the doctrinal debate concerning hell to expose the inadequacy of naïve inerrantist approaches to Scripture. Put simply, we cannot reliably settle doctrinal disputes by sifting through the Bible to find the answer in some passage or other. The Bible is not a book of doctrinal theology, and efforts to turn it into one are routinely stymied by the ambiguity, complexity and seeming contradictions in the text.[11]

What we wish to treat more fully at this point is the claim that human reason is ill-equipped to adequately address the issue of the fate of humans after death, and that we should therefore rely instead on divine revelation. Certainly, human reason *divorced* from any theological tradition, or any view of divine revelation, *is* ill-equipped to address this issue; but we do not intend to use unaided reason in this way. On the contrary, our intent is to reason from the starting points that are central to Christianity.

Furthermore, there is something naïve about claiming we should rely on revelation instead of reason. This claim assumes we can identify divine revelations without reason's help – a dangerous assumption that opens us to a credulity ripe with the potential for exploitation.[12] Careful discernment with the aid of our rational faculties strikes us as our only guard against the errors and heresies peddled by false prophets. It may well be true that reason, at least narrowly conceived, can only derive truth from other truths already given and, hence, cannot give us knowledge apart from the content provided by sources outside of reason, such as our senses. However, this does not mean that reason is unequipped to reflect on these sources on which it depends. Without reason, we would never know when our senses are deceiving us – for it is reason that discerns when a given sense experience, however vivid, is incompatible with a broader set of experiences and stable judgments.

Likewise, it is reason which tells us when a certain reading of Scripture, however plain it may seem, is incompatible with broad scriptural themes and stable doctrines derived from centuries of critical engagement with Scripture.[13] This is precisely what we want to say about those who have derived DH from their reading of Scripture: even though certain scriptural texts seem to teach it, DH is at odds with broad scriptural themes as well as broadly-affirmed doctrines that have emerged from hundreds of years of scripturally informed reflection and debate within Christian communities. To say this is not to place our finite intellects *against* Scripture, but rather to use reason as a tool to help decide which doctrine – DH or DU – best fits with Scripture's holistic message.[14]

If Scripture is indeed revelatory – if studying it can offer insight into the divine nature and will – then the content of Scripture itself rules out the naïve idea that these revelations are to be identified with the literal sense of each isolated proposition found in the text. Instead, the analogy to sense perception is apt. While sense perception, when taken as a whole, enables us to gain an understanding of the world around us, individual observations can be, and often are, deceptive. Sometimes some very consistent surface impressions (such as the apparent solidity of tabletops and rocks) must be qualified by the lessons learned from a rational study of the implications of our most systematic and detailed observations (leading, for example, to the conclusion that apparently solid objects are actually mostly empty space, within which miniscule particles are suspended by a range of dynamic forces). Likewise, systematic rational study of the Scriptures taken holistically can reveal implications that force us to qualify or radically revise our understanding of isolated passages and even of pervasive surface impressions.

Putting our reason to use for such purposes is no guarantee against error; but only a fool would suppose that one is less likely to err *without* reason's guidance than with it. As do Aquinas and Leibniz, we assume that revealed truths cannot contradict truths known by unaided reason. From this perspective, the claim that some doctrine is rationally incoherent *implies* that it is not revelatory. And while a product of careful reasoning is always a tentative product that is susceptible to revision, we do not do the cause of truth a service by dismissing the fruits of reason without argument simply because they conflict with some preexistent view concerning the substance of revelation.

The second chief concern about our approach turns on its comparative character. Why is a *comparative* philosophical approach necessary? Sometimes disputes between rival perspectives can be resolved simply by focusing critical philosophical attention on *one* of the rivals: either by deducing the preferred perspective from appropriate starting points or by decisively refuting the other perspective and embracing the preferred perspective by way of a disjunctive syllogism. Suppose it could be shown that DU follows logically from central Christian teachings. If that is true, and if DU is incompatible with DH, then could we not show that DU is the fitting doctrine without ever having to subject DH to any sustained attention? Or suppose it could be shown that DH violates central Christian teachings, then – assuming that DU is the only viable alternative – we could conclude that it is the correct Christian doctrine without having to perform a sustained comparison. Why think such a 'one-sided' examination is insufficient?

We think there are two problems with it. The first rests with the fact that some contemporary defenders of DH – most notably William Lane Craig – have devoted considerable attention to the task of showing not that DH is true or even plausible given the broader context of Christian belief, but only that it cannot be decisively *proven* to be logically incompatible with broad Christian doctrines and other things that are known to be true. In fact, when Thomas Talbott uncovered a series of unsupported and seemingly unlikely assumptions underlying Craig's defence of DH,[15] Craig responded by pointedly insisting that his project was simply to show that DH might be true in the *epistemic* sense (i.e. *for all we know* it might be true), and that highlighting the implausibility of his assumptions is therefore beside the point.[16]

In short, Craig offers what, in contemporary philosophical jargon, amounts to a 'defence' of DH rather than a 'theodicy'. The strategy, roughly, is this: someone argues that DH is incompatible with some set of doctrines about God, doctrines the hellist does not want to abandon. The hellist notes that the incompatibility does not exist between DH and the other doctrines taken *alone*, but emerges only when we deny the truth of some further proposition, P. That is, the argument against DH based on the theistic doctrines relies (either implicitly or explicitly) on asserting not-P. If P is true, then there is no contradiction. Since, as far as we can *know*, P is possibly true, it follows that, given the relevant doctrines about God and other things we know to be true, DH could be true.[17] In this case, 'P' serves as what might be called a 'reconciling proposition' for DH and the relevant theistic doctrines, in the sense that DH and these doctrines are compatible if P is true.[18]

But what if not-P has great intuitive plausibility and P seems preposterous? That is, what if P – although we do not *know* it to be false in some strong sense of 'know' – defies an enormous body of inductive evidence, or would require us to abandon an explanatory hypothesis that is not only consistent with our experience, but offers the best unifying explanation for what we know? Or what if P, to put it baldly, just seems crazy in light of the intuitions of reasonable people who take the time to reflect on it? In such cases, we would likely say that believing not-P is far more reasonable than believing P, and if DH can be reconciled with some relevant set of theistic doctrines *only* on the supposition of P (or if all other available reconciling propositions are similarly outlandish), the proper conclusion seems to be that affirming both DH *and* the relevant theistic doctrines is presumptively unreasonable.

In other words, that one has offered a 'defence' of DH in the indicated sense is consistent with belief in DH being profoundly unreasonable in light of all the available arguments and evidence. A defence of DH is not a defence of its *reasonableness*, but only a demonstration that there exists a way for theists committed to DH and the relevant theistic doctrines to avoid an outright logical contradiction in their belief-set – because there is some reconciling proposition out there, however outlandish, whose truth is not impossible (or at least not known to be impossible) and which has not been *shown* to be false.[19]

If this is what Craig's efforts to 'defend' DH amount to, the result is an almost unassailable position in defence of a conclusion that is not especially interesting.[20] For in even the most compelling and persuasive arguments against DH from central Christian teachings, we are likely to be able to find at least one premise which *could* be rejected on the condition that some highly implausible, but epistemically possible, assumption were adopted. But what does this prove? Not that Christians should adopt DH, nor that adopting DH is not unreasonable. The only thing that follows is that those Christians who do adopt DH can avoid an outright logical contradiction in their belief set by embracing a certain claim rather than its negation. However, the same can almost certainly be said of those Christians who adopt DU. If we are to move forward – that is, if we are going to make progress towards actually deciding which doctrine is more reasonable for Christians to embrace – we need a comparative examination of the relative merits of the cases for and against DU and DH.

In short, so long as each doctrine – DH and DU – enjoys even the remotest epistemic possibility of being true in light of the broader Christian context, the task of determining which doctrine Christians ought to accept cannot be completed by a one-sided defence of, or attack on, either doctrine. What is required is a comparative treatment of the rival doctrines to ascertain which is *more* plausible and defensible in light of the entire body of evidence that Christians find authoritative.

Our goal here, therefore, does not involve refuting Craig's contention that some version of DH *might* be compatible with central Christian teachings. Rather, our goal is to show that central Christian teachings render DU *more reasonable* than DH, and this requires a comparative approach.

There is a further reason why a comparative defence of DU, rather than a one-sided defence, is required. The problem with any one-sided examination of religious doctrines is that all such doctrines – DU and DH being no exception here – tend to resist simple explication, insofar as they are typically expressed using religious terminology that is subject to competing interpretations (often in the light of alternative understandings of related doctrines).

These facts render a simple deduction or disjunctive syllogism unsatisfactory for settling doctrinal disputes. Even if a doctrine such as DU is deducible from more central Christian doctrines under *one* interpretation of those doctrines, it may not be deducible under other interpretations. Hence, anyone who is resistant to DU might reject a valid deduction of DU from central Christian doctrines by reinterpreting those doctrines so as to render the deduction invalid. (The supralapsarian Calvinists might be taken to have made such a move when they provided their own novel interpretation of the doctrine of God's perfect goodness – a doctrine that, together with their view that sinners contribute nothing to their own salvation but are saved by God's grace alone, might otherwise have been taken to imply DU.)[21] Furthermore, if a doctrine such as DH is shown to be *problematic* in light of central teachings, it might be rendered unproblematic through a reinterpretation of these teachings. If *this* cannot be done, then the problematic doctrine – say DH – might *itself* be reinterpreted to avoid the problems while remaining sufficiently similar to the original to qualify, not as a new doctrine, but as a less problematic 'version' of it. This appears to be what has happened over the last few centuries, as the classical doctrine of hell – holding that God eternally rejects some creatures – has been gradually replaced with the doctrine that some creatures eternally reject God despite His best efforts to save them. In short, rival doctrines almost never mutually exhaust the possibilities, since each rival admits of numerous variants that typically emerge only through criticism of both.

A few points of clarification are called for here. Above, we refer to 'doctrines', 'interpretations' and 'versions' of doctrines as if these notions were unproblematic – but that is hardly the case. One way to make sense of the idea that a doctrine admits of numerous interpretations is to treat a doctrine as nothing more than an ambiguous sentence, and an interpretation of a doctrine as one proposition that the ambiguous sentence might express. However, a doctrine, as traditionally conceived, is not a sentence but rather something expressed *by* sentences. When religious believers affirm their allegiance to some doctrine, they are not affirming their allegiance to a *sentence* that might express many different propositions, some true and others false; rather, they are affirming the truth of some proposition. Furthermore, when we speak of better or worse ways of *expressing* a doctrine, we are clearly treating the doctrine as a proposition that can be expressed, more or less perfectly, by a sentence. But how can a *proposition* – which, properly conceived, is the *meaning* of an expression – admit of alternate interpretations?

One solution is to treat doctrines as 'ill-defined' propositions. Ambiguous sentences are often such that there is a cluster of related propositions that the sentence might plausibly be taken to express. Sometimes when we utter such a sentence we are affirming not that one particular proposition in the cluster is true, but that *some* proposition in that cluster is true. Hence, when we utter the sentence we do not intend to express a single proposition, but rather a cluster; and we do not intend to affirm the truth of the whole cluster (which would typically land us in contradiction), but rather that there is some true proposition somewhere in the cluster of propositions plausibly expressed by the sentence we utter. This loose and imprecise mode of expression may be exasperating to philosophers and other academics, but it is quite typical in ordinary discourse. There is a sense in which we do not always 'know what we mean' when we speak – or better, that we do not know *precisely* what we mean – and yet we affirm the truth of what we mean. This is possible because we are committing ourselves not to the sentence uttered (which is hardly coherent), nor to *one* of the meanings of that sentence, but rather to the view that *something* in the cluster of plausible meanings is true. We are waving in a general direction, saying, in effect: 'the truth is somewhere in this vicinity'.[22]

Such imprecision is often perfectly satisfactory for ordinary discourse, but it is not satisfactory when the relative merits of rival doctrines are being examined. In such an examination one must inevitably explore questions of logical implication and consistency – and these questions require that precise meanings be assigned.

However, here is where the difficulty arises. While DH (or one version of it) might be deducible from (or refuted by) one understanding of central Christian teachings, DU may be deducible from (or refuted by) a different understanding. Hence, given the 'ill-defined' character of much doctrine, a one-sided examination of the issue at hand is likely to be unsatisfactory.

A comparative examination may prove far more satisfactory. While rival doctrines may both be deducible from alternative interpretations of Christian teachings, a comparison of these deductions may reveal, for example, that one deduction relies on doctrines that are more *central* (where a central doctrine is one whose removal from the body of Christian belief would require that the majority of theologians redefine, more or less radically, their understanding of Christianity), or on more *defensible* interpretations of those doctrines (e.g. interpretations that are closer to the ordinary meaning of the religious terminology in question, or interpretations that can be more readily integrated into the larger context of Christian belief, or ones that are more logically coherent in themselves). Hence, even in the case where rival doctrines may both be deduced from Christian teachings, a comparative examination can provide us with measures – such as the relative centrality of the teachings, and the comparative defensibility of their interpretations – for deciding between them.

Given this understanding of what a comparative defence of DU over DH involves, it should be apparent that any such defence is an enormous undertaking. In fact, it would be nothing short of hubris to suppose that any single work, written by a pair of authors, is the definitive comparative treatment of a set of rival doctrines. As such, even though the scope of the comparative defence we launch here is deliberately ambitious, it can (and should be) understood as our contribution to an ongoing comparative project to which many other scholars have already contributed, and will continue to do so.

That said, our hope is to offer a contribution that is powerful enough to shift the burden of proof onto the shoulders of those who would say DH is more philosophically defensible in the light of broader Christian teachings than is DU. We think that, when confronted with the choice between DH and DU, DU is, simply put, the better philosophical fit with the most plausible understandings of the most central teachings of the Christian tradition. Our aim in what follows is to explain why.

CHAPTER 2

HELLISMS: THE SPECIES OF DH

2.1 The Role of Definitions in a Comparative Treatment of DH and DU

We begin our comparative case by enumerating the various species of both DH and DU. This definitional work is important, first, because arguments that may work against some species of DH may not work against others. For example, the argument that it would be unfair of God to punish a person forever for a temporally finite sin, while applicable to species of DH that regard damnation as retributive punishment for earthly sins, has no force against species of DH that regard damnation as the natural outcome of forever rejecting God's love. A comprehensive case against DH must therefore distinguish species of DH and show why *each* is either indefensible or less defensible than some alternative theory (in our case DU).

A second reason this definitional work is important is that while some species of DU may be objectionable from the standpoint of theism in general, or Christianity in particular, other species might not. Recall that we are *not* claiming that every version of DU is superior to any version of DH, but that for any version of DH some version of DU is preferable. As noted in Chapter 1, our conclusion is disjunctive insofar as we resist taking sides in the theological controversy over whether God can legitimately extend efficacious grace to the unregenerate. Instead of resting our case on one answer or another, we distinguish and defend species of DU based on which answer is presupposed.

2.2 A Generic Definition of DH

Before distinguishing the species of DH, we offer a general definition that captures what the species have in common. We propose the following: *every doctrine of hell holds that some created persons, while preserved forever in being, will never be saved.*[1]

To clarify this definition we first need an account of what Christians mean by 'salvation'. That salvation involves perfect, eternal bliss is generally agreed, but to *define* salvation as just this is too superficial. In light of both Scripture and tradition, it should be clear that the primary element in salvation is the *clear or direct ongoing experience of the divine essence* – that is, the beatific vision.[2] Bliss is only *one* consequence of the beatific vision. Moral sanctification – the purging of all sinful dispositions – is another.[3]

This point deserves elaboration. Christianity takes God to be, *objectively*, the highest good; and God's objective value imposes an obligation on our subjective values: if we fail to value God above all things, our subjective values are defective, and our moral character is more broadly compromised.[4] In failing to order our values appropriately, we inevitably fail to act in ways that respect the inherent worth of things.

Given traditional Christian moral theology, then, rational creatures are perfectly good only when God is the object of their highest devotion. Loving God above all else completes their moral nature, perfecting them in both intellect and will so that all their inclinations and actions are in accord with right reason. However, on the traditional view, this rightly ordered love of God can only be *fully* achieved by a direct vision of the divine essence.[5] Thus, Philip Melanchthon asserts that: 'although the law points out what God is like, such righteousness cannot be in anyone unless God himself dwells in him and gives him his light and glory. Thus the law is entirely fulfilled in us only in eternal life, in eternal righteousness, when we have eternal joy in God, and God has become all in all.'[6]

In summary, 'salvation' means a spiritual union with God that produces both eternal moral perfection and perfect happiness. Given this notion of salvation (and remembering human fallenness), to say that some are *never* saved means that some are never granted *the only thing that will complete them as rational creatures* – namely, the beatific vision. Their intellects are thus eternally darkened by false notions of what is true and good, leading to disordered desires that overvalue some things and undervalue others. They will never properly love God, their neighbours, or themselves.

This disorder in the desires has traditionally been called *concupiscence*, and has been thought to involve selfishness that prioritizes carnal desires but that, *in a sense*, lacks self-love.[7] As Aristotle would put it, those who are good love that which is best for themselves, namely virtue, while the wicked reject virtue (which is to their soul what health is to their body) in favour of such lower goods as fame, wealth, power and sensual pleasure – thereby eschewing the very thing their souls need in order to be healthy.[8]

All species of DH agree, then, that hell's essence is the eternal privation of the beatific vision and consequent sickness of the soul. However, some species hold that hell is also characterized by further ills of body and/or soul. Among the ills of the soul that have been historically listed are such things as never-ending pangs of conscience, hatred of God, continual frustration at the inability to satisfy perverse desires, and so on.[9] Among the ills of the body (also called external pains) are torment at the hands of other fallen creatures (particularly devils), never-ending burning produced by an infernal fire, and so on.[10] However, though some versions of DH list these as punishments which accompany t‑c

damnation, not all do. What all forms of DH share is the view that some are eternally deprived of the beatific vision and so endure the unending moral and spiritual vitiation which necessarily follows.

However, if this is correct, then every species of DH holds that God either allows or causes some persons to be eternally confirmed in two evils: the loss of the *joys* of heaven and, more significantly (we think), *eternal moral wickedness*. To be deprived of the beatific vision is to be deprived of the only thing that can *eradicate* sin.

Thus, the question becomes: why would a perfect God, Who not only loves His creatures but *hates sin*, permit (or bring it about) that some of His creatures are eternally marred by both misery and sinfulness, and so fall eternally short of the end for which He made them? *Why would a perfect God allow sin to reign forever victorious over His divine purposes in creation, at least in the souls of the damned?*

If God is morally perfect and omnipotent (in the sense of being capable of doing whatever is metaphysically possible[11]), then there must be either (a) some morally sufficient justification for permitting or inflicting these evils, or (b) some metaphysical impossibility associated with saving the damned from them. While (a) strikes us as more plausible than (b), we do not want to rule out (b) in advance. In either case, God would be *justified* in not saving all – either because He has a morally sufficient reason not to do so or because He cannot do so (and so cannot be morally required to do so). In either case, as we argue in what follows, God's failure to save all would have what the Protestant Scholastics called an 'impelling cause'.

As they used the term, an 'impelling cause' is a kind of 'reason' that motivates God to will a certain act or course of action – either a *motive* for God to will some particular act or end (what they called an *internal* impelling cause), or an external state of affairs that 'activates' an essential divine moral attribute, thereby 'generating' a motive for God's willing something (what they called an *external* impelling cause). For example, the divine volition to destroy Sodom would have its internal impelling cause in God's justice, and its external impelling cause in the Sodomites' wickedness.

Hellists have historically proposed various impelling causes, both internal and external, for damnation – these typically correlate with different ideas about the *nature of the evils* that the damned endure. Suppose that one thinks God has an internal impelling cause for *imposing* damnation – namely, the righteous desire to fulfil the demands of retributive justice – which is 'activated' by the external impelling cause of human wickedness. In that case, one would likely think the damned suffer from torments *inflicted* by God as punishment for sin. By contrast, suppose that one thinks God has an internal impelling cause for *permitting* damnation – namely, His respect for creaturely autonomy – 'activated' by the external impelling cause of the creature's free rejection of God. In that case, one would be less inclined to think God heaps suffering on the

damned and more inclined to think their suffering is restricted to what naturally accompanies alienation from God.

In short, we have two interrelated ways whereby species of hell might be distinguished: in terms of the impelling causes of damnation, and in terms of the
nature of the sufferings of the damned. In the next two sections we will flesh out
species of DH in terms of these two parameters, attempting to provide an exhaus-
tive portrait of alternatives consistent with supposing God to be perfectly good.

2.3 The Nature of the Sufferings of the Damned

We begin with the nature of the sufferings of the damned, or NH. Here, we see
two main options:

> NH1: The evils suffered by the damned include not only the privation of
> the beatific vision and whatever positive evils result necessarily from that
> privation, but also certain other positive evils that do not so result (here-
> after *ancillary evils*).

> NH2: The evils suffered by the damned do not include any evils other
> than the privation of the beatific vision and whatever positive evils result
> necessarily from that privation.

In order to better understand NH1, we must recall that Christians have historically held that the welfare (and very being) of creatures is constituted by God's
presence to them. At least since Augustine, the biblical notion that death is a
punishment for sin has been interpreted to mean that sinners, by turning away
from God, are cut off from the 'spiritual light' that they need in order to flourish.[12] Their intellects are thus darkened, leading to both ignorance and error;
and they come to love some things more than they ought (especially themselves
and carnal goods), and others less than he ought (especially God and their
neighbours).[13] Some theologians also thought that losing God's light so diminished the soul's vital powers that even the body was harmed – resulting in illness
and physical death.[14]

Whatever the positive evils resulting necessarily from privation of the beatific
vision, the more important question is whether the sufferings of hell are *limited*
to such evils. One's answer to this question is what establishes our distinction
between NH1 and NH2. As such, it is important to think about which evils are
really ancillary to the loss of the beatific vision, and which are essential. To
determine this, we think it helpful to make a further distinction between what
we will call *objective* and *experiential* evils.

By an objective evil, we mean an evil whose existence is independent of the
awareness of the afflicted subject. Cancer that has yet to be discovered or to

manifest overt symptoms is nevertheless a bodily affliction, and an objective evil in our sense. A sinful disposition remains a part of a person's character, and hence is an objective evil, even while the person is asleep and so experiences no active urges of that disposition. It remains an evil even though the person is ignorant of its wickedness and so lacks the experience of being afflicted by sin.

With most objective evils, it is possible for the subject to become conscious of these evils as evils: to experience them for what they are. When this happens, the conscious experience of objective evils becomes an additional evil afflicting the subject – an intrinsically undesirable conscious state. This is what we have in mind when we speak of *experiential* evils. Broadly speaking, they are equivalent to actual conscious suffering. They are *pains*. Physical pain is an immediate experience of an objective bodily evil, even if not mediated by a conscious awareness of the nature of the objective evil and its significance. Such aware-ness, if the cause of pain is a degenerative illness, might well generate a further psychological pain atop the physical, but both pains are experiential evils. Mor-phine might eliminate, for a time, the physical pain, but not the underlying objective evil that is its cause. Unconsciousness might remove the psychological distress, but not the disease.

The point of drawing this distinction is this: while someone might well hold that privation of the beatific vision necessarily generates *objective* evils, it is harder to maintain that it necessarily generates *experiential* evils. Conscious awareness of loss does not seem to be a necessary concomitant of being denied the beatific vision. Hence, while alienation from God may produce objective evils that afflict the soul and even the body, it does not necessarily produce suf-fering. The conscious suffering generated by an awareness of being deprived of the beatific vision, or by an awareness of the various positive evils that immedi-ately result from being so deprived, is *ancillary*. They are not *necessary* concomi-tants of being denied the beatific vision – both because one who lacks the beatific vision might not be aware of it as *a loss*, and because such a person might not be conscious at all.

This means that those who embrace NH2, and so deny that the damned are subjected to *ancillary* evils, must also deny that the damned are afflicted by experiential evils; that is, by any evils constituted, at least in part, by conscious awareness. They must hold, in short, either that the damned are plunged into everlasting unconsciousness or, if conscious, that none of their conscious states add to the evils they endure (e.g. they will have no awareness of being separated from God, if such awareness causes pain).

In either case, someone might reasonably suppose that for the damned to avoid all such ancillary experiential evils, God would need to shield them from the awareness of the objective evils they endure by truncating or extinguishing their conscious awareness. Such loss of consciousness (either selective or total) might *itself* be viewed as an evil which God would have to *inflict* on the damned to prevent their suffering. In this view, NH2 becomes untenable: God must choose among ancillary evils, either permitting suffering that is not strictly necessary or inflicting oblivion. Even if unconsciousness in the damned is not an evil, there may be reasons that preclude God from imposing such unconsciousness even for the sake of relieving suffering. Once again, the existence of such constraints would be a reason to reject NH2 in favour of NH1.

While NH1 holds that the damned do suffer ancillary evils – most significantly, the experiential evil we call suffering – these need not go beyond what immediately accompanies conscious awareness of privation of the beatific vision (and whatever further objective evils follow). That is, the ancillary evils affirmed in NH1 might be limited to those that result from conscious awareness of the *non*-ancillary evils. They need not include pains inflicted by God for retributive reasons; but, then again, they might. These alternatives are significant enough to warrant distinguishing sub-species of NH1, as follows:

> NH1a: The evils suffered by the damned include not only the privation of the beatific vision and whatever positive evils necessarily result from that, but also certain ancillary evils that *are* inflicted by God as retribution for sin.

> NH1b: The evils suffered by the damned include not only the privation of the beatific vision and whatever positive evils necessarily result from that, but also certain ancillary evils that, while willed or permitted by God, are *not* inflicted as retribution for sin.

NH1a holds that the ancillary evils of damnation have their ultimate cause in God's retributive justice: God wills that the damned suffer ancillary evils because it is intrinsically fitting that the unregenerate suffer in this way. NH1b, by contrast, does not commit itself to any particular motive that God might have for willing or allowing the damned to suffer ancillary evils; it simply denies that He positively wills such pains for retributive reasons. We suspect that in most cases, allegiance to NH1b would entail the view that the ancillary evils suffered by the damned are limited to the suffering that comes from consciously experiencing the non-ancillary evils. It is hard to imagine what else might motivate God to allow or inflict evils beyond this once retributive motives are off the table. Conscious awareness of the objective evils that one endures might be justified, however, if awareness of the truth is better in itself than the lack of such awareness. The intrinsic worth of such a connection with the truth, as opposed to retributive motives, would be what justified the suffering attending conscious awareness of non-ancillary evils.

2.4   *The Impelling Causes of Damnation*

To be fully characterized, a species of hell must not only identify the nature of the suffering endured by the damned, but also why they suffer damnation at all. That is, one needs an account of the impelling causes of damnation (CH). Such impelling causes will take one of two forms: (a) they will give an account of why

God *cannot* save the damned; or (b) they will give an account of why God either *permits* or *wills* their damnation, even though it is within His power to save them. Both alternatives, as we shall see, presuppose that the impelling causes of damnation, whether internal or external, are intrinsically related to the *choices of agents*: either the damned are responsible for their fate through their own choices, or God is responsible for their fate through His choices, or some combination of the two.

That this is so is perhaps clearest in the case of (b), in which case God's choices play the decisive role in damnation. In the case of (a), the primary impelling cause of damnation must be an external one that limits what God can choose – but what could this external impelling cause be other than the choices of the damned? Christianity affirms that the damned are not different in their fundamental nature from the saved, and so the view that God cannot save them will not be explicable by reference to a difference in their nature. It must, rather, be accounted for in terms of a difference in their will. If God cannot save them, it will be because they make choices which take them out of the class of those God can save. The most obvious candidate for such a choice is the decision to reject God – that is, the refusal to willingly experience the beatific vision. Given God's presumed omnipotence, to say that God cannot save those who make such a choice is coherent only if the experience of the beatific vision essentially involves the creature's free participation. Perhaps 'the beatific vision' describes a relational state involving God and the creature, and perhaps the creature's contribution to the relation can only exist through an exercise of libertarian freedom which God cannot bring about even in Alvin Plantinga's weak sense. If so, God would be unable to save those who wilfully reject Him, despite a divine moral disposition (love) which would otherwise provide an internal impelling cause for God's acting to save all.

One could, however, ask if this means that under option (a) there is *no* internal impelling cause of damnation. After all, given that (a), God's moral dispositions do not motivate damnation, and rather than being triggered or activated by an external state of affairs, they are stymied by one. However, the external state that stymies God's moral disposition might still be viewed as an external impelling cause of damnation insofar as it impacts how God's moral dispositions manifest in divine action (or, in this case, inaction). Furthermore, even in the case of (a) there is something God does that contributes to damnation: *He preserves the damned in being.* Christianity traditionally teaches that if God ceases to sustain something in being, then it ceases to exist.[15] Thus, given (a) God could presumably still annihilate the damned (sparing them hell's torments) even if He could not save them. God's decision to preserve the damned in being would, it seems, be best accounted for in terms of, first, the external impelling cause of the intrinsic value that attaches to the essential nature of the damned and, second, the internal impelling cause of God's 'complacent' love – a love which moves God to preserve what has intrinsic value.

In case (b), the assumption is that God can save the damned but chooses not to do so. However, since God has a prima facie good reason to save all, the damnation of some must be explained by the presence of a more impelling internal impelling cause for God's not saving all. Simply put, option (b) implies that to save *all*, God would have to do (or refrain from) something that it is impermissible for Him to do (or not do).

This moral impediment to saving all could manifest itself at the level of either means or ends. To say that it manifests at the level of means is to say that, at least sometimes, the actions that God would need to perform in order to save a creature would be morally impermissible. Thus, even though there would be no internal impelling cause motivating God *not* to will the salvation of a creature *as an end*, He is barred from achieving this worthy goal because the available means of doing so are impermissible. Alternatively, to say that the moral impediment manifests at the level of *ends* is to say that the salvation of a creature ceases to be a goal that God ought to pursue. That is, God's moral dispositions, triggered by relevant facts about the damned, become an internal impelling cause for His not willing their salvation. Put simply, it would be wrong, all things considered, to seek their salvation (despite God's prima facie reasons to do so), even were the means of doing so morally permissible.

Consider the following analogy: suppose that Eric has good prima facie reasons to financially support his son through college; that is, to bring it about that his son gets to go to college without having to work full time in order to pay for it himself. Suppose, however, that the only way Eric could do this would be by stealing money. In this case, there would be a moral impediment at the level of means. Suppose also that Eric's son has proven irresponsible with the use of opportunities given to him by others, and displays responsibility only when the opportunity arises through his own efforts. In that case, Eric may have compelling moral reasons not to bring it about that his son gets to go to college without having to work for it. Were his son's character different, Eric's prima facie reasons for bringing about this state might be decisive (his son would be able to focus more fully on his studies and pursue more extracurricular educational opportunities). However, given his son's character, it would be wrong for Eric to pursue this end even if he could do so without stealing money (or doing something else impermissible). In this case, we have a moral impediment at the level of ends.

If God were morally barred from saving the damned at the level of means, the likely reason would be that, with respect to at least some of the damned, saving them would require action that failed to properly respect or love them; though saving them would clearly not display a lack of concern for their *welfare* (since it would promote it). So in what would the lack of respect lie? The common answer is that it would fail to respect their freedom or autonomy. That is, were God barred from saving the damned at the level of means, it would presumably be because He could only save them by violating their autonomous choices in morally impermissible ways. While God could save them, and while He could respect their autonomy, He could not do both – and respect for the latter (it is supposed) is more important.

In other words, if God is morally barred from saving the damned at the level of means, we find ourselves with a theory about the impelling causes of damnation very similar to what we encounter in the case in which God is taken to be *unable* to save the damned: in both cases, the free rejection of God by the damned takes them out of the pool of creatures that God can legitimately save. Either He cannot save them at all, or (perhaps more plausibly) He cannot save them in a morally legitimate way. In either case, it makes sense to say that the damned's free choices put them in hell – that is, that the *external* impelling causes of damnation are so powerful that God is simply left with no legitimate choice but to let them suffer their fate.

However, if God fails to save the damned because He no longer wills their salvation as an end, the situation is different. In this case, if God willed the salvation of the damned, He would have available to Him a means of doing so that, in itself, was not morally objectionable. What most directly keeps God from saving the damned under this view, then, is His own rejection of them, in the sense that He simply does not will (all things considered) that they be saved. While their rejection of Him may be the external impelling cause of God's rejection of them, it is His rejection of them that is the more immediate impelling cause of damnation.

It is one thing to say that, because the damned reject God, God's hands are tied and He cannot save them even though He still wants to. In that case, God is *not* willing their damnation, let alone inflicting damnation upon them. They are damned by what *they* will, not by what God wills – even if God wills His own obedience to moral principles which happen to preclude Him from performing acts that might have saved the damned. In the latter case, however, God's will intervenes in a more direct way between what the damned will and their fate. The internal impelling cause of damnation – usually thought to be retributive justice – is the more crucial cause, even if the external impelling cause of God's will that the damned not be saved is the fact that they freely rejected Him.

Some Christian theologians, however, have held that something other than the sinner's rejection of God motivates God to reject the damned. Consider the supralapsarian Calvinist view that God willed Adam's fall in order to manifest the glory of His justice in damning some sinners, and that of His mercy in saving others.[16] Here there is *no* external impelling cause of damnation, but only an internal one, as becomes clear when the supralapsarians insist that there is nothing about those whom God elects which makes them more worthy of election than those He rejects, and nothing about those He rejects that makes them more worthy of rejection. Even though God has an internal impelling cause for saving some and damning others, His choice about who to save and damn is *arbitrary*.

This view is almost the opposite of the view that God cannot save the damned due to their free choice to reject Him. On that view, the external impelling cause of damnation is the essential thing; but even on that view, as we have seen, damnation requires that God will the continued existence of the damned – which would presumably be an internal impelling cause rooted in God's complacent love. Thus, even on species of DH which hold that the external impelling cause of damnation is the metaphysical impossibility of God's saving those who reject Him, God's motives and will are, albeit indirectly, causes of damnation. Hence, no doctrine of hell can fail to provide *some* internal impelling cause of damnation.

For all these reasons, we find it helpful to distinguish the impelling causes of damnation according to the following alternatives:

> CH1: The damned freely reject God, and although God never stops willing their salvation as an end, He cannot save them either because: (a) it is metaphysically impossible for Him to do so, or (b) all of the metaphysically possible means of securing their salvation are morally impermissible.

> CH2: If God willed the salvation of the damned as an end, it would be metaphysically possible for Him to achieve this end through means that were morally permissible; but He does not will their salvation as an end, either for (a) morally good but not compelling reasons, or (b) morally compelling reasons.

Several observations should be made about this division. First, there are really four alternative accounts of the causes of damnation here. However, the first two and the last two are so closely connected that they can and will be typically dealt with together.

Second, it is possible to imagine a hybrid theory of DH according to which *both* the end of saving the damned *and* the available means are taken to be morally objectionable. To our knowledge no one has embraced this view, but even if someone did it would not significantly influence our critical assessment of DH. A conjunction would be defensible only if CH1 and CH2 are defensible individually. If both CH1 and CH2 are problematic – as we argue – then so too would be their conjunction.

Third, we should say a few words about the distinction between CH2a and CH2b. While both stress that God ceases to will the salvation of the damned as an end – and it is this fact, rather than any inability to achieve that end, that stays God's hand – the nature of God's motive in each case is different. In the case of CH2b, the motive is a morally compelling one: if God saved the damned, He would be achieving an immoral end. Put another way, His moral character impels Him to reject the sinner. In CH2a, however, the causes for God's refusing to grant salvation to the damned would be motives upon which He might legitimately act but *need not*. Under this view, God would be doing nothing strictly wrong were He to save all. Universal salvation would be compatible with any moral standards – including justice – employed to judge the fittingness of that end. Even so, God does *not* will this end. While God *does* have reasons for rejecting the damned, these reasons do not morally *compel* Him to act.

This view strikes us as puzzling, and we include it mainly because it seems to be the view of Aquinas.[17] One way to understand it is as follows: while God has a prima facie reason to save all, He also possesses reasons not to – but these latter reasons are neither more compelling nor less compelling than His reasons for saving all. Therefore, God is free to act on them or not and just so happens to act on those reasons which dictate against saving all.

Finally, in relation to CH2 we should note that the most common reason for Christians believing that God would actually cease to will the salvation of the damned as an end (instead willing their damnation) is that the damned deserve hell as a matter of retributive justice. As such, we expect that most would elaborate CH2 in these terms. In this view, meeting the demands of retributive justice is *as pressing as* (CH2a), or *more pressing than* (CH2b), any prima facie reasons God might have for the saving of all. Thus, given what the damned deserve, He ceases to will their salvation – either because it would conflict with His perfect moral character to do otherwise (CH2b), or because it is consistent with His moral character to go either way, and He just so happens to choose to cease willing their salvation (CH2a).

2.5 Complete Species of DH

A complete account of DH would spell out both the nature of the sufferings of the damned and the impelling causes of it, thus combining some species of NH with some species of CH. We think any such combination is at least prima facie coherent. First, NH2 (which holds that the sufferings of hell are limited to what necessarily accompanies loss of the beatific vision) can be combined with any form of CH. Even if God is morally required to reject the damned (CH2b), justice might demand nothing more than the infliction of the set of evils naturally flowing from loss of the beatific vision (which might be viewed as a very harsh punishment in itself). However, if NH2 is compatible with a retributive requirement to reject the damned, then it is a fortiori compatible with reasons for rejection that fall short of requiring it, and hence with CH2a. If God is not morally required to punish the damned at all, why think the punishments cannot be merely privative? By similar reasoning, NH2 is compatible with the idea, expressed in CH1, that God would save the damned if He could do so legitimately, but tragically cannot.

That NH1a and NH1b are also compatible with every form of CH might appear more controversial. If God wills the salvation of the damned as an end but is barred from realizing this end by their rejection of Him (CH1), it may seem that God would not then will on them evils which do not flow necessarily from that rejection as NH1a posits Him to do (especially if we suppose that God continues to will their salvation due to His continued love for them). Nevertheless, some have held that, though God does continually desire to save the damned, He nevertheless continues to inflict retributive pains on them which go beyond loss of the beatific vision and its necessary concomitants. While God desires their salvation and would save them if He could do so in a permissible way, He also desires that retributive justice be done – and so, insofar as the damned deserve additional pains, He inflicts them.

However, if this is right, then NH1a can also be combined with CH2. After all, if it is possible for God, even though He loves the damned and desires their salvation, to will upon them – for retributive reasons – suffering that does them no good, then a fortiori it seems He could will such suffering if He has decisively rejected them because they no longer deserve to be saved.

Finally, if NH1a can be combined with either CH1 or CH2, then so too can the more moderate NH1b. The more controversial issue in this case is combining NH1b with CH2. If God rejects the damned because they no longer deserve salvation, why would He limit their suffering to what accompanies the conscious awareness of their loss? We have already argued that NH2 – which denies any actual experiential suffering at all – is consistent with CH2, and so it seems that NH1b would be for similar reasons.

NH1b also seems to be compatible with CH1. One might hold that the only way to shield the damned from conscious suffering would be for God to actively cast them into a state of perpetual sleep or cause them to be deluded about their state – acts arguably inconsistent with the love or respect that God has for them as rational beings. This means that someone who endorses CH1 could readily endorse NH1b, even while denying that God inflicts pain out of retributive justice.

Hence, we have six complete versions of DH:

> (DH1) The conjunction of NH1a and CH2;
>
> (DH2) The conjunction of NH1b and CH2;
>
> (DH3) The conjunction of NH2 and CH2;
>
> (DH4) The conjunction of NH1a and CH1;
>
> (DH5) The conjunction of NH1b and CH1;
>
> (DH6) The conjunction of NH2 and CH1.

DH1 is the version of hell most commonly embraced by popular imagination: God not only casts the unregenerate from His presence, but heaps torments on them for eternity. DH2 and DH3 are variants of this view, and together with DH1 comprise versions of what we will call the Classical Doctrine of Hell (since

this is the perspective most commonly expressed in medieval Catholic and Protestant Orthodox theology), with DH1 being the Classical Doctrine in the strict
or narrow sense. What all variants of the Classical Doctrine share is their insistence on CH2 – the view that God rejects the unregenerate and would damn
them even if He could legitimately pursue their salvation.

DH5–DH6 have emerged as the most popular contemporary expressions of
DH among Christian philosophers and theologians, and might be dubbed versions of the Liberal Doctrine of Hell. Both reject the idea that retributive
motives contribute to God's failure to save the damned. What the damned suffer, they suffer because their free choices produce outcomes that God cannot
negate, at least not without doing something wrong.

DH4, which we will call the Retributive Doctrine of Hell, amounts to a *via
media* between the Classical and the Liberal views. In this view, God continues to
will the damned's salvation but, given their rejection of Him, has no (legitimate)
means of saving them; however, their rejection of Him also means that they
deserve to suffer more than loss of the beatific vision and its attendant evils. If
God could save them they would be sanctified and no longer deserve these ancillary afflictions; but since God cannot save them they continue to sin in ways that
demand retribution. Thus, while perhaps anguished by His inability to save
them, God nevertheless imposes on them additional retributive pains.[18]

2.6 Challenges Faced by the Species of DH: A Preliminary Assessment

With these species of DU in place, we want to offer a preliminary overview of
the difficulties associated with each, since these difficulties are what justify a
critical reassessment of the traditional Christian endorsement of DH.

While the most significant problems for any species of DH arise from the
impelling causes of hell, there are also some interesting concerns relating to
the nature of the evils endured by the damned. Consider the species of DH
(DH3 and DH6) that endorse NH2, thus denying that the damned endure any
ancillary evils. As already noted, those deprived of the beatific vision do not
need to be conscious, and so the evils of hell that require consciousness are
ancillary. It follows that DH3 and DH6 must deny that the damned have any
conscious experience of the evils they are subject to, and so must deny that the
damned *suffer*. If so, we can ask whether DH3 and DH6 are really species of DH
at all, insofar as suffering is typically understood as an integral part of damnation. Perhaps DH3 and DH6 describe a kind of *via media* between DH as it is
ordinarily conceived and DA (the doctrine of annihilation). However, even by
setting this worry aside, problems still remain.

First, since consciousness seems essential to our nature as rational beings
(we cannot exercise any of our intellectual or spiritual powers in its absence),

perpetual unconsciousness would be a decisive vitiation of that nature. As such, the loss of consciousness needed to prevent active suffering would itself be an objective evil – but not the kind of evil that would result necessarily from loss of the beatific vision. Hence, it is an objective evil that God would presumably have to inflict on the damned, perhaps out of mercy. If so, then God can be seen as having to choose from among ancillary evils: He must either permit suffering that is not strictly necessary, or inflict oblivion.

If this is right, then no species of DH that included NH2 would be possible at all, since no matter what God did, the damned would endure one kind of ancillary evil or another. To avoid this outcome, the defender of DH3 or DH6 would need to make the case either that perpetual unconsciousness would be a necessary consequence of being cut off from the beatific vision, or that the damned are so lost in sin that the deep vitiation of their souls caused by sin causes them no pain, even if they are conscious.

Whatever we think of this issue, there is another that is at least as important. As already noted, being deprived of the beatific vision entails being cut off from a clear understanding of the objective order of values, resulting in disordered desires that overvalue some things and undervalue others. Put more simply, damnation confirms the damned in moral degeneracy. This will be true even if they are put into a state of perpetual unconsciousness. They may be sleeping villains, but they remain, in character and dispositions, villainous. Even if suffering is not a necessary consequence of losing the beatific vision, perpetual moral degeneracy is.

If it is true, given NH2, that the damned are forever mired in wickedness, then it is true a fortiori for all species of DH. This fact thus highlights a global feature of DH: for every species of DH, one of the evils that necessarily accompanies damnation is eternal moral degeneracy. What is troubling here is that this degeneracy is not the rationale for damnation – that is, it is not some fact about the creature which justifies God in permitting or imposing damnation – rather, it is an *effect* of being deprived of the beatific vision. God either cannot, or will not, provide what amounts to a necessary condition for overcoming wickedness. Therefore, all versions of DH commit one to the view that God is either defeated by sin or complicit in its perpetuation – thus raising serious questions about God's sovereignty, goodness, or both.

This line of thinking becomes even starker when considering the difficulties arising from the alternative impelling causes for damnation – especially if we grant the pervasive Christian conviction that God's fundamental moral property is a love that extends universally to each of his creatures, regardless of their worth (the species of love called *agape*). Those who defend a version of DH falling under CH2 must maintain that, despite God's love for every sinner, there are moral considerations that would inspire God *not* to will the salvation of some of His creatures – even though love involves (at least prima facie) willing what is best for them. Defenders of CH2 face the challenge of providing an adequate account of what these moral considerations are.

We believe that the magnitude of this challenge is routinely overlooked. Defenders of CH2 must overcome the prima facie absurdity of the following conjunction: God loves every one of His creatures with a profound and unwavering benevolence; and He wills upon some of these creatures the very worst kind of evil conceivable, and He wills that they suffer it for all eternity, even though it cannot possibly do them *any* good, since it never culminates in anything but more of the same.

Defenders of a version of DH falling under CH1 face different challenges. Because they hold that damnation originates in the creature's own rejection of God, they must accept that some creatures freely reject God forever, and that God cannot legitimately overcome this free rejection of Him (despite potentially infinite time in which to work on their intransigence). That someone created in the divine image, and hence naturally ordered towards the good, should eternally reject the perfect good strikes us as prima facie unlikely, especially if God continues unremittingly to seek the creature's repentance. Furthermore, that an omnipotent and omniscient God should *eternally* fail to find a morally legitimate way to transform an unwilling creature's heart strikes us as prima facie dubious.

However, the problem runs deeper, as can been seen when we focus on the fact that a necessary feature of every species of DH is that the damned are eternally confirmed in moral degeneracy. This is troubling in its own right, but becomes even more troubling when combined with CH1 – which entails that, in God's war against sin, God confronts *ultimate* defeat in the souls of the damned. Despite all of His infinite resources, despite infinite time in which to work, despite His perfect knowledge of every nuance of the souls of the damned, despite His unrelenting love, His efforts will be for naught. At least in some human souls, sin will prove more powerful than God.

This rather staggering implication seems unavoidable for any of the 'liberal' versions of DH, and is one that we imagine most Christian theologians historically would have responded to with cries of blasphemy. This may be the main reason that the Classical Doctrine of Hell has not disappeared despite its drawbacks. If God's salvific aims simply do not include the damned, then we are no longer driven to the conclusion that God's aims are, in some human souls, ultimately defeated. In the various forms of the Classical Doctrine, the eternal alienation of the damned is directly intended by God and so cannot be viewed as God's failure or defeat. In this view, God prevails over sin in different ways: in the saved, through their sanctification; and in the damned, through their punitive expulsion from the goods of heaven.

However, this way of thinking obscures deep problems that, once again, become evident when we recall that being confirmed in wickedness is a necessary consequence (perhaps the only necessary one) of being deprived of the beatific vision. In the Classical Doctrine, the damned are punished for their wickedness at least in part by being eternally confirmed in wickedness.

To see the magnitude of the difficulty, it may help to reflect on what is so bad about sin. At root, sin is a failure to appropriately value what ought to be valued, and so to fail to express, in actions and dispositions, due reverence for the inherent worth of things. The most significant element of sin, in classical theology, is the failure to do this with respect to God, who has infinite inherent worth, and thus ought to be valued above all else. Failure to do so is a moral affront akin to the sociopath's failure to properly value his victim, only magnified in severity by God's infinite worth.

According to the classical doctrine of hell, God responds to this infinite affront against his dignity by deliberately acting to ensure that this affront continues for all eternity. While He could stop it from continuing, He chooses instead to make sure that this most intolerable of all evils persists forever in the souls of the damned by deliberately withholding the necessary condition for bringing it to an end.

Therefore, the defender of any form of the classical version of DH must explain why it would be a demand of justice to bring it about that a criminal never stop committing his crime. We, at least, cannot conceive of any coherent conception of justice under which this would make any sense.

CHAPTER 3

UNIVERSALISMS: THE SPECIES OF DU

3.1 The Essence of Salvation

We turn now to a discussion of DU and its species. As already noted, DU is the doctrine that all rational creatures are ultimately saved, where salvation in the Christian sense essentially consists in union with God, which produces perfect bliss and moral sanctification. While this understanding of salvation is largely sufficient for our purposes, there may be some value in a brief survey of how several important Christian thinkers have elaborated on this general understanding.

Consider, first, how the Lutheran Scholastic David Hollaz explains salvation's essential piece–namely, the beatific vision:

> Our eternal and highest blessedness consists in the perfect sight and enjoyment of God ... The beatific sight of God is an act of the intellect illumined with the light of glory, by which it perceives God clearly and immediately, and as He is in Himself. The enjoyment of God is an act of the will, by which the blessed ... most eagerly embrace God as the highest good, most delightfully comprehend Him, and are most fully satisfied with Him. ... Inseparably accompanying the beatific sight and enjoyment of God, will be the most ardent love to God, the most complete joy ... immunity from the danger of sinning, and the most constant holiness.[1]

In short, the beatific vision engages the whole self, intellect and will, and so consists in both knowing God and delighting in Him and His perfect goodness.

The tradition has generally held that experiencing the beatific vision produces an array of related goods. The seventeenth-century Lutheran John Andrew Quenstedt summarizes most of these under two headings: privative goods and positive goods. Under privative goods he lists 'the absence of sin and the causes of sin ... and of the punishments of sin such as various calamities ..., temporal death ..., and eternal death', as well as 'immunity from the affections and actions of the animal body as such', including immunity from 'hunger, thirst, eating, drinking, the use of marriage, etc....' Under positive goods, he first considers internal goods, divided into those that apply to soul or body, or to both. Goods of the soul include: (1) 'the perfect enlightenment of the intellect' (2) 'complete rectitude of will and appetite' and (3) 'the highest security concerning the perpetual duration of this blessedness'. Goods of the body include: (1) 'Spirituality' (2) 'Invisibility' (3) 'Impalpability' (4) 'Illocality' (5) 'Subtility' (6) 'Agility' (7) 'Impassibility' (8) 'Immortality and incorruptibility' (9) 'Strength and soundness' (10) 'Brilliancy' and (11) 'Beauty'.

Finally, under 'external' goods – namely, goods that 'the blessed experience deeply outside of themselves' – Quenstedt lists 'the most delightful intercourse with God ... and the angels ... and all the blessed ... consisting in mutual presence and most agreeable conversation, and rendering of mutual honor joined with mutual love; and a most beautiful and magnificent abode'.[2] In short, the blessed in heaven participate in a morally perfect community with one another, and with God.

While details of this picture may strike contemporary readers as puzzling, it has the virtue of highlighting the significance that moral sanctification played in traditional understandings of blessedness. One of the striking features of Quenstedt's portrait of blessedness is that one of its chief joys – the joy which seems to most enliven Quenstedt's prose (one gets the sense he is especially excited about the prospect of experiencing it) – is a direct outflow of the moral sanctification that the beatific vision produces. By virtue of it, the blessed can participate in the most perfect and satisfying sort of community conceivable – what might be called the Kingdom of God, or, following Martin Luther King, Jr., 'the beloved community'. If the essence of the moral law is love, this connection makes sense: heaven is about persons being perfected in love by a direct encounter with the God who *is* love. Since love is essentially relational, the fruits of being perfected in love will also be relational.

We suspect it is partly because this aspect of heaven is overlooked that so many not only accept DH, but (like Peter Berger) find it appealing. DH looks much more appealing when we think of heaven – as Thomas Hobbes did[3] – as but a reward for virtue consisting in wholly non-moral goods, and of hell as a punishment for vice that withholds these goods. However, when we conceive of heaven as essentially including the perfection of a rational creature's moral state, and hell as its unending vitiation, DH becomes more troubling.[4] Not only does it thus imply, as already noted, that what is intolerable to God (namely sin) continues to exist in all its intolerability for all eternity, it also implies that by virtue of this intolerable sinfulness some of God's beloved creatures are forever cut off from participation in the beloved community, thereby truncating the scope of the Kingdom of God – a fact which might delight those prone towards bitterness, resentment, vengefulness, or a wrath that cannot distinguish sinner from sin, but which we imagine could only be a source of sadness and regret for those perfected in love (a point we explore in Chapter 5).

With this understanding of salvation in mind, we offer our definition of DU as a genus as follows: *Every version of DU holds that all creatures will eventually come to enjoy the beatific vision and its attendant blessings, chief among them being their own moral perfection and participation in the beloved community.*

3.2 Impelling Causes of Universal Salvation

In considering the determinate species of DU, for our purposes it is most helpful to distinguish them in relation to two questions often posed as challenges to DU: first, given that some sinners remain unrepentant at death and that God is not only loving but just, what impelling causes would motivate God to will universal salvation? Second, how does God achieve the salvation of all in light of human freedom and the fact that some persons seem to stubbornly reject God's goodness and grace? In other words, given that voluntary participation in the joys of blessedness is an element of salvation, how does God achieve the conversion of the unregenerate?

With respect to the first question, we identify five possibilities:

> IU1: God is impelled to save all by His perfect benevolence.
>
> IU2: God is impelled to save all by virtue of the all-sufficient Atonement of Christ.
>
> IU3: God is impelled to save all by His complacent love for His own majesty.
>
> IU4: God is impelled to save all by His complacent love for rational creatures as created in His image and essentially ordered to Him as its ultimate objective end.[5]
>
> IU5: A combination of some, or all, of the above.

Before explicating each of these, we should note that the version of DU we prefer is the sub-species of IU5 that incorporates *all* of the impelling causes identified in IU1–IU4. Hence, as we discuss each possibility we will not only clarify its meaning but indicate why – given the broad stream of Christian teaching – we think each can be conceived as an impelling cause for God's willing the salvation of all. We also hope it will become clear how each impelling cause connects to and reinforces the others.

IU1: Divine Benevolence

God's benevolence is perhaps the most obvious impelling cause for God's willing universal salvation, and Christians generally agree that God is indeed benevolent. Although strict Calvinists have endorsed doctrines that are hard to reconcile with God conceived as *universally* benevolent, this strikes us as a point where strict Calvinism is most out of step with both the broad stream of Christian teaching and the New Testament portrait of God – according to which God seeks the good of each creature even to the point of becoming human, suffering, and dying so that sinners might be saved. This unmerited love is what theologians refer to as God's *agape*.

Such radically inclusive benevolence can, by itself, provide a powerful motive for universal salvation; and belief in God's benevolence is not limited to Christianity. Hence, the species of DU that are characterized by IU1 alone constitute a form of universalism with appeal beyond Christianity.[6] In these species of DU God's benevolence is not motivated by the moral worth of creatures, but is a free gift bestowed because of who *God* is. There is nothing outside God's moral character inspiring Him to save creatures. Hence, nothing they do or think – no matter how wicked – can impact God's decision to save them. That decision is motivated by His nature, defined in terms of agapic love. To use Protestant Scholastic terminology, IU1 teaches that God's willing the salvation of all does not depend on any external impelling cause, but only on an internal one.

In this regard, consider Aquinas's statement of God's universal benevolence:

> since to love anything is nothing else than to will good to that thing, it is manifest that God loves everything that exists. Yet not as we love. Because since our will is not the cause of the goodness of things, but is moved by it as by its object, our love, whereby we will good to anything, is not the cause of its goodness; but conversely its goodness, whether real or imaginary, calls forth our love, by which we will that it should preserve the good it has, and receive besides the good it has not, and to this end we direct our actions: whereas the love of God infuses and creates goodness.[7]

Here, Aquinas characterizes God in terms of a love that does not *depend* on some pre-existing worth in its object, but rather *bestows* worth. On this basis many Christian thinkers have taught that there is in God no distributive justice, because whatever good is in the creature is there because God, out of love, first put it there.[8] IU1, then, holds that God is motivated to save all by virtue of this creative and universal benevolence or *agape*.

While we think a strong case can be made for the species of DU that appeal to divine benevolence alone, our comparative case for DU will not appeal to them because we think that, within a Christian context, a version of DU that appeals to additional divine motives is more powerful. When looking for the best *Christian* species of DU, IU1 strikes us as incomplete precisely because it leaves out the motives identified in IU2 through IU4.

IU2: Christ's Atonement

The first and most obvious reason why IU1 might be incomplete from a Christian perspective is that it makes no appeal to Christ's Atonement. Christians might worry that appealing to God's 'naked' benevolence to account for salvation risks making Christ's work irrelevant. We have already noted a problem with this worry in Chapter 1: one may be convinced that God wants to save all, can do so, and hence will, without considering the specific steps that God might take or need to take *in order* to do so – and hence without considering whether the means He used (or had to use) are those Christians affirm. In other words, one might take God's *motive* for saving all to be nothing but His benevolence, but then argue that the Atonement is the necessary *means* of saving all.

While this move does ensure that Christ's work is *not* irrelevant, it is not the whole story because, in some of the most influential theories of the Atonement,

Christ's work is a 'means' of salvation only in a special sense. More specifically, it serves as the means whereby God becomes *reconciled to sinners* so as to be able to will their salvation as an end, rather than serving as the means whereby God converts them so as to render them subjectively fit to enjoy heaven's blessings.[9]

There are important understandings of the Atonement which take Christ's work to serve primarily as a means of converting sinners. For example, the 'moral influence' view of the Atonement seminally promulgated by Abelard treats Christ's life, crucifixion and resurrection as offering a moral lesson intended to awaken sinners to the gravity of their sin and so inspire repentance. In this construal, the Atonement might be understood as a means of bringing about conversion; but if so, either this is *efficacious,* in the sense that it irresistibly brings about conversion (at least when God fully employs it by, for example, vividly presenting the full significance of Christ's death on the cross), or it is resistible by the exercise of the sinner's free choice and can only be used as one strategy among others. These alternatives exactly parallel the means of salvation that we will explicate in the next section. Hence, if the Atonement is construed in this way, it can be understood as one of the means God uses to bring about the conversion of sinners. We discuss these in section III of this chapter.

However, the most historically influential Atonement theories have conceived of Christ's work not only as a causal *means* used by God to *convert* sinners, but also as a means whereby *God's motives* for rejecting sinners – which would otherwise impede Him from acting on His prima facie will to save sinners – are done away with. In other words, the most influential Atonement theories presuppose that God has morally compelling motives which *conflict* with the benevolent ones that would otherwise motivate him to save all. While these Atonement theories posit such conflicting motives, they also conceive of the Atonement as a means of overcoming the conflict, and hence of clearing the way for God's benevolence to operate unimpeded.

And so there might be a distinctively Christian species of DU according to which there is more than one impelling cause for God's willing the salvation of all. In addition to the internal impelling cause of salvation found in God's unmerited benevolence (IU1), there is the external impelling cause found in the all-sufficient Atonement of Christ (IU2). What this external impelling cause does, however, is *do away with* a divine reason *not* to save all – what we might call a 'salvation-impeding divine motive'.[10]

The historically dominant view of the Atonement follows Anselm in taking the salvation-impeding motive in question to be God's justice – often conceived as a separate attribute from His love that places limits on the appropriate expression of the latter. Put simply (and overlooking differences of detail), the broadly Anselmian or 'penal-substitutionary' view is that sinners *deserve* eternal punishment because, in offending an infinite God, they have committed a crime of infinite severity. Christ's Atonement, in this view, serves as God's means of vicariously meeting the demands of justice, thereby sweeping away a moral impediment that would otherwise have barred Him from willing the sinner's salvation.[11] Because Christ was fully God, what He endured on the cross had the infinite worth necessary to atone for sins of infinite gravity. Being fully human, what He endured could be offered up on behalf of humanity as payment for human sin; and because Christ's atoning work fully satisfies the demands of justice, God is free to act on His benevolent desire to save sinners without offending justice (a reconciliation of motives that itself has its origins in God's love).[12]

Does this Anselmian doctrine, with its introduction of divine justice as a distinct trait separate from God's love, rule out DU? On the contrary – we argue in Chapter 6 that those who seek to justify DH by appeal to divine justice actually confront a compelling challenge to their view in the Anselmian theory of the Atonement and its later development (especially among the Lutheran Orthodox). In the briefest terms, we argue that there can be a distinctly Anselmian species of DU, holding that – because Christ satisfied the demands of justice on the cross – God is free to act on His limitless benevolence to pursue the salvation of all.

However, to say that an Anselmian version of DU falling under IU2 is *possible* is not to say that such a version is the best Christian version of DU. In fact, many Christians have harshly criticized Anselm's understanding of the Atonement and, as such, would be loathe to accept IU2 if it meant allegiance to a variant of the penal-substitutionary theory. The reasons for criticizing it are numerous.[13] Some reject it on the basis of its separation of divine justice from divine love, holding instead (with, for example, Schleiermacher[14]) that divine justice should be understood as an expression or manifestation of divine love.[15] Others object to it because the theory makes the crucifixion into something orchestrated *by* God in such a way that we can no longer treat it as we ought to; namely, as a wrong done *by* humanity *to* the incarnate God. Still others argue that this model of the Atonement is premised on the moral acceptability of retributive violence, and so is at odds with important New Testament themes testifying to an ethic of non-violence.[16]

While we sympathize with all of these objections, we also think it is possible to construct a variant of the Anselmian theory that avoids them – a variant we find nascent in some of the things said by Luther and later Lutheran theologians. On this neo-Lutheran theory, the key impediment to saving sinners is not that justice demands of God the *infliction* of retributive suffering; rather, the key impediment lies in the moral character of reformed sinners.[17]

The idea, roughly speaking, is that sinners cannot come fully into God's presence – which entails both truly understanding *and* aligning ourselves with the good – without both (a) becoming perfectly conscious of the full magnitude of our past sinfulness (our guilt), and (b) becoming the kind of people who take responsibility for our past errors (who do *penance*, which is what divine justice *really* calls for, as opposed to the mere external infliction of hardship). That is, when we are morally perfected through the beatific vision, our past sins do not and cannot just go away as if they never existed. On the contrary, for sinners such as ourselves to become sanctified means, in part, coming to fully understand our guilt and feeling a pressing moral need to make it right – and so to diligently pursue penance for the wrongs we have done.

However, we *cannot* make it right because as finite beings nothing we can do would be sufficient to atone for wronging the infinitely benevolent creator. As such, the guilt we bear is more than we *can* bear. So, to be brought into the sanctifying presence of God (which, of course, is the essential element of salvation) is to experience a weight of guilt too great to endure, and to recognize (and feel an urgent need to fulfil) an obligation of penance infinitely greater than we can perform. Therefore, in the absence of some kind of profound divine intervention, coming into the presence of God would lead us to care so much about the good and to take such responsibility for our sins that we would toil for eternity to make up for offences we could never succeed in making up for. Therefore, paradoxically, for anyone who has sinned – in other words, for all of us – *salvation would be hell.* Put simply, the guilt we have accrued for our sinfulness is too great for us to bear ourselves. Thus, God, in His perfect benevolence, finds a way to bear it for us.

Our purpose here is not to explain how Christ can vicariously bear our guilt and perform on our behalf the penance we would otherwise feel compelled to attempt despite its fruitlessness – our point is simply to highlight another version of vicarious, 'substitutionary' Atonement, one in which the brutality of the crucifixion is *not* conceived as something orchestrated by God on the grounds that penal *violence* is morally required to satisfy a divine justice divorced from His love. In this view it is quite possible to see the crucifixion as being something that we do to Christ in response to His sanctity and benevolence, precisely because we cannot bear the burden of guilt we would experience were we to internalize what it means to be as good as we ought to be, as good as Christ calls us to be, as good as we intuitively recognize Him to be. We reject and nail Christ to a cross rather than face the magnitude of our sin. This is not something God does to Christ to satisfy the demands of justice, but something we do to Christ to avoid having to bear the burden of our sin.

What *God* does, in response, is turn our violence on its head, making of it a penance on our behalf. Because we cannot bear our guilt, we nail Christ to the cross; and Christ makes of that crime an opportunity to bear our guilt in truth. The ultimate sin of killing the Incarnate God is transformed into the sufficient atonement for that very sin. By deciding to treat our crime against Him as a penance for that very crime, Christ makes it possible for us, through the 'wedding ring of faith' to be 'married to Christ' and thus able to 'put on' His righteousness (to borrow Luther's language)[18] as we come into the presence of God, and so to experience the beatific vision without being overwhelmed by guilt.

There are many details which would need to be worked out in order for such a view of the Atonement to be wholly defensible. Our point here, however, is that like the Anselmian theory, this neo-Lutheran variant holds that a vicarious Atonement clears away an impediment to God's willing the salvation of all. For Anselm, the impediment is the moral demand that an infinite punishment be imposed in response to sin. In the neo-Lutheran view, the impediment is that sinners who become sanctified experience a responsibility and need for penance too vast to bear. God's *love* inspires Him to wish to impart the beatific vision on His creatures; but that same love precludes Him from imposing on us a burden we could never conceivably bear – and that is what granting us the beatific vision would entail in the absence of a vicarious Atonement. What the Atonement does, then, is lift away a moral impediment to God's willing that sinners be granted the beatific vision – an impediment *rooted in* divine love, conflicting with *another* urging of divine love, and overcome *by* divine love.

What this shows is that even universalists who object to Anselm's theory might nevertheless embrace a version of IU2 that takes seriously a *kind* of substitutionary Atonement. Furthermore, the Anselmian theory is not the only Atonement theory which might ground a species of IU2. IU2 could also be grounded on the oldest Atonement theory, endorsed by many Church Fathers and sometimes called the 'Ransom' theory, which views Christ's suffering and death as a ransom paid to the forces of evil to liberate sinners from bondage to those forces.[19]

While there are different ways of working out this theory, including Gustav Aulen's 'Christus Victor' approach,[20] one possibility (metaphorically promulgated by C. S. Lewis in *The Lion, The Witch and The Wardrobe*) is to see the forces of evil as having acquired a legitimate claim over sinners. We have used the freedom God gave us – the freedom to make decisions about the disposition of our lives – in the most self-destructive way imaginable: handing ourselves over to *das Nichtige* ('the Nothingness', Barth's term for the palpable force of non-being that is God's ultimate adversary[21]) in exchange for ephemeral or imaginary goods. Insofar as God has given us a real right over our own lives, our act of giving those lives over to the forces of darkness thereby confers upon them a claim on us that God cannot legitimately ignore.

To pursue our salvation in defiance of that claim (which an omnipotent God would certainly have the power to do) would be less than morally perfect. Therefore, God becomes incarnate and offers Himself to be crucified in exchange for releasing humanity from bondage. Once released, the moral impediment to God's pursuit of our salvation is lifted. In fact, the universalist could argue it is *wholly* lifted – thereby endorsing a species of IU2 according to which, by virtue of the ransom Christ paid for our souls, there is nothing that impedes God from willing the salvation of all.

In short, several ways of understanding the Atonement could be incorporated into a species of DU falling under IU2 – but not, we think, divorced from IU1. For even if Christ's Atonement is conceived as influencing God's motives rather than serving as a conversion tool, the *way* it does so is by clearing away a conflict in God's motives such that God's benevolence becomes free to operate unimpeded.

Of course, many sincere Christians take the Atonement to function solely as a means of converting sinners, playing no role in God's motivation to save all.[22] Thus, we do not insist that the only legitimate Christian version of DU includes IU2. However, we are personally drawn to what we think of as the richest understandings of the Atonement, those in which Christ's work operates on multiple levels, including some of those sketched above.[23] As such, the species of DU that we personally favour includes the impelling causes identified in IU2. More importantly for our comparative case for DU, a version falling under IU2 calls attention to the following fact: if God does indeed have motives (such as those flowing from divine justice) that would conflict with His prima facie benevolent desire to save all, then Christianity has consistently paired belief in the existence of such motives with a theory of the Atonement according to which the cross provides a pathway for benevolence to prevail. Hence, it is hard from a Christian standpoint to justify DH over DU by appealing to such motives.

IU3: God's Complacent Love for Himself

Beyond the issue of incorporating the Atonement into our account of DU, there remain reasons why Christians might not want to take benevolence as the sole basis of God's desire to save all. Much here hinges on what one means by 'benevolence'. Barth thought love really *does* exhaust God's moral attributes, but that the divine love also includes the divine holiness, justice and even wrath, and is not to be thought apart from them.[24] In this view, an understanding of divine benevolence is incomplete if it excludes the point that God's love is opposed to sinners *insofar as they are sinners* – but *for* sinners insofar as they are much more than sinners. God hates everything in us that is sinful precisely because He loves *us* in an unconditional way, and because sin is the most fundamental harm we can endure. God must therefore destroy the sinner, *qua* sinner, in order to save the human soul that has been shackled and distorted by the power of sin. He 'kills' the false self to raise up the true.[25]

If we conceive of God's benevolent love in this way, much of what conservative theologians say about God's holiness and justice can be interpreted as flowing from His benevolence: a holy benevolence that cannot even conceive of making the wicked 'happy' apart from making them good. However, even in this view of benevolence, we think it may be a mistake to understand divine love solely in terms of benevolence. For in much traditional Christian theology, God's love consists in more than the sheer benevolence (or agape) directed to creatures irrespective of their intrinsic worth. God also has what has traditionally been called a 'love of complacency' – that is, a love directly responsive to the merits of its object, one which delights in what is intrinsically good. In addition to being a *bestower* of value, God is also a *respecter* of it. He recognizes and honours the intrinsic worth that something possesses because of what it is. While God's benevolence is directed outward, creatively bringing goods into existence and bestowing further goods on what He has created, His complacent love is directed to anything with intrinsic worth – especially the most intrinsically valuable thing of all: God Himself.

In speaking of God's complacent love of Himself, we must stress that there is nothing self-seeking or egotistical about it. God loves His own essence not out of narcissism, but because doing so is objectively right.[26] Part of what it means to be morally perfect is to respond appropriately to what is intrinsically valuable – to value it in proportion to its worth; but insofar as God's objective worth is infinite, this means it would be a moral failure on God's part to fail to love Himself with anything but the most perfect delight and respect for His own merit.

However, *what* renders God worthy of being the object of such limitless respect might well be His boundless agapic love, the unwavering and life-giving benevolence that does not wait on worth. It seems to us that God would not *be* benevolent unless He *valued* benevolence. By implication, God would not be benevolent *above all else* without valuing benevolence – and its most perfect embodiment – above all other moral goods. Hence, one might think that the reason God loves Himself most of all (with the love of complacency) is precisely because He values agapic love above all other things, and because it is God Himself who most perfectly embodies such love.[27]

To value something means, in part, standing up for it, insisting that its value be respected. Those who show disdain for, or indifference to, God (at least if they have anything approaching a proper understanding of God's essence) are showing disdain for, or indifference to, *benevolent love itself.* God cannot be perfectly benevolent without being angered by such disdain for, or indifference to, perfect benevolence.

These considerations lead us to the importance of including in a complete Christian account of DU some reference to IU3 – that is, God's complacent love for Himself. This love for His own perfection has been – and, we think, justifiably should be – considered a fundamental basis for God's opposition to sin, insofar as sin involves a failure to value God as He ought to be valued. The failure to love God as one should is the failure to appreciate and value the ground of all love, all benevolence and all goodness; and insofar as God's worth is infinite, this shortfall is inevitably infinite in degree.

This is what is meant, we think, by the traditional claim that sin is an affront to God's majesty – not in the way that disobedience is an affront to the pretensions of a tyrant, but in the way that slavery is an affront to a person's real objective worth. To be in God's presence while persisting in sin is like being in the presence of another human being and treating that person as a mere thing. It is a failure to respond appropriately to the objective worth of the person with whom one is confronted.

This is something that a morally perfect being cannot tolerate. Hence, just as a morally good person becomes rightly angry when a human being is treated like a thing, God becomes rightly angry when He is treated in a manner that falls short of what is fitting with respect to the ultimate source of all good and value.[28]

While this love of God for His own essence is often put forward as a reason why God might be so wrathful at sin as to cast sinners into hell, we think it is more coherently invoked as a divine motive for willing universal salvation. If God loves His own essence, then He loves the love of it and hates the hatred of it (or even indifference to it).[29] Hence, God would have a powerful motive to expunge all hatred of His essence and replace it with love. That is, He would have a powerful motive to convert every sinner, *especially* those who most flagrantly offend His majesty. As Thomas Talbott has pointed out, insofar as DH implies that the damned never repent and forever reject God, DH commits one to the view that hatred of God is never fully stamped out, *but persists forever in the souls of the damned.*[30] This outcome would seem to be an intolerable affront to God's majesty. Hence, God's majesty (a term often used to refer to all of God's perfections, whether moral or metaphysical, taken as a whole) may be an external impelling cause occasioning in God the production of an internal impelling cause – a cause rooted in God's complacent love for whatever has intrinsic worth – for a volition to save all.

While we can imagine a species of DU that invokes nothing other than God's love of Himself as His motive for saving all (that is, a species of DU falling under IU3), we do not find this the most defensible Christian version, in part for reasons already noted in our discussion of IU1 and IU2. However, beyond these considerations, there is another – for in addition to His complacent love for Himself, Christian theologians have widely recognized another complacent love working on God's motives and which would, it seems, provide a further impelling cause for a divine volition to save all.

IU4: God's Complacent Love for Creatures

In traditional Christian theology, all creatures participate in God's goodness, especially rational creatures who were made in God's image.[31] This brings us to IU4, according to which God is moved to save the unregenerate because of the nature of the rational creature. The rational creature is, essentially, a being bearing the divine image and ordered towards union with God. The idea is this: God can no more cease to value rational creatures – even if they fall into sin – than He can cease to value Himself, because rational creatures are a reflection of His own essence.[32] Therefore, He is always faithful to them, even when they are unfaithful to Him,[33] and must seek to destroy their sin. When rational creatures fail to love God, they fall short of their own nature as beings ordered towards union with God. A respect for what the creature essentially is would thus motivate God to seek to overcome this corruption of it.

Even if we are correct that (as argued in the previous section) God must love His own essence and therefore seek to be glorified by the creature, it is not for *His own good* that He seeks to be so glorified. While it is intrinsically fitting for the creature to glorify God, and while that is itself a reason for God to demand it, He also demands it for the sake of the creature's good. As Walther puts it:

> God has created all to His honor, says Holy Scripture. By this it does not mean to say: God is a being who seeks honor, and that He needs creatures in order to be properly honored; but God is a friendly, loving God. He did not wish to be alone in His glory; He wished to draw other human beings into His glory. But this can occur only if they recognize His glory and so give Him all honor. To the extent to which man truly recognizes God he is blessed; to the extent that God remains hidden from him he is miserable and wretched.[34]

While God might be taken to will the creature's good purely out of His own benevolence – that is, purely because of who *God* is, we think there are good reasons to suppose that God also wills the creature's good out of respect for what the *creature* is.

This point has been neglected by many recent Protestant theologians, particularly the so-called Neo-Orthodox, such as Karl Barth, Anders Nygren and Gustav Aulen. The dominant Christian view of creation not only holds that the good of creation is from God, it also holds that God has really instilled in creatures a certain imitation of His glory.[35] John Gerhard argued that while creatures' goodness does not come from their own essence but from God's creative act, the essence that God created is good in itself. In Gerhard's terms, creatures are not *essentially* good, but they are *intrinsically* good.[36] Although they do not have their goodness *from* themselves (*a se*), they do have goodness *in* themselves (*in se*). In short, rational creatures have an intrinsic worth – one that demands respect – which cannot be lost so long as they exist. God would fail to respect the very goodness that flows from Himself if He failed to respect the intrinsic worth of creatures.

How does one show respect for *what* a creature is? If the creature has, as part of its nature, a teleology – if it is naturally ordered to the attainment of a certain end, the realization of which constitutes its good – then respect for it seems to involve at least some desire for the attainment of the creature's end. However, the Christian tradition holds that the end of the rational creature is union with God. As Dorner puts it: 'human nature finds its only true reality, or realization, in union with God. God's uniting act does not violate or unmake it, but rather first causes it to be what, in God's idea, it was meant to be.'[37]

Although Dorner and other exponents of this view do not explicitly draw any universalist implications, we may rightly ask how God could fail to have a motive to save all rational creatures if their natures are completed only in salvation, and if their natures have a value that demands respect. In short, God may be bound *in duty* to save (if He can) even the most recalcitrant of sinners out of respect for their intrinsic worth.

However, we must stress that even if God has a duty to save the rational creature (at least if doing so is possible and would not contravene any other moral obligations that God has), such a duty must not be supposed to rest on anything the creature *does*, but on what it *is*. God gives the creature what is due to it based on what He has already given it, in effect crowning His own work; but if creatures exist as beings that God has created distinct from Himself, and are not merely facets of God, then it seems God can have duties towards creatures. One such duty may be to save even the worst sinners, just as a father has a duty to save, if he can do so legitimately, even his most erring child – even if he had no duty to bring the child into being in the first place.

The tradition has been reluctant to speak of any duties on the part of God to creatures, holding with Baier that God's distributive justice must ultimately be recalled to benevolence since the creature only exists out of God's benevolence.[38] Nevertheless, the tradition has also asserted that once God does create, He cannot fail to act in a way that befits the creature's essence. To do so would be contrary to His own nature.[39] For as He loves Himself He loves all creatures proportionate to their degree of similarity to Him.[40]

When Christian thinkers have held that God has no duties to creatures, this seems to be because they were thinking of duties arising from a *debt* owed to another. God cannot owe creatures such a debt, since creatures get all they are from God, while God gets nothing from them. Even so, the rational creature's intrinsic perfection may still ground in God an obligation based on the respect that any intrinsically valuable thing demands – analogous, perhaps, to the respect a creature owes itself. This respect does not arise from any debt the creature owes itself, but out of respect for its own worth (as well as gratitude to God).

A similar point holds of the respect every rational creature owes every other rational creature. Even apart from the divine command enjoining us to love one another, and apart from the duties we have to some arising from the good they have done us (such as duties to our parents), it seems we have duties to others simply because their natures command respect.

Hence, it seems highly reasonable to suppose that God not only possesses a complacent love for creatures, but that this love generates a motive for saving those that He cannot legitimately ignore, even in the case of the most wicked. In short, this motive seems to have a universal scope that would entail, barring any contravening obligation, a divine will to save all that God can save.

IU5: A Grand Synthesis

The foregoing suggests that IU1, IU3 and IU4 all identify motives that, even within a fairly conservative Christian theology, would give God reason to will the

salvation of all. Furthermore, IU2 identifies a distinctly Christian basis for concluding that any divine motives which might *conflict* with those identified in
IU1, IU3 and IU4 have been done away with. Therefore, a species of DU that
combines all the motivations identified in IU1–IU4 would provide an essentially
conservative Christian basis for asserting that God has overlapping and mutually reinforcing motives to save all if He can, and no extant motives barring His
willing that end.

In fact, the variant of IU5 encompassing IU1–IU4 is so compelling that complete species of DU falling under it are (as we argue in Chapters 5 and 6) far
more plausible than those species of DH (namely DH1–DH3) that locate the
chief impediment to universal salvation in God's motives. As such, our disjunctive case for DU will focus exclusively on species of DU that fall under IU5.
Where our argument becomes disjunctive is in relation to God's *means* of saving
all (in the sense of converting them). We think it is on this front that philosophical advocates of DH have their strongest case. Specifically, defenders of a
'liberal' doctrine of DH can argue that, despite having moral motives that uniformly impel God to will universal salvation as an end, God will ultimately not
save all because the available *means* for achieving that end – means of converting and redeeming sinners – are either unavailable or morally impermissible. It
is at this point that our argument becomes disjunctive.

Before turning to an explicit treatment of the species of DU distinguished in
terms of the means employed by God to convert and redeem sinners, we want
to briefly summarize the specific synthesis of IU1–IU4 which we endorse
through the remainder of this book. In brief, this version of IU5 holds, first,
that whatever goodness is possessed by either the wicked or the just comes from
God Himself, thus finding its source in a divine benevolence that is not responsive to the worth of its object, but that bestows such worth. Such benevolence
would, likewise, not be conditioned by the moral worth of creatures but would
respond to the sinfulness of creatures by bestowing good where it is lacking –
that is, by seeking to redeem the wicked, since their wickedness is a vitiation
that fundamentally impedes their capacity to enjoy the ultimate human good;
namely, union with God. Hence, no conception of divine benevolence towards
the creature could include any sort of *indulgence* towards sin, but would be committed to its *eradication* – something that can only be achieved through salvation.

In the version of IU5 we favour, however, this motive for saving all is rein-
forced by God's complacent love – a love that responds to the intrinsic worth
both of creatures and Himself. In both cases, this complacent love involves
seeking to cure sinners of their wickedness. In the case of creatures, this is so
because no real love seeks to further the good of a being by enabling it to
achieve what is contrary to its ultimate end.[41] In the case of God's complacent
love for Himself, the same conclusion follows, though for different reasons.
Since God's complacent love for Himself is essentially a love of goodness, it

involves love of *whatever* is good and hatred of *whatever* is evil. Included in the love of the good is the love of the love of the good, and the hatred of the hatred of (or even indifference to) it.

God's moral nature, then, makes Him truly angry at wickedness. For all its virtues, nineteenth-century Liberal Protestantism tended to neglect this point either by taking the old doctrine of God's impassivity to its logical conclusion (Schleiermacher), or by appealing to God's eternity (Ritschl). By contrast, the subspecies of DU that we favour, IU5, sides with the more Orthodox idea that God's love involves hatred of sin and anger at sinners *insofar as they sin*. However, unlike the view that treats this wrath as a justification for damnation, IU5 asserts that God's will to save all *flows from* His judgment against wickedness (as well as from other motives). For it is only when all are saved that wickedness is stamped out entirely.

However, insofar as God's wrath against sin demands that He not merely denounce sin but also seek to overcome it, a Christian approach to universalism cannot ignore the fundamental Christian belief that this victory over sin was won on the cross. A fully Christian Universalism would therefore explain God's motive for saving all by appealing not only to the 'wrathful love' that seeks to eradicate sin in every human soul, but also to the atoning work of Christ.

A species of DU conceived in terms of these converging divine motivations, then, is what we defend in the rest of this book. What remains to be discussed is the means whereby God might achieve His will.

3.3 The Means to Save All

We turn, then, to the means God might use to save all (MU). According to this parameter for distinguishing species of DU, two possibilities present themselves:

> MU1: God saves the wicked by efficacious grace.
>
> MU2: God saves the wicked by preserving them indefinitely and working on their salvation inhibitors until such time as they accept the offer of salvation.

Because we treat each of these in detail in later chapters, (Chapters 7 and 8), we discuss them only briefly here. According to MU1, God exercises His omnipotence to directly produce the conversion and repentance of even the most recalcitrant sinners. This exercise of His power can be understood to work in various ways, which we will later explicate. Here we will only note that, whatever one thinks of efficacious grace, it must not be supposed that partisans of efficacious grace conceive of such conversions as *forced*, even in a secondary sense.

In the primary sense, one is forced to act when one has no volition in support of performing the act (and, usually, volitions opposed to it). An example might be that X has a computer chip implanted in his brain by mad scientist Y, and Y uses the chip to cause X's body to kill Z against X's will. In a secondary sense, an action can be said to be forced if it is done under duress. Take, for example, the case of the father who betrays his country because his children are being held at gunpoint by an enemy (supposing he does not *want* to betray his country). Aristotle calls such acts 'mixed' but holds that, in the circumstances in which they are done, they are voluntary because the person doing them has chosen to do so, though the person would rather not be in such circumstances.[42] The father in the case would rather not have to choose between betraying his country and letting his children be killed, since both clash with deeply held desires.

Conversions brought about by efficacious grace are not forced in either sense. They are completely voluntary: those who convert under the influence of efficacious grace do so because they want to, not due to any undesirable consequences of refusal. Their will is so wholly ordered to God by God's grace that no impulses conflict with their will to choose union with God.

It is true, however, that those who are converted by efficacious grace could not have chosen otherwise. Having received grace, they cannot summon any motive inclining them not to convert. Even so, the grace that impels conversion also renders it wholly voluntary. Furthermore, receiving efficacious grace is not something the creature *does*. Thus, a fortiori, it is not something the creature does under compulsion or duress; it is, rather, something that happens *to* the creature.

Of course, the same is true of rape, and we still want to say that a rape victim was forced. Rape is not merely something that happens to you (like catching a cold); it is something *done* to you, and so can be described as something that you are forced to *submit* to. Why can the same not be said of efficacious grace – at least in the case of those who actively resist receiving it before it has a chance to take hold?

Consider an alternative example. Suppose that you set out to contract cancer by smoking six packets of cigarettes a day, as a passive-aggressive way of committing suicide. Your lung cancer is diagnosed, friends pray for a miracle, and God intervenes to cure you. However, imagine that the reason you were suicidal was because of an undiagnosed brain tumour. In miraculously curing the lung cancer God simultaneously cures the brain tumour, and all the suicidal impulses that caused you to seek out cancer and resent your friends' prayers disappear. You are overjoyed by your new lease on life.

This case seems far closer to the imposition of efficacious grace than does the rape case. Do we want to say that, since a rape victim was *forced* to submit to sex, the cancer victim was forced to submit to the miraculous cure? The answer hinges on several factors: the scope of your right to choose what happens to you, the difference between something that is done *to* you and something that merely happens to you, the conditions under which you could be said to have really chosen at all, and the unique scope of God's authority to make decisions on your behalf (analogous, perhaps, to parents' authority to make similar decisions affecting their children). These are issues we take up in Chapter 7. For now, we simply want to note that there are views one can adopt with respect to these factors such that the bestowal of efficacious grace does *not* qualify as something to which the unregenerate are *forced to submit.*

Despite all of this, however, we acknowledge that some will have serious worries about the moral legitimacy of God's bestowing efficacious grace on creatures in order to save them – especially those who have a strong libertarian view of freedom and who attach great value to the exercise of such freedom. MU2 avoids these worries by making the case that God can guarantee the salvation of all even while strictly respecting the libertarian freedom of every creature. In Chapter 8, we argue that by preserving the unregenerate indefinitely in being while using the vast array of divine resources to liberate them from the delusions and entrenched bad habits that lead them to choose against their own good, God can bring it about that universal salvation amounts to a kind of mathematical certainty.

3.4 Complete Species of DU

We now consider how IU and MU are logically related. Our own position is that any species of the former can be combined with any species of the latter, but this is not an uncontroversial matter. It may in fact be our chief point of disagreement with those who defend the Liberal Doctrine of Hell, who would likely deny our position in one of two ways: they would deny either that a combination of IU with MU would generate a version of DU, or that IU and MU can coherently be combined at all.

The history of DH is marked by a radical shift – beginning in the seventeenth century – from the Classical Doctrine of Hell (according to which God does not will the salvation of the damned) to the Liberal Doctrine (according to which God is either morally or logically unable to save the damned despite His willing it). This shift can be conceived as a change in which aspect of a complete version of DU is being denied – IU or MU. Since, in the classical view, God does not will that the damned be saved, defenders of this view must deny that the potential motives identified in our discussion of IU are actually impelling causes for universal salvation – by denying either the veridicality of these potential motives (e.g. by denying that God is truly loving), or their impelling power (e.g. by denying that God's love gives Him reason to will universal salvation).

However, defenders of the Liberal Doctrine deny neither. They typically accept that God wills the salvation of all. What they deny is the availability to

God of a *means* for saving all – either God *cannot* save all, or He morally *may* not. While most recent defenders of DH favour the latter, Eleanor Stump appears to embrace the former:

> If, as I think and has been well argued elsewhere, it is not logically possible for God to make human beings do anything freely, and if heaven is (the state of willing only what is in accordance with God's will), then it is not within God's power to insure that all human beings will be in heaven, because it is not in his power to determine what they will.[43]

Stump's position here appears to deny both MU1 and MU2. MU1, which holds that God can, through efficacious grace, transform the will of the sinner, is declared *impossible*; and while Stump does not deny that some means, like MU2 (indefinitely pursuing the conversion of the damned), are available to God, she does deny that any such means could *guarantee* the salvation of all. However, if MU1 is impossible and MU2 is no guarantee of universalism, then neither could be combined with a species of IU to generate a version of DU – the former would express a logically impossible doctrine and the latter would express a doctrine that falls short of DU.

For those who hold that the means of saving all are *morally* impossible for God, their rejection of DU typically amounts to a denial of our claim that species of IU can be *coherently* combined with any species of MU. This point is particularly evident in the work of Jonathan Kvanvig, who defends a so-called 'issuant conception of hell', by which he means a conception of hell according to which the very same moral nature that explains God's will to save sinners also explains the damnation of some. Kvanvig insists that 'any adequate account of hell must begin with an understanding of the nature of God and present the possibilities of heaven and hell as flowing from this one nature'.[44] He then argues that such an issuant conception of hell can be generated in two ways: first, both heaven and hell could be explained by reference to the same divine attributes; second, while heaven and hell are explained by different attributes, some explanation could be offered 'as to why the attribute generating hell must predominate when the attribute generating heaven cannot'.[45]

Kvanvig himself opts for a version of the former, arguing that divine love for creatures grounds both God's desire to save all and His failure to save some.[46] Those who are damned are damned by their own choice to reject God forever; and this is a decision that God could override only by violating their self-determination – an act that would fail to love them in the appropriate way. In short, the same divine attribute that generates the impelling motive for saving all renders the means of saving all morally unavailable.

As such, Kvanvig would deny that any species of IU can be coherently combined with any species of MU. It is precisely his denial of this claim that makes possible his own 'issuant' conception of DH. While other recent defenders of DH are less explicit about the need for this sort of 'issuant' conception, the versions of DH they favour involve the same implication: an account of DU that coherently integrates a motive for universal salvation with a means to achieve it is impossible – and they embrace DH for this reason.

Hence, we cannot *assume* here that a coherent version of DU, which combines species of IU and MU, can be formulated. Showing this must be an integral part of our case for DU. Nor do we at this point wish to enumerate every possible combination of IU and MU, since we have already argued that the most satisfactory Christian conception of DU would fall under the variant of IU5 that combines all the motives identified in IU1–IU4. Hence, we content ourselves here with identifying the two complete versions of DU that will be our focus in later chapters:

> DU1: The conjunction of (the most inclusive species of) IU5 and MU1.

> DU2: The conjunction of (the most inclusive species of) IU5 and MU2.

DU1 holds that God wills universal salvation for all the reasons mentioned in IU1–IU4 and achieves this will through bestowing efficacious grace. DU2 holds that God wills universal salvation for all these reasons and achieves this will by preserving the unregenerate indefinitely in being, working on the various inhibitors to their freely accepting the offer of salvation until they accept it and are saved.

Our argument is that, depending on which assumptions are made by defenders of DH, either DU1 or DU2 is superior to the most defensible form of DH. From the foregoing discussion concerning challenges to the coherence of any form of DU, it becomes clear that this case for DU must include each of the following elements:

1. Against the Classical Doctrine, we must show that the impelling causes of universal salvation outlined in IU really have the impelling power we ascribe to them.
2. Against the Retributive Doctrine, we must show that God would not, out of retributive justice, heap on the damned pains which do not necessarily accompany loss of the beatific vision.
3. Against Stump and others who deny the possibility of God guaranteeing the salvation of all, we must show either that MU1 is metaphysically possible, or that MU2 guarantees universal salvation, or both.
4. Against Kvanvig and others who deny the moral possibility of God guaranteeing the salvation of all, we must show that there is at least one metaphysically possible means of guaranteeing universal salvation – either MU1 or MU2 (or both) – that is also morally legitimate.

In mounting our comparative defence of DU, we address each of the above in detail. In doing so, it will become clear that the problems which defenders of

DH have attributed to DU are either not problems at all, or are problems that can be resolved without requiring us to compromise central Christian teaching. However, DH does not fare as well. In its classical forms, DH thrusts upon its adherents commitments that are utterly at odds with fundamental Christian doctrines; and in any of its forms it confronts its adherents with deeply disturbing implications.

In the end, it will thus become clear that to favour DH over DU is to favour the less defensible over the more defensible, and to unnecessarily threaten the very coherence of Christianity. It is to affirm, needlessly, that God falls short either in the power that is necessary to save the unregenerate, or in the benevolent and complacent love that would inspire Him to will this end. To embrace DH over DU is therefore to confront a choice between two conceivable views of God, and to favour the view in which God is *less* loving or *less* powerful than he might be; a view in which God is needlessly denied His final and triumphant victory over sin.

CHAPTER 4

UNIVERSALISM AND THE 'PLAIN SENSE' OF SCRIPTURE

4.1 Michael Murray on the Authority of Scripture's 'Plain Sense'

Surely the most significant reason that so many Christians have favoured some version of DH over any version of DU is because they have believed Scripture clearly teaches DH. C. F. W. Walther, for example, was conscious of a deep philosophical tension between DH and his core Lutheran precepts – but because he thought that both had strong scriptural support, he resolved the tension by deliberately sacrificing philosophical consistency (even if that meant he and his fellow Missouri Synod Lutherans would be 'classified as stupid people who have abandoned all the intellectualism of their native Germany').[1] While philosopher Peter Geach was not sure that Scripture clearly supported DH, he was sure it opposed DU: 'If the Gospel account (of Christ's teachings) is even approximately correct, then it is perfectly clear that according to that teaching many men are irretrievably lost.'[2]

More recently, in his essay 'Heaven and Hell', Michael Murray has insisted that 'the most natural reading of the text of Scripture and the words of the Lord' supports a version of DH.[3] He invites readers to follow the dictum that 'if the plain sense of the text [Scripture] makes good sense, seek no other sense'.[4] He then argues that the version of DH that most closely conforms to Scripture's plain sense can be successfully defended against the charge of *not* making good sense.

Murray's invocation here of the 'plain sense' of Scripture represents an approach to deciding doctrinal questions that is common among Christians. It is, in effect, a sophisticated variant of biblical literalism which treats the literal meaning of biblical passages as prima facie authoritative: non-literal understandings are justified only if the literal sense proves untenable (or if it is clear from the text itself that a non-literal reading is intended). Since such an invocation of Scripture's 'plain sense' is likely to be the first line of response to a sustained philosophical case for DU, a deeper understanding of it will be helpful. As such, a closer look at Murray's argument may be instructive.

In reviewing Murray's argument, our primary aim is to uncover and assess the role that Scripture plays in it. We do so because we think Murray's argument offers the most plausible variant of *this* kind of appeal to Scripture – and, if acceptable, it would essentially render our arguments in later chapters irrelevant. We mean to show that such an appeal will not work for two reasons: first,

Scripture simply does not have the 'plain sense' on this matter that Murray and others attribute to it; second, even if it did, the nature of Scripture itself dictates against invoking it in the way Murray does.

Murray thinks Scripture's plain sense supports not just *some* doctrine of hell, but the view that 'those who die without Christ are judged and assigned to hell for eternity'.[5] The phrase 'to die without Christ' is ambiguous. There is a sense in which many Christians think no-one *can* die without Christ, because Christ is the companion and saviour of *all* humans whether or not they acknowledge this or subjectively enjoy its fruits. However, Murray presumably takes 'dying without Christ' in a different sense, to refer to those who do not *explicitly* embrace Christ as Lord and Saviour before death. Murray's view then becomes this: Scripture's plain sense teaches that everyone who dies without explicitly accepting Christ as Lord is immediately assigned to eternal hell. It is this view (hereafter the 'Exclusivist Elaboration' of DH) that he defends against objections.

To see how Scripture plays into Murray's argument, we need to understand two things: first, what he means by the 'plain sense' of Scripture; second, what kind of authority this plain sense carries in settling doctrinal disputes. We begin with the first issue. Does Scripture *as a whole* have a plain sense, and is this what has authority? Or does the authority also attach to discrete passages? If the former, can the plain sense of the whole conflict with the plain sense of discrete passages – and would it then trump them? If the notion of plain sense attaches to discrete passages, do these passages gain some of their plain sense from how they are related to the whole? Or is their plain sense whatever meaning most immediately emerges apart from such contextual reading?

Since Murray makes no effort to indicate what 'the whole' says about our eternal destinies (instead merely referencing three one-verse Scripture passages and one two-verse passage in a footnote[6]), he clearly attaches authority to discrete passages and not just to the whole. Also, since he makes no effort to understand isolated passages in terms of how they relate to the whole, it seems he thinks discrete passages have a plain sense *apart from* such a holistic interpretation. While he does not preclude such interpretation, it does not seem to be what gives a passage its *plain* sense; rather, such interpretation is presumably what is done when the 'plain sense does not make good sense'.

What we have, then, is an understanding of Scriptural authority which holds that the plain sense of a discrete passage, read in isolation, is authoritative unless it can be shown not to make good sense – in which case an interpretation of the passage, perhaps in the light of Scripture's overarching themes, is warranted. The question then becomes what it means for the plain sense to 'make good sense'. In other words, what are the conditions under which the plain sense of a scriptural passage is *not* authoritative?

In answering this, it might help to examine how Murray addresses objections to the coherence of the Exclusivist Elaboration of DH (which he takes to be taught by Scripture's plain sense). For us, the most striking observation is just how light Murray takes his burden of proof to be. Specifically, he believes this burden has been met, and the plain sense of Scripture vindicated, just in case he has shown that allegiance to Scripture's plain sense does not force one to affirm something known to be false – even if it *does* force one to affirm some staggeringly improbable claims.

Consider Murray's response to an important objection to the Exclusivist Elaboration of DH – what we will call the Objection from Human Ignorance. According to it, a policy of damning all who fail to explicitly accept Christ is unjust in a world where so many who have lived over the last millennia have never even *heard* of Christ. Given the Exclusivist Elaboration, God has made avoiding hell contingent on a choice that many were in no position to make. In short, the objection affirms the following:

> HI1: It is unjust to condemn someone to eternal suffering for failing to choose something that they would have chosen had they been able to choose.

While Murray accepts HI1, he notes that it does not entail the injustice of God in the Exclusivist Elaboration without a further premise, which can be articulated as follows:

> HI2: At least some of the millions who died never hearing the gospel message would have accepted it had they heard it.

Taken together, HI1 and HI2 entail that the Exclusivist Elaboration of DH is incompatible with God's perfect justice. Murray sketches out three responses to this objection – but his primary response, following a strategy proposed by William Lane Craig, calls into question HI2.[7] 'For all we know,' Murray says, 'those who never hear are such that were they to hear, they would not believe anyway.' Under this assumption 'God has not done anything unjust or unloving in not letting them hear in the first place. He has just allowed to happen what would have happened no matter what'.[8]

In other words, *if* we assume that none of those who never heard would have believed had they heard, God's justice is reconciled with the Exclusivist Elaboration. Granted this, what Murray takes to be the plain sense of Scripture is vindicated.

But what, precisely, does granting this assumption involve? Historically, the gospel has been more widely disseminated in some parts of the world than in others and more widely available at some times than at others. In all those times and places where the gospel message was not heard, Murray asks us to assume that not a single person among the millions would have come to believe.

The truth of this assumption would be impossible to test – something Murray happily acknowledges, noting that 'we can never have evidence' that 'those who *never* hear' the gospel 'would respond if they heard'.[9] Nor (we might add) can we ever have direct evidence that they would not. On inductive grounds, however, the assumption that Murray invokes is decidedly improbable. In each place that Christianity has been introduced, there have been converts. Murray would have us assume that in every generation *before* the Europeans arrived in the New World to begin their evangelistic efforts, not a single Native American would have been successfully evangelized. This seems far less plausible on the inductive evidence than the contrary assumption that at least some would have been converted had evangelistic efforts started sooner.

Furthermore, if we assume (as Christians do) that there is an intrinsic appeal to the gospel message given its divine source, it is hard to imagine that in any large population, selected entirely in terms of temporal and geographic location, the gospel message would not encounter a single receptive ear. What could explain universal and total resistance to the power of God's Word by an entire population of people in a particular geographic location at a particular time, when fifty years later that same population admitted of a more receptive audience? It seems to belittle the power of divine grace operating through the gospel proclamation. Furthermore, such universal rejection in such a large population would defy common sense *unless* there was something about the environment in that time and place which determined the population in its fixed resistance to the gospel's appeal. In that case, however, they would not have been free to believe – and the same problems of injustice would thus arise in a different form.

Furthermore, there are distinctly moral objections to Murray's assumption. Through most of Christian history, East Asia, Africa, and the Americas have been largely or wholly cut off from exposure to the gospel message. Where there was extensive exposure to it (as in Europe), Christianity became the dominant religion. If we add to these facts Murray's assumption – to the effect that no single East Asian, African or Native American would have been successfully converted in the centuries prior to European colonial expansion – it is hard to avoid the conclusion that there is something essentially different between Europeans and others which renders Europeans somehow more intrinsically responsive to God's Word. Such an implication is morally appalling.

In short, inductive, theological, and moral arguments all speak against Murray's assumption. In brief, we might say it defies common sense. Nevertheless, there is no way to prove that it is false. Thus, we have two unprovable alternatives – although one is vastly more appealing to common sense and, if accepted, would lead us to reject the Exclusivist Elaboration of DH.[10] Murray defends the Exclusivist Elaboration by asking us to reject common sense in favour of an assumption that verges on preposterousness. Of course, our common sense *could* be mistaken, but that hardly justifies ignoring it. We need more than that: an authority greater than common sense telling us that our common sense *is* mistaken. Without such an authority, Murray's response to the Objection from Human Ignorance is untenable.

Murray, however, thinks he has such an authority – namely, the 'plain sense' of Scripture. This, ultimately, is what justifies such a weak reply to the Objection from Human Ignorance: while its conclusion is endorsed by common sense, the contrary conclusion is endorsed by Scripture's plain sense. Thus, it becomes clear that when Murray says that we should follow Scripture's plain sense unless it does not make 'good sense', he is assuming a difference between *good* sense and *common* sense as conceived here. If Murray is right about what the plain sense of Scripture teaches, then its plain sense requires us to set aside otherwise strong inductive, theological and moral concerns. What, then, could lead us to conclude that Scripture's plain sense *does not* make good sense? It seems that the plain sense of Scripture can be rejected only on the basis of valid arguments whose premises are derived from a source *at least as authoritative* as the plain sense of Scripture. Indeed it turns out – given the above analysis – that little qualifies as such a source. Presumably basic principles of logic – such as the principle of non-contradiction – *do* qualify; but what else might? The only other obvious candidate would be Scripture itself. If the plain sense of one passage conflicts with that of another, we are forced to interpret one or the other in a way that deviates from its plain sense.

What if the plain sense of a passage conflicts with an established theological principle that, while not directly posited in a scriptural passage, became established because of its utility in *interpreting* and *unifying* numerous scriptural passages? What about doctrines *implied* by such principles? Or what about the 'self-evident' principles – such as the principle of sufficient reason – used so extensively by medieval theologians?

Clearly, Murray's dictum concerning Scripture's plain sense needs elaboration. However, even apart from such elaboration, this dictum clearly lends such authority to the plain sense of discrete scriptural passages that – if Murray and others are right that 'the plain sense of Scripture' univocally supports some version of DH – even a very strong philosophical case favouring DU over DH will prove uncompelling. 'You have shown that DU is far more likely to be true *on the non-scriptural evidence*,' Murray might say, 'But so what? So long as DH *could* be true (as far as we know), we should embrace it on the authority of Scripture's plain sense.'

Thus, if we want our arguments to speak to those who, like Murray, give Scripture's plain sense such weight, we must establish one of three things: (1) based on principles that even someone with Murray's views must agree have more authority than Scripture's plain sense, DH cannot be true. (2) The plain sense of Scripture cannot carry the degree of authority that Murray and those like him wish to attribute to it. (3) The plain sense of Scripture is not as plain on this issue as Murray and others contend.

While we are strongly tempted to claim that the arguments presented in subsequent chapters succeed in establishing (1), the ease with which thinkers such as Murray are willing to saddle themselves with intuitively implausible assumptions in order to save what they take to be the plain sense of Scripture suggests that what appears to us to be incontrovertible may not appear so through the lens of this view of Scripture. Thus, relying on (1) alone is ill-advised.

Point (2) is an appealing approach, since we think there are few good reasons to embrace Murray's view of scriptural authority and many reasons not to do so. This is not to say that we do not accord great authority to Scripture; rather, it is to say that its authority should be conceived differently than Murray conceives it. However, rather than pursue (2) on its own, we will do so as an outgrowth of pursuing (3). An unbiased review of Scripture will, we think, reveal that the relevant scriptural passages, in their plain sense, are hardly unanimous in supporting DH. On the contrary, many have a plain sense that supports DU.

4.2 A Review of Scripture

One difficulty with assessing the plain sense of Scripture is this: if anything has authority, it is the plain sense of the original Greek, Hebrew and Aramaic texts. Translation involves interpretation. As such, any attempt to discuss the plain sense of Scripture in modern Christian communities, in which only a few experts have the language skills to access the original texts, is immediately suspect. Relying on any English translation of the Bible is relying on the authority of a group of experts who can and do disagree, as evidenced by variations among the English translations produced by scholars who were commissioned based on their expertise.

Questioning those experts and their translations has played an important role in challenging the hegemony of DH over DU. Consider the only text from Paul's epistles whose plain sense seems to support DH; namely 2 Thessalonians 1.8-9: 'He will punish those who do not know God and do not obey the gospel of our lord Jesus. They will be punished with everlasting destruction and shut out from the presence of the Lord and from the majesty of his power.' Several scholars suggest that this passage's apparent support for DH may result from a series of unfortunate translational decisions. Here is how one biblical scholar sums it up:

> The Greek simply says, 'they will be punished with eternal destruction *from (apo)* the presence of the Lord.' The word *apo* could be translated as 'away from' ... or 'coming from', depending on context. Following Gene Green and Tom Talbott, I suggest that the context favours the translation 'coming from' – the destruction comes from the presence of Jesus.
>
>   Second, the punishment is 'eternal destruction' (*olethron aiōnion*). How are we to understand this expression? Well, we note first that the adjective *aiōnion* suggests that the destruction referred to is the 'destruction of the age to come' (not *everlasting* destruction), and thus the phrase need not carry any connotations of eternal conscious suffering. Second, the word *olethron* can mean 'ruin' or 'destruction', depending on the context.[11]

The argument continues with the observation that while Paul uses *olethron* rarely (and in different ways) his use of it in 1 Corinthians 5.5 is clearly meant to describe a punishment that is intended to be good for the person being punished, even if it is painful.[12] The result is that a passage which has a plain sense supporting DH in standard English translations does not have such a plain sense in the Greek. It *could* be referring to a punishment that *comes* from the Lord and which may *not* be everlasting and may *not* involve total destruction (and may even be reformatory in nature) – hardly an unambiguous endorsement of DH.

Nevertheless, our strategy here will not be to systematically question the correctness of the translations of the relevant 'hell texts', for several reasons. The first is humility: we cannot even pretend to have the language skills of the scholars who developed the NIV translation (upon which we rely here) and other standard translations. Second, we mean to offer arguments that can be assessed by any intelligent English speaker, not just a few qualified specialists. Third, Scripture's plain sense can guide us only if it is accessible. If it is not sufficiently accessible even to those reputable scholars who are trusted to offer translations to the English-speaking world, then that fact alone undercuts the claim that we can verify DH by an appeal to Scripture's plain sense.

None of this means that translational difficulties are irrelevant; but, at the end of the day, even the most subtle exegesis of the 'hell' texts in light of the original languages will leave *some* passages whose plain sense supports DH. Our point is that this is hardly decisive support for DH, since there are other texts whose plain sense clearly supports DU.

Before turning to these passages, we should note that many passages commonly invoked to support DH do not actually do so. The judgment that they do is based on several mistakes. The first is to confuse passages that clearly imply that some will experience post-mortem suffering or punishment with passages that support DH. A doctrine maintaining that some will, in a post-mortem state, suffer either punishment for sin or alienation from God is entirely compatible with DU – so long as the post-mortem suffering is *finite*. To support DH on scriptural grounds, one needs passages whose plain sense indicates that some are *never* saved – that some endure *eternal* punishment.

One supposed 'hell' text that suffers from this problem is the parable of Lazarus and the rich man in Luke 16.22-26. When the rich man, who refuses to help the beggar Lazarus, dies and finds himself in a place of torment, his pleas for succour are rejected, and he is informed that 'between us and you a great chasm has been fixed, so that those who want to go from here to you cannot, nor can anyone cross over from there to us'. To suppose that this 'chasm' image supports the notion of *eternal* hell is clearly to read more into the parable than is given by its 'plain sense'. While it is obvious that *so long as the chasm is in place* the rich man cannot join Abraham and Lazarus in heaven (nor will the blessed be able to reach down to him), that this chasm will be in place *forever* – while widely assumed – is nowhere indicated. This assumption is imposed on the text by those already convinced that the sufferings of hell are eternal (perhaps based on other texts – though if so, it is these other texts that support DH, not the Lazarus parable).[13]

Another common 'hell' text that suffers from a similar problem is the parable of the wheat and the weeds in Matthew 13.24-43. While this parable indicates that the weeds – which represent 'everything that causes sin and all who do evil' – will be thrown 'into the fiery furnace, where there will be weeping and gnashing of teeth', it does not indicate that the suffering will be eternal. Although Jesus offers a partial interpretation of the parable, considerable ambiguity remains. The image of weeds suggests something fragile that would be utterly destroyed by fire. If this is given weight, a doctrine of annihilationism would follow. However, this conclusion is belied by the image of 'weeping and gnashing of teeth', which suggests ongoing existence in the flames.

To highlight the problem with saying that the plain sense of this passage supports DH, it may help to consider a universalist reading of it, according to which the 'weeds' represent those so in bondage to sin that they *identify* with their sinful dispositions. The 'wheat' represents those who, while corrupted by sin, no longer identify with it. Both are subjected to the purging fire of divine love which rejects and burns away their sin. For those in the latter group, the purging is a welcome liberation. For those of the former, it is torment because it feels as if *they* are being burned; that by rejecting their sin God is rejecting *them*. Eventually, however, that fire of rejection utterly consumes the false identity, allowing the true identity to emerge from the ashes. The 'evildoer' is destroyed. In their place stands the purified Child of God.

Is this reading of the parable any less true to the text's plain sense than one which takes 'wailing and gnashing of teeth' to be the permanent state of those who remain in bondage to sin on judgment day? Both interpretations go beyond the plain sense, attaching meaning in terms of a more richly developed theology. While the elaborations implying DH have support in other scriptural texts, the same can be said for those elaborations which imply DU (consider Psalm 30.5).

The second major mistake when using Scripture to assess this issue is to assume that DH is implied by passages imposing conditions on entry into the Kingdom of Heaven. Claiming that entry into heaven is barred to those who fail to meet certain conditions is consistent with universal salvation, since it is possible that eventually everyone will meet the indicated conditions. While 1 Corinthians 6.9-10 (and, similarly, Ephesians 5.5) indicates that certain classes of sinners 'will not inherit the kingdom of God', Paul is quick to point out, in 1 Corinthians 11 (and, similarly, in Ephesians 5.8), that his readers were once classed among such sinners. Thus, being classed among such sinners, while a bar on entry into God's Kingdom, is not a fixed state – the bar can be lifted.

The third mistake is to assume that passages referring to God's power to inflict eternal punishment imply, by themselves, that God will use that power to eternally damn anyone. Consider Matthew 10.28: 'Do not be afraid of those who kill the body but cannot kill the soul. Rather, be afraid of the One who can destroy both soul and body in hell.' Although this passage is suggestive, it is a straightforward logical error to take it to imply, in isolation from other passages, that 'the One who *can* destroy both soul and body in hell' *will* ever do so (which DH denies in any event, since it holds that God *preserves the creature in being* while it endures damnation – in this sense the passage seems more in tune with DA).[14]

Of course, one might argue that this text's immediate context justifies reading it in hellist terms, since the immediate context has the form of a warning; but if we use context to shape our interpretation, why stop at the immediate context? Why not note that the larger context is one in which Jesus is speaking encouragement and comfort to His disciples? (v. 31 reads, 'So don't be afraid; you are worth more than many sparrows', referencing v. 29, in which Jesus notes that God uses His power to hold the sparrows aloft). Better yet, why not interpret the passage in terms of Scripture as a whole – including the redemptive arc of the gospel story, and Paul's apparent universalism (sketched out below)? If we do *that*, will it still be obvious that the passage should be read to say God that *will* destroy some 'in both soul and body in hell'?

Put another way, advocates of a 'plain sense' reading of Scripture want to attach authority to the plain sense of *isolated* texts – but is there really such a thing, or is the plain sense always partly a *function* of context? If so, we must always look to context to discern meaning, and as soon as we do this we must ask how much context is enough. This pushes us in the direction of a holistic understanding of Scripture in which isolated passages always need to be read in the light of the whole (which is the view we ultimately defend). In any event, Matthew 10.28 has no clear implications for DH apart from context – and the implications of context depend partly on how much context we invoke.

Therefore, none of these passages have an isolated 'plain sense' that supports DH. Are there any that do? We think so. Aside from 2 Thessalonians 1.8-9, three passages in particular deserve mention:

> Matthew 25.31-46 (sheep and goats parable), esp. 32-33, 41, and 46: All the nations will be gathered before him, and he will separate the people one from another as a shepherd separates the sheep from the goats. He will put the sheep on his right and the goats on his left ... Then he will say to those on his left, 'Depart from me, you who are cursed, into the eternal fire prepared for the devil and his angels ...' Then they will go away to eternal punishment, but the righteous to eternal life.

Luke 13.23-28: Someone asked him, 'Lord, are only a few people going to be saved?' He said to them, 'Make every effort to enter through the narrow door, because many, I tell you, will try to enter and will not be able to. Once the owner of the house gets up and closes the door, you will stand outside knocking and pleading, "Sir, open the door for us." But he will answer, "I don't know you or where you come from." Then you will say, "We ate and drank with you, and you taught in our streets." But he will reply, "I don't know you or where you come from. Away from me, all you evildoers!" There will be weeping there, and gnashing of teeth, when you see Abraham, Isaac and Jacob and all the prophets in the kingdom of God, but you yourselves thrown out.'

Revelation 14.9-11: A third angel followed them and said in a loud voice: 'If anyone worships the beast and his image and receives his mark on the forehead or on the hand, he, too, will drink of the wine of God's fury, which has been poured full strength into the cup of his wrath. He will be tormented with burning sulfur in the presence of the holy angels and of the Lamb. And the smoke of their torment rises for ever and ever. There is no rest day or night for those who worship the beast and his image, or for anyone who receives the mark of his name.' (See also a similar passage in Revelation 20.10-15).

A straightforward reading of these passages would suggest that some are *never* saved – that some are *forever* shut out of God's Kingdom. Of course, even these passages could be *interpreted* in ways amenable to DU.[15] However, whatever interpretation we might give in the light of Scripture as a whole, their plain sense, taken in *isolation*, supports DH. Does it therefore follow that the plain sense of *Scripture* supports DH?

No. What follows is that the plain sense of these texts, *taken in isolation*, supports DH, but we need not look far to find passages whose isolated plain sense supports DU. Consider the following:

Lamentations 3.22 and 3.31-33: Because of the Lord's great love we are not consumed, for his compassions never fail ... For men are not cast off by the Lord forever. Though he brings grief, he will show compassion, so great is his unfailing love. For he does not willingly bring affliction or grief to the children of men.

John 12.30-32: Jesus said, 'This voice was for your benefit, not mine. Now is the time for judgment on this world; now the prince of this world will be driven out. But I, when I am lifted up from the earth, will draw all men to myself.'

Romans 5.18-19: Consequently, just as the result of one trespass was condemnation for all men, so also the result of one act of righteousness was justification that brings life for all men. For just as through the disobedience of the one man the many were made sinners, so also through the obedience of the one man the many will be made righteous.

Romans 11.32: For God has bound all men over to disobedience so that he may have mercy on them all.

1 Corinthians 15.22. For as in Adam all die, so in Christ all will be made alive.

1 Corinthians 15.28: When he [God] has done this [subjected all things to him], then the Son himself will be made subject to him who put everything under him, so that God may be all in all. (or, in the Revised Standard Version: 'that God may be everything to every one.')

Colossians 1.19-20. For God was pleased to have all his fullness dwell in him [Christ], and through him to reconcile to himself all things, whether things on earth or things in heaven, by making peace through his blood, shed on the cross.

Of course, these passages can be interpreted in ways that defy their immediate universalist meanings. John Murray, for example, seeks to place restrictions on the scope of 'all' in 1 Corinthians 15.22 and Romans 5.18 so as to make them fit with DH – by, among other things, arguing that the second 'all' refers only to those 'who are Christ's'.[16] Thomas Talbott, in turn, forcefully challenges the adequacy of Murray's interpretive efforts.[17] However, for the point we are making here, these interpretive disputes are not telling.[18] Whatever else can be said of John Murray's interpretations of Romans 5.18 and 1 Corinthians 15.22, they clearly defy the *plain sense* of these passages. If we look to *that*, without bringing prior commitments to the text, the straightforward message is that all are saved. In the most direct reading, the phrase 'in Christ' in the Corinthian passage qualifies *how* all are saved, not (as Murray wants to say) that only those who are in Christ are saved. The non-universalist reading of this text seems to rest on the failure to acknowledge that literally all humans might be reconciled to Christ, and that it is on account of this universal reconciliation that all will be made alive. On the assumption that of course only *some* will be reconciled, the *plain sense* of both Romans 5.18 and Corinthians 15.22 is distorted.

Such distortion is unavoidable if we seek to bring these passages into harmony with others whose plain sense supports DH. In fact, John Murray comes to his interpretation of Paul's universalist texts with the assumption that Paul could not have intended the clear universalist reading, since other passages in Paul clearly support DH (most notably 2 Thessalonians 1.8-9). However, one might as readily come to the interpretation of 2 Thessalonians 1.8-9 (especially given the translational issues already discussed) with the assumption that Paul could not have intended the most obvious non-universalist reading, since so many passages in Paul clearly support DU.[19] This is the point we want to make about approaching this issue by appealing to Scripture's plain sense: among the texts which have an obvious 'plain sense', we find contradictory messages. At best, the plain sense of *some* passages support DH, while that of *others* supports DU.[20]

4.3 Implications for Scriptural Interpretation and Authority

It is therefore evident that if we take the plain sense of Scripture as our authority, we are left without a solution to our question because the relevant passages are at odds. Thus, we *must* interpret some texts in ways that deviate from their plain sense – but which texts should be interpreted, and how, and on what basis? Simply looking at isolated texts will not give us the answer. We need a biblical hermeneutic.

Here is the crucial point: in order for the interpretive hermeneutic demanded by conflicts among Scriptural passages to have the authority to adjudicate among the competing passages by interpreting (or even rejecting) some of them, the hermeneutic *must have the authority to override Scripture's plain sense.* Such authority, however, cannot be piecemeal – we cannot consistently invoke this hermeneutic to adjudicate conflicting passages unless we are willing for it to override the plain sense of Scripture *in all cases where that is called for by the hermeneutics' own logic.* This means that it is not the *plain sense* of Scripture that has authority, but the sense attained by subjecting the text to the appropriate hermeneutic (although the appropriate hermeneutic might be derived from a comprehensive reading of Scripture, and may have to be continually refined in the light of careful scriptural study).

Simply put, a careful study of Scripture's substance reveals that its plain sense cannot coherently carry the authority biblical literalists want to attach to it – thus forcing us to look beyond the plain sense of isolated texts for guidance on what to believe. We have already seen this in relation to clashing texts on universalism and hell; but it is also apparent on a broader reading, which reveals Scripture to be a disparate collection of writings – literary, historical, theological and mythological. Treating their 'plain sense' as the most fundamental authority threatens to generate a fragmented and disjointed theology with no clear centre – turning the Christian gospel into but one fragment – one patch in a patchwork quilt – rather than the thread that binds everything together.

In fact, the same problem emerges if we adopt *any* view of Scripture according to which every passage of the Bible has the same kind of revelatory significance. As Andrew Fairbairn puts it: 'To attempt to make a multitude of books, into a single uniform authority, when almost all the books are, from the nature of the case, of different values, is the surest way to discredit even the most authoritative.'[21] Gustaf Aulen asserts that it is 'really very obvious' that not every passage of Scripture is equally revelatory. Aulen notes that 'if every syllable in the Bible is equally inspired, all statements have the same binding authority, since there can be no different degrees in divine authority'. The outcome, Aulen thinks, is the dissolution of Christianity itself:

> When the theory of verbal inspiration breaks down and proves itself useless for the validation of the Christian affirmations of faith, the reason is that, consistently applied, it does not lead to a verification, but rather to a dissolution, of the Christian character of that theology which builds on this foundation. If the theory of verbal inspiration were taken seriously, it would obviously imply that the divine revelation in Christ is equated with every other 'biblical revelation'. But this would also mean that the revelation in Christ ceases to be what the Christian faith affirms that it is, namely, that standard by which all divine revelation is measured and judged.[22]

While Aulen's insight here is important, it may not undermine *any* version of plenary verbal inspiration. Clearly, to preserve the Christian character of Scripture, some passages must be given a central authority not given to others; but one might hold that every passage of Scripture is what God wanted written without insisting that every passage propositionally expresses a divinely revealed truth. A liberal thinker might, for example, affirm plenary verbal inspiration while denying inerrancy by, for example, insisting that God inspired some biblical authors to express mistaken cultural biases in order to ensure that reverence for Scripture does not degenerate into idolatrous Bible worship. A more moderate thinker might endorse plenary verbal inspiration while acknowledging that Scripture encompasses diverse literary forms – and that inspired poetry has a different function than inspired theology, and both have a different function than inspired parables.

The mistake, then, is not so much accepting verbal inspiration as it is assuming that every Scriptural passage has the same kind of *status*. It would be as much a mistake to treat every scriptural passage as a theological proposition whose content must be included in one's theology, as it would be to treat every scriptural passage as poetry whose literal sense must be subordinated to its aesthetic and emotive content. Even if God inspired every passage of Scripture, it does not follow that every passage expresses a Christian doctrine, let alone one that is literally veridical. That way of equating all scriptural passages clearly falls prey to Aulen's criticism.

Whether or not one accepts some modified form of verbal inspiration, Aulen's remarks embody two important insights. First, if the goal is to develop genuinely *Christian* theology, one cannot treat every passage of Scripture as having the same revelatory significance *for theology*.[23] Second, even among passages that are roughly theological in character (which might be determinable only through a critical and holistic reading of Scripture), devotion to Christ demands that some passages be afforded a normative centrality lacking in others, with the former employed to interpret the latter.

But if we can neither simply accept the plain sense of scriptural texts nor assume that each has the same revelatory significance, how should we determine an appropriate hermeneutic? Such a hermeneutic must offer the resources to decide which passages must be interpreted to fit with others, and (perhaps) which should play no role at all in developing doctrine.

In making his point about the inadequacy of a strict biblicism, Aulen was reaching back to Martin Luther. Perhaps, then, a solution can be found in the same place.

Luther revered Scripture, regarding it as the fundamental authority for the Christian understanding of God's revelation to the world. As Paul Althaus notes, Luther took Scripture to serve the crucial function, in the life of the church, of preserving the 'normative apostolic message' that might otherwise be 'heretically distorted' over time if the gospel were transmitted by word of mouth alone.[24] Scripture thus serves as the 'standard by which (congregations) may criticize and correct' those human teachers who may 'fail and become false teachers'.[25] This is precisely the function that Scripture served for Luther as he challenged the Roman Catholic teachings of his day – and it could not have done so had he not respected it as a profound authority.

However, for Luther, the reverent insistence that Scripture is our ultimate authority was juxtaposed against a critical perspective that even included a willingness to disparage whole books of the Bible (such as the epistle of James). Reinhold Seeberg offers a telling catalogue of Luther's critical remarks about Scripture:

> (Luther) asserts that the text of the prophesies has fallen into confusion; the discourses were presumably not committed to writing until afterward, and then by redactors (63. 57, 74; 62. 123). The prophets were often in error (*fehlten*), when they prophesied of worldly events (*von weltichen Lauften*) (E. 8. 23). The books of the Kings are more trustworthy than the Chronicles (62. 132). By whom Genesis was composed, is a matter of indifference (57. 35). It would be better if the book of Esther were not in the canon (op. ex. 7. 195. E. 62. 131). The composition of Ecclesiastes by Solomon is doubted (E. 62. 128). The reports of the synoptic gospels are not of uniform value (30. 314, 331; 14. 319). The Epistle of Jude is derived from the second Epistle of Peter (63. 159). The Epistle of Hebrews errs, in denying a second repentance (ib. 155), 'and is apparently composed of many parts'. James wrote 'a right strawy epistle ... for it has certainly no evangelical character about it' (ib. 115), *i.e.*, 'he teaches nothing' about Christ, and connects righteousness with works (156 f.). He even says: 'James talks wildly' (*delirat*) (op. ex. 4. 328. W. 2. 425).[26]

This is only a partial catalogue. What these remarks reveal is a scholar approaching Scripture in much the same way that a scholar might approach *any* text – willing to question received conventions about authorship, prepared to challenge theological claims, and so on. How can such a critical approach be reconciled with a reverent commitment to scriptural authority? The answer lies in the fact that Luther viewed Scripture's authority as derivative. Luther's ultimate allegiance was to Christ, and he took Scripture to have authority only to the extent that it testifies to Christ:

> as Christ himself says in John 15, 'You shall bear witness to me'. All the genuine sacred books agree in this, that all of them preach and inculcate Christ. And that is the true test by which to judge all books, when we see whether or not they inculcate Christ ... Whatever does not teach Christ is not apostolic, even though St. Peter or St. Paul does the teaching. Again, whatever preaches Christ would be apostolic, even if Judas, Annas, Pilate, and Herod were doing it.[27]

Christ, then, becomes the focus for all biblical interpretation. As Richard Muller puts it: 'The center of Scripture – the rule by which the message of Scripture is known to be authoritative – is the redemptive significance of Christ at the very heart of God's saving revelation.' For Muller, as for Luther and others, the 'work of Christ' becomes 'the heuristic key to the unity of the authoritative or canonical Scriptures'.[28]

In fact, there seems to be no better *Christian* principle for biblical interpretation. If the problem with crass biblicism is that it fails, as Aulen notes, to do justice to Christ's centrality to the Christian faith, then the solution is to build a

hermeneutic around precisely that centre. If one's understanding of Scripture
is to be a *Christian* one, one must look to the central Christian story of Christ
crucified and resurrected for humanity's redemption. When we do this, our
understanding of the nature of scriptural authority diverges radically from that
of the literalist. As Seeberg puts it in relation to Luther:

> There thus results an entirely new conception of the authority and inspiration of the
> Scriptures. Their specific content, in both the Old and the New Testaments, is Christ,
> with his office and kingdom. It is this content in which faith is interested, and which faith
> verifies by inner experience. This is therefore the important thing in the Scriptures. It
> must accordingly be the impelling motive in the special divine agency which gave the
> Scriptures their peculiar character. In other words, the testimony of the Holy Spirit in
> the Scriptures is the testimony to the great facts of salvation and redemption. This is the
> purpose of their inspiration, and in proportion as they fulfill it do they substantiate their
> claim to be regarded as an authority in matters of religion.[29]

The Lutheran view of Scripture as a *means* of grace, alongside the sacraments,
emerges quite naturally out of this view. Scripture's authority does not reside in
the supposed inerrancy of every passage, but in its suitability as a means of
bringing believers into relationship with Christ. What believers encounter in
Scripture is *Christ*, not merely a series of infallible propositions – and Scripture
can facilitate such an encounter even if it contains propositions that are unclear,
misleading or false (although it would surely fail to do this if its content were
largely unclear, misleading or false). Thus, Luther likens the Bible to the manger in which the baby Jesus lay. It contains the gospel – but it may also contain
straw. Indeed, there may be whole 'epistles of straw'. Nevertheless, Luther sees
Scripture as the final Christian authority because it is, in Seeberg's words, 'the
primitive and original testimony to Christ and his salvation'.[30]

Many Christians may be troubled by Luther's willingness to disparage whole
books of the Bible. In this regard, the thoughts of Althaus on Luther are helpful
– he notes that for Luther 'Christ is the Lord and the King of the Scripture, and
the individual passages of Scripture are his servants ... And one should not be
loyal to the servants but rather to the Lord.'[31] Still, it seems that Christians
should presume, at least prima facie, that Scripture is a *loyal* servant which
authentically furthers the master's cause. Otherwise Scripture would fail to
provide what, according to Luther, Scripture is intended to provide: a normative apostolic expression of the gospel that can both bring believers into relationship with Christ and prevent distortions of the gospel message that might
lead them away from Christ.

Luther did not deny this. His point, rather, was this: if we have to choose
between master and servant, we must choose the master. Thus, Althaus understands Luther's dismissal of James in the following way: '[Luther] explains that
he had been previously accustomed to interpreting the Letter of James according to the meaning of the rest of Holy Scripture ... Since, however, some did

not allow the validity of his interpretation of this passage, he simply said, "Away with James."'[32] Althaus takes the disparagement of James as a symbolic act of allegiance – a dramatic portrayal of the precept that it is better to disparage a whole book of the Bible than to disparage Christ.

In general terms, if we find ourselves unable to find an interpretation of a scriptural passage that is consistent with the core message that we are saved through Christ's redemptive work, Luther would advise us to leave it out of our theology rather than distort the gospel. Where interpretation fails us, *criticism* is preferable to blind appropriation; but both interpretation and criticism express a deeper devotion to Scripture *as a whole*. Thus, Luther took Scripture to be *its own* interpreter and critic: he thought it was Scripture itself that provides the Christocentric hermeneutic by which individual passages are interpreted, criticized or even jettisoned if that is what is required. For Luther, it is more true to Scripture to cling to its Christocentrism than to its inerrancy.[33]

Of course inerrantists can argue that *criticism* of Scripture, as opposed to interpretation, is called for at all only due to shortcomings in our interpretive resources. However, Luther's point is that we are *more* faithful to Scripture when we reject those passages that, given our best interpretive efforts, conflict with the gospel message of redemption through Christ than we are when we allow devotion to inerrancy to distort this message.

Whatever else might be said about inerrancy, once Scripture is seen fundamentally as a means of bringing us into a personal encounter with the Christ of the gospel story, the need for inerrancy wanes. While Scripture would have to be reliable *overall* as a witness to God's redemptive work in order to mediate a transformative encounter with Christ, such reliability does not demand that every passage be inerrant, and it certainly does not require that the plain sense of each passage be prima facie correct. If the heart of Scripture is the message that God has acted in history through Christ to save a fallen humanity and reconcile the world to Himself – and if the purpose of the Scriptures is to mediate a personal encounter with this saviour who was not defeated by death and so is not merely a character in history but a living presence in whom we can place out trust – then the question of whether, for instance, Samson *really* slew a thousand Philistine soldiers wielding nothing but a donkey's jawbone becomes of little importance.

4.4 *Significance*

What are the lessons of this essentially Lutheran approach to Scripture for our task of assessing the relative merits of DH and DU? First, the kind of authority Scripture possesses in Luther's scheme does not *depend* on inerrancy. If there are reasons to ascribe to inerrancy, the need to uphold scriptural authority is not one of them. Whatever one thinks of inerrancy, the view that the plain sense of Scripture is inerrant cannot be sustained in the light of passages that, in their plain sense, conflict with one another. Thus, we cannot settle the controversy between DU and DH by a simple appeal to scriptural texts.

Second, the central Christian revelation in Scripture is not the isolated propositions expressed *by* the text but the *person of Christ* and the saving work of Christ encountered *through* the text. In George MacDonald's words, the Bible 'nowhere lays claim to be regarded as the Word, the Way, the Truth. The Bible leads us to Jesus, the inexhaustible, the ever-unfolding revelation of God. "It is Christ in whom are hid all the treasures of wisdom and knowledge", not the Bible, save as leading to Him.'[34]

What emerges here is a view in which Scripture's primary function is not establishing doctrine, but a living relationship with God. If so, then given the project of this book – to examine the merits of rival doctrines – one might think the proper lesson is that the Bible should be set aside entirely, since settling this sort of matter simply is not what the Bible is *for*. However, this is not our position. If Scripture mediates an encounter with Christ, it does so by presenting the reader with the story of Christ, the religious and historical context out of which Christ emerged, the teachings of Christ and – in Paul's writings – a seminal theological account of the significance of Christ's life, death and resurrection. We encounter Christ not as an abstract figure, but as a concrete person with a history, purpose and significance for our lives.

To say that the Christ encountered through the text is more than just a description on a page is not to deny that there is indeed a description. To say that Scripture mediates an encounter with a saviour that transcends the page is not to say that this encounter has no implications for how we understand what is *on* the page. Out of such living engagement with Scripture, Christian doctrine is born. Even if the Bible's revelation cannot be reduced to a series of static propositions, it does not follow that the lessons drawn from vital engagement with the text cannot be formulated into doctrines which we can meaningfully say that 'Scripture has revealed'.

The task of Christian theology is the task not only of drawing doctrines from Scripture and from the encounter with Christ that it mediates, but of coordinating these propositional revelations into a coherent system of ideas that can help us make sense of (and hopefully deepen) our relationship with Christ. This theological enterprise evolves in constant conversation with Scripture – interpreting texts whose meanings are unclear in order to fit them into the core understanding of God and humanity that emerges out of our scripturally mediated encounter with Christ; setting aside (as 'straw') those texts that we simply cannot integrate into this understanding (always conscious that if these 'straw' texts become too numerous we should be ready to rethink our holistic reading). The criticism can run both ways: sometimes Scripture calls us to recognize ways in which our initial attempts to formulate our experience of the divine into doctrines, or to organize those doctrines into a system of thought, have fallen short.

However, it is not the mere meaning of an isolated text that forces such a change. Luther again offers a cogent example: through his compulsive study of Scripture, he found himself confronted vividly with an understanding of the significance of Christ's Atonement that forced him to radically alter his inherited theology. He did not piece together the doctrine of justification by grace through faith by simply extracting the relevant verses from Paul's letters and the gospel of John. Rather, through the study of Scripture he *encountered* God's grace in a ways he never had before. This encounter in turn guided him to a deeper reading of the relevant scriptural passages, allowing him to see their broader significance for Christian doctrine and theology.

In short, Christian doctrine is not 'lifted' straight from the text of Scripture. Rather, it emerges out of theological reflection on an encounter with Christ that is mediated through Scripture, but which cannot – and must not – be identified with the 'plain sense' of each scriptural text.

Furthermore, theological reflection is not a purely individual process. Christianity has always understood its revelatory inheritance as being public and communal – as something intended *for* the community of believers and, more fundamentally, aimed at *forging* this community. Thus, theological reflection should develop communally, as individual Christians enter into dialogue with one another over the understanding of the Christ they encounter in and through Scripture.

In fact, it is at least in part the theological task itself – broadly conceived as the conversation among Christians over how to understand Scripture in relation to reason and experience (especially their experience of relationship with God) – that transforms individual revelatory experiences into communal ones, and so helps bring together disparate Christians into a community of faith. If God's revelation was essentially propositional – if doctrine were simply handed out in the plain sense of Scripture – then the forging of community through the theological struggle to formulate Christian doctrine would become unnecessary, and a key function of divine revelation would be lost.

The idea that revelation works in and through the community of faith – such that the meaning of revelatory texts cannot be given, apart from the community's experience (and theological reflection *on* that experience) – has a powerful advocate in Albrecht Ritschl. Consider, for example, Ritschl's treatment of the scriptural revelation concerning the forgiveness of sins:

> Now it is not sufficient for my purpose to bring out what Jesus has said about the forgiveness of sins attached to His Person and His death. For even if His statements might seem perfectly clear, their significance becomes completely intelligible only when we see how they are reflected in the consciousness of those who believe in Him, and how the members of the Christian community trace back their consciousness of pardon to the Person and the action and passion of Jesus. For thus we are made aware that Jesus' purpose of pardon has not failed. Its success, however, not only serves to make clear what His purpose was: it also forms an essential condition of our religious and theological interest in

this matter. We should pay no special attention to this purpose of Jesus, nor should we seek to discover its value and its meaning, did we not reckon ourselves part of *the religious community* which first attested, through the writers of the New Testament, its possession of the forgiveness of sins as effected by Christ.[35]

Finally, the task of Christian theology is not isolated in time and so can help establish a community that is not limited to the present age but extends into the past and reaches towards the future. For theology to do this, however, it must be *conversational.* Conversation does not move in one direction in the manner of a transfer of information. The only way for one generation to converse with another is if later generations not only *receive* the teachings of the past – in the sense of listening respectfully – but also question, challenge, supplement and refine these teachings. Earlier generations must pass on the outcomes of their theological conversation to future generations with the implicit question, 'What do you think?'

In short, for theology to forge community over time it must be dynamic and evolving, which is possible only if revelation is not limited to a static text. The Lutheran approach achieves this by insisting that God's fundamental revelation is not the *text* of Scripture but the person of Christ encountered *in* Scripture (and in the life of the Church). Through this approach, we establish doctrine not by extracting the plain sense from isolated texts, but by critically reflecting on those texts in light of a communal and historic conversation based on faithful meditation on the Christ and gospel story seminally encountered in Scripture. Whether such an approach to Scripture can be reconciled with inerrancy or verbal inspiration we leave to those who favour such doctrines to decide.

In short, we think that the way in which Scripture contributes to the formation of doctrine is far more complex than the 'plain sense' view would have us believe. The whole text must be read in light of what is central, namely Christ, and in light of the theological tradition that has struggled, and continues to struggle, to integrate the experience of the Christian community and its members as they have endeavoured to live out their understanding of what it means to be the body of Christ. Reading the text in the light of these things requires a practice of receiving inherited theological conclusions with respect and honour; but it also requires critical engagement with that inheritance.

Careful philosophical reflection is an important part of that respectful, critical appropriation of the Christian theological inheritance – especially insofar as it engages seriously with principles that have emerged historically as Christians have sought to understand Scripture through the lens of the Christ discovered in Scripture and in the life of the community. Philosophical methods can help show the *implications* of these principles, and hence which interpretations of Scripture best cohere with them. In fact, we think no other discipline is better equipped to do so.

In the rest of this book, we aim to use this philosophical approach to argue, in effect, that a universalist reading of Scripture coheres best with core Christian principles. What we hope to have shown in this chapter is that, even if this outcome means we must set aside the plain sense of isolated scriptural texts, it does not follow that our method is opposed to Scripture. Rather, we think the kind of philosophical engagement we pursue here is a vital part of the approach to Scripture that, as we see it, is most true to (a) the complex content of Scripture (in which, among other things, passages in their plain sense often conflict), (b) the Christian commitment to the centrality of Christ and (c) the role of the evolving, historical Christian community in testing and refining its understanding of Scripture through a living engagement with it.

Chapter 5

A Prima Facie Case for DU

We begin our comparative case for DU with an initial prima facie case in the form of three general arguments supporting DU. Not surprisingly, these arguments focus on God's love – the first on His benevolent love for rational creatures, the second on His complacent love for them, and the third on His benevolent love for the blessed.

5.1 An Argument from Divine Benevolence

In philosophical arguments for DU, appeals to God's benevolence – though hardly exhausting the universalist case – deserve pride of place. We therefore begin our prima facie case for DU with what we will call the Argument from Divine Benevolence (hereafter AB):

1. Benevolence is an essential divine attribute.
2. If (1) then God's benevolence roots in Him an internal impelling cause to will what is best for every rational creature.
3. Therefore, God's benevolence roots in Him an internal impelling cause to will what is best for every rational creature (1, 2).
4. If (3) then unless there is a divine attribute that could root in God an internal impelling cause not to will what is best for every rational creature, God does will what is best for every rational creature.
5. There is no divine attribute that could root in God an internal impelling cause not to will what is best for every rational creature.
6. Therefore, God wills what is best for every rational creature (3, 4, 5).
7. If (6) then God wills that every rational creature be saved.
8. Therefore, God wills that every rational creature be saved (6, 7).
9. If God wills that every rational creature be saved, then all will be saved unless *either* it is metaphysically impossible for God to bring this about *or* all the means available to God for bringing this about are morally impermissible ones.
10. It is not metaphysically impossible for God to bring it about that all rational creatures are saved, and there are some means God could use to do this that are morally permissible.
11. Therefore, all rational creatures will be saved (8, 9, 10).

Because we will, in later chapters, defend (5) and (10) in the course of considering and critiquing species of DH, we do not defend them in this chapter. Instead, we focus on objections targeting other premises.

First Objection to AB: Premise (2) is false because the notion of a finite creature existing in a best possible state is incoherent

The first objection to AB runs as follows: though it would be better for Hitler to be saved rather than damned (whether or not it is better *that* he be saved), it would be better still for him to participate in the beatific vision to the same degree as the Virgin Mary; and, arguably, Mary herself could be united with God more fully than she is. If God is infinite and creaturely comprehension of God merely finite, then any creature could experience the beatific vision more fully than she actually does – and thereby be better off. Hence, not even God could bring about what is *best* for a creature.

There are several responses to this argument. The first, favoured by some Protestant Scholastics, is that the blessed all enjoy the same degree of union with God, because salvation consists in the beatific vision and its outcomes, and one either 'sees' God or does not.[1] This response, however, is inconclusive. Suppose that both a child and a botanist see a tree. Does the botanist's expertise enable them to see more of the tree than does the child? Or suppose an opera neophyte and an experienced opera lover listen to a recording of Rossini's *Semiramide* together. Though both would be *hearing* the same opera, the opera lover would *perceive* more about it. Similarly, some of the blessed might perceive more of God's infinite essence than others.

However, these analogies are imperfect, especially if we grant the traditional view that the 'light of glory' – the union of God's essence to the soul – is necessary for the beatific vision. This light has been thought to elevate the soul so that it *can* perceive (though not by the senses) God's essence as adequately as a creature can (conferring the equivalent, if you will, of the botanist's knowledge or the opera lovers trained ear).[2] Furthermore, God's spiritual nature makes analogies with perception of physical things problematic. Arguably, we never perceive the *substantial essence* of a tree but only its accidents. Perhaps this explains why one person can perceive more of it than another: they have access to more of its accidents. If so, were two persons given the power to perceive the *substantial essence* of something, degrees of perception might make no sense – one either perceives this singular essence, or not.

However, our critic might here insist that finite creatures cannot *comprehend* the infinite even if they perceive it, and that part of the joy of heaven actually consists in forever coming to know God better; but is the idea that creatures *cannot* comprehend the infinite (even when aided by the light of glory) as obvious as many suppose? Denying it does not seem to imply a contradiction; and if the light of glory can enable creatures to perceive God, why couldn't it enable them to *comprehend* God? Furthermore, supposing that some of heaven's joys would be lost if the blessed fully comprehended God *from the start* seems not only intrinsically implausible (would the blessed get bored with comprehending God?), but to imply, quite implausibly, that *God's* joy would increase were He never to fully comprehend Himself but always come to know Himself better.

Let us grant that no finite being can comprehend the infinite, and that the joy of the blessed partially consists in growing eternally in their comprehension of God. Does it follow that there are degrees of blessedness? No – if growth in appreciation of God's infinite essence is endless, then from the standpoint of eternity there is no degree of such appreciation had by one of the blessed (for example, Mary) that is not also had by another (Sue), who will eventually achieve that level of comprehension even if Mary starts out and remains perpetually ahead. As such, endless growth in comprehension of God can be what is best for rational creatures, a good which – from the standpoint of eternity – is not a matter of degrees.

Furthermore, for those who accept the notion of individual essences, differences in the degree of apprehension of God can be readily reconciled with each rational creature apprehending God as fully as their essence allows, and hence with each rational creature being in the best state they can enjoy.[3] However, even if there are no *individual* essences, most in the Christian tradition have held that there are natural kind essences (oak, horse, human, etc.).[4] In this view, either the human (or angelic) essence allows infinite growth in the apprehension and comprehension of God – in which case that endless growth is the 'best state' which the saved can enjoy – or there is a maximal scope of apprehension and comprehension of the divine essence that the human or angelic essence permits (in which case *that* is the 'best state').

Second Objection to AB: Premise (4) derogates from God's sovereignty

AB(4) implies that God has essential moral attributes that put Him 'under' the moral law, such that there are things it would be morally illegitimate for God to do. Those who hold to an extreme view of divine sovereignty, however, maintain that there is nothing of this sort – that there is nothing God might will which, were God to will it, would render Him less than morally perfect. This is so because, they think, God's will *establishes* whatever moral constraints there are.

In short, some might reject AB(4) because they embrace theological voluntarism. There are numerous troubling problems with this theory, but since these problems have been widely discussed we sketch out only a few highlights here.

As many great theologians have pointed out, this theory confuses might with right,[5] and appears to be a form of moral nihilism since it robs actions of any *intrinsic moral nature.* If nothing (neither murder nor hatred of God) is bad in itself, then nothing can become so simply by being forbidden.[6] After all, unless there is something intrinsically right about obedience to the *one* who issues a command or prohibition, how could the mere act of someone issuing it generate an obligation? That it is God who issues it becomes morally significant only if there is something *intrinsically right* about obeying God because of who God is.[7]

This is not to deny any *positive* law, whereby an authority may oblige those who owe obedience to perform (refrain from) actions which are not in themselves morally obligatory (prohibited). However, morally binding positive laws are related to an intrinsic moral demand – one which the dominant stream of the Christian tradition has identified as 'the natural law'.[8] For example, states enact speed limits to make it less likely that someone will drive in ways which recklessly threaten lives – and driving so as *not* to do so is a demand of the natural law, even if the precise speed limit set by the state is not. Even in cases where an action is commanded or forbidden solely to test trust (as some have taken to be the case with God's command to kill Isaac), some non-arbitrary good – namely, *the good of trusting one who should be trusted*, is involved.[9] Positive law is always grounded in a morally significant relation rooted in the intrinsic characteristics of the relata. In the case of God, our duty to obey is rooted not simply in His power, but in His goodness and wisdom. Otherwise, an all-powerful devil would warrant obedience. While obedience to such a devil might be prudent – though one could not trust him to 'reward' the obedient – it could never be a *moral* duty. All of this is true even if God may legitimately command what no human may command.

Moreover, we do not see what divine attribute could remove God from the sphere of morality. Is it power? The power to do a good act does not remove the duty to do it, but is a requisite for having the duty. Is it knowledge? Those who – through no fault of their own – cannot understand their duty, or who are nonculpably ignorant of morally relevant facts, might be exculpated for their moral failings, but *not* those who *know*. Is it God's independence coupled with our dependency? A mother is not relieved of duties to her children simply because they depend on her. Finally, is it God's perfect goodness? His goodness makes Him unable even to be tempted to do what is wrong or less than optimal, but that does not put Him *beyond* the ethical; it makes Him its archetype.[10]

5.2 An Argument from Divine Complacent Love

Our second argument for DU, the Argument from God's Complacent Love (AC), runs as follows:

1. Perfect complacent love is an essential divine attribute.
2. If (1) then there is in God an internal impelling cause of His willing that every rational creature has the necessary prerequisites for achieving what it is naturally ordered to achieve.

3. Therefore, there is in God an internal impelling cause of His willing that every rational creature has the necessary prerequisites for achieving what it is naturally ordered to achieve (1, 2).

4. If (3) then – unless there is in God an attribute which could root in Him an internal impelling cause not to will that every rational creature has whatever is necessary for it to achieve what it is naturally ordered to achieve – God does will that every rational creature has these necessary prerequisites.

5. There is no attribute in God which roots in Him an internal impelling cause not to will that every rational creature achieve what it is naturally ordered to achieve.

6. Every rational creature is naturally ordered towards union with God.

7. A necessary prerequisite for a rational creature to achieve union with God is that it experiences the beatific vision.

8. Therefore, God wills that every rational creature experience the beatific vision (3, 4, 5, 6, 7).

9. If (8) then – unless either: (a) it is metaphysically impossible for God to bring it about that every rational creature experiences the beatific vision, or (b) all the means God could use to achieve this are morally impermissible – every rational creature will experience that beatific vision.

10. It is not metaphysically impossible for God to bring it about that every rational creature experiences the beatific vision, and there are some means God could use to do this that are morally permissible.

11. Therefore, every rational creature will experience the beatific vision (8, 9, 10).

12. Every creature that experiences the beatific vision is saved.

13. Therefore, every rational creature is saved (11, 12).

Unlike AB, AC does not assume that a creature could be in a best possible state. However, AC does assume the essentially Aristotelian view that what is good *for* a thing (what promotes its welfare or flourishing) is determined by its nature. In brief, the view is this: things have natures that root in them powers, which in turn make it such that they are *intrinsically directed* towards performing certain activities, being in certain states and relations, and having certain dispositions. Put another way, things have a teleology determined by their *nature*, and this teleology (not God's arbitrary will) determines which activities, states, relations and dispositions are good for them. Just as God could not make it good *that* John torture an infant, so He could not make it good for the infant (granted its nature) to be tortured (or for John to commit torture).[11]

This teleological understanding of welfare has, we think, broad intuitive appeal. Consider loving parents. At least in general, such parents do not merely want their children to have lives in which pleasant states outweigh painful ones. They want, additionally, that their children cultivate and exercise their natural capacities. Intuitively, loving parents seem to discern that this is what will bring their children true happiness ('fruition', as the Protestant Scholastics put it). Furthermore, this notion of what is good for a thing has been generally endorsed in the Christian tradition and so fits our dialectical aims.[12]

With this in mind we turn to an examination of AC's premises. As with AB, two of AC's key premises – (5) and (10) – are challenged by defenders of DH in ways we will explore carefully in Chapters 6–8. Hence, we do not take them up here. Likewise, we make the case for (12) in Chapter 7 – which, combined with what we take to be its intuitive plausibility, means that we need not address it here.

This leaves (6) and (7), though (7) is uncontroversial: while a creature might have an *attenuated* relationship with God under conditions of divine hiddenness, genuine *union* is not possible without God's unmediated presence; that is, without the beatific vision. This leaves (6), which clearly *is* controversial. While classical Protestant theologians (Lutheran and Reformed) would accept it, classical Catholic theologians would not.[13]

Before sketching the controversy, it will help to highlight the points of agreement in classical Catholic and Protestant theological anthropology – their shared 'Augustinian assumptions' (so-called because these points of agreement can be traced to Augustine's profound influence on both). These shared assumptions include each of the following: (a) God instilled into Adam intellectual and moral virtues that made him 'able not to sin' (the 'concreated righteousness' of Adam); (b) Adam's ability not to sin included his motives – that is, he had an instilled love of God above all things, including himself; (c) these instilled virtues intrinsically ordered him to heaven so that, had he remained upright during the time of trial, it would have been intrinsically fitting for God to grant him the beatific vision; (d) humans living now do not possess the concreated virtues of Adam; (e) Adam's fall is part of why we do not have those virtues; and (f) only God's power can create in us the virtues that Adam possessed before the Fall.[14]

Despite this substantial agreement, classical Protestants and Catholics differed sharply over whether union with God was humanity's *natural* end. While the classical Catholic position is complicated, the essential idea is this: no creature, not even a rational one capable of moral action and worshiping God, can be *naturally* ordered to union with the infinite Good.[15] As such, God has no obligation to give humans what they need in order to achieve such union (in the way He possesses a prima facie obligation to provide, for instance, a physical environment in which they can survive and flourish during their mortal lives[16]).

Of course, as already noted in Chapter 3, there is a sense in which most Christians deny that God owes creatures anything – namely, in the sense of owing a debt. Most, nevertheless, agree that *once* God has created them His moral nature requires that He respect them in accord with their intrinsic worth (which attaches to *what they are*, that is, their essential nature). Combined with the doctrine that what is good for a thing is what completes its nature, we see why the tradition held it would be inconsistent with God's complacent love to fail to bring it about that creatures are able to attain the ends towards which their natures direct them.

Insofar as classical Catholic theologians deny that creatures could be *naturally* ordered to union with God, they take humanity's natural ends to consist in the same goods Aristotle identified: activity in accord with virtue, friendship, life in a well-ordered polis, abstract contemplation and worship of God, and so on.[17] The concreated virtues that God gave unfallen humans were thus given out of sheer grace and taken as unmerited favour. They were not only graciously given but *intrinsically supernatural*.[18]

The Protestants disagreed with this Catholic view in two ways. First, they argued that union with God is necessary for perfect human happiness. Humans, as rational beings, can conceptually grasp goodness *and* conceive of the Being who *is* Goodness. This draws the human will to God. Because of their distinctive capacities as rational beings, humans will not rest until they rest in God. In other words, *their rational nature orders them to union with God.*[19] This means, for the Protestants, that those concreated virtues of intellect and will that characterized unfallen man were natural to him as they were necessary for him to achieve his end (union with God), and hence that God could not, in justice, have denied them. While it was through sheer grace that humans were created, once they were created they possessed a nature and worth that God could not but respond to out of complacent love. This is why unfallen man was concreated with those virtues that made it possible for him not to sin.[20]

Second, the classical Protestants found the concept of *created* supernatural virtues incoherent, since only God is supernatural. Of course, they admitted that the *source* of the virtues possessed by unfallen man was supernatural – and in this sense some spoke of these virtues as supernatural – but this did not mean they were *intrinsically* supernatural.[21] While only God could, by sheer will, change water into wine, that fact *alone* would not make the miraculously produced wine intrinsically supernatural.

In short, we see a sharp divide between Protestants and Catholics on whether union with God is a natural human end. Insofar as AC(6) asserts that it is, we must defend the Protestant view against the Catholic one. We begin with a prima facie argument in its favour – that is, an initial case for the truth of AC(6). The argument takes its cue from Aquinas's argument that only union with God can make a rational creature happy:

> It is impossible for any created good to constitute man's happiness. For happiness is the perfect good which lulls the appetite altogether; else it would not be the last end, if something yet remained to be desired. Now the object of the will, i.e., of man's appetite, is the universal good, just as the object of the intellect is the universal true. Hence it is evident

that naught can lull man's will, save the universal good. This is to be found, not in any creature, but in God alone; because every creature has goodness by participation.[22]

Classical Protestant theologians embraced this argument but added a premise: 'If humans cannot achieve perfect happiness unless united with God, then humans are naturally ordered to union with God.'[23] From an Aristotelian perspective this premise seems irresistible. If happiness is defined in terms of achieving the ends for which one's nature orders one, then it would be incoherent to assert that human beings can be happy only through union with God but that such union is not natural to them. [24] The Protestants thus accused the Catholics of being inconsistent in teaching *both* that humans cannot be happy unless they enjoy union with God *and* that they are not naturally ordered to God.

Unsurprisingly, Roman Catholic theologians did not take this Protestant attack lying down. They argued that it was not their doctrine but the Protestant one which was incoherent, and in so doing mounted what amounts to an attack on AC(6).

First Objection to AC: Premise (6) entails absurdities

The Catholic argument runs as follows: if rational creatures are naturally ordered to union with God, and if the concreated virtues that humanity lost at the Fall are needed to make humans fit for union with God, then the concreated virtues lost at the Fall are necessary for creatures to realize their natural end. However, if these virtues are necessary for rational creatures to realize their natural end, God would not have created humans without them (since that would involve doing something unjust); but God has, since the Fall, created humans without such virtues. Since God would do this only if such virtues are not naturally due humans, it follows that such virtues are not naturally due humans. However, since such virtues are necessary for union with God, it follows that humans are not naturally ordered to union with God.[25]

While this argument is, at first glance, quite powerful, it is open to several responses. First, one might challenge the Augustinian assumptions on which it is based, attempting to construct a coherent version of the Protestant view by invoking instead, as Ritschl did, a broadly Irenaean theology that denies any special virtues possessed by unfallen humanity but lacking in us.[26] We will not pursue this line of argument here, however, since we think Ritschl's alternative understanding of sin's origins leads to some of the same problems the Catholics were highlighting, only in a different guise.

The Catholic argument faces a more telling response. Neither Augustine nor his Catholic followers denied that human beings after the Fall could come to experience union with God. Thus, even if one accepts a strong Augustinian understanding of the Fall, it does not follow that what was lost to humans in the

Fall *precludes* achieving union with God. Hence, it does not preclude the view
that such union is natural to humans.

Consider the following analogy: that a person is born with defective lungs
does not entail that they have no need of oxygen for the attainment of their
(terrestrial) ends. It does, however, entail that a surgical procedure restoring
normal lung function may be necessary for achieving their natural ends. If God
would be unjust in denying the person what they need to achieve their natural
ends, this injustice is avoided not merely by God giving them healthy lungs, but
also by making the surgery available. It is only if some of those born with
this disability are *denied* access to the surgery that a presumptive injustice has
been done. In other words, the Catholics are wrong to infer, from their understanding of the Fall, that God would be guilty of injustice if human beings were
naturally ordered to God. This follows only on the presumption that *God does
not extend to all* that which is required for salvation after the Fall. As such, it begs
our question here.

This line of argument can be strengthened by considering it in the light of
the orthodox Lutheran understanding of the Fall, characterized by the following theses: (i) the virtues that God gave Adam were not removed as a punishment for the first sin; rather, their loss was a natural result of Adam's turning
from God to an inordinate love of created things;[27] (ii) all Adam's descendants,
as 'emanations' from him, lack the virtues that Adam lost since *no one can give
what they do not have* (a view called 'traducianism');[28] (iii) God does not account
Adam's descendants responsible for Adam's individual sin;[29] (iv) God regards
the 'original sin' of infants in the manner of a disease: He does not hold them
to be *morally* at fault for it and does not damn infants who die unbaptized;[30] (v)
all humans born with original sin will commit actual sins, but they have control
over their degree of sinfulness;[31] (vi) none of the good works of fallen humans,
whether regenerate or not, will be purely good since they will not proceed from
a properly ordered love of God and neighbour;[32] (vii) God offers to all grace
that is truly sufficient for their salvation.[33]

Is this account of the Fall and original sin susceptible to the Catholic argument that, were one to view humans as naturally ordered to God, we would
need to conclude that God is unjust to humans after the Fall? No, because the
above account is entirely consistent with the following additional thesis: (viii)
the chances of humans achieving union with God are as great now as before the
Fall (that is,100%), but God now employs an even more marvellous and powerful means of salvation.

Nevertheless, this perspective is not without problems. How is it consistent
with God's goodness and justice to allow children to be born in a sinful state –
even if we assume that God intervenes to ensure that this defect does not
impede their achieving their natural ends? First, there are reasons to suppose
God could not, morally speaking, have simply restored to the first humans the
virtues lost by sinning. As we will see in the next chapter, much of the tradition

has held that every sin against God, as a sin against an infinite being, required an infinite good to make up for it. On Anselmian theories it required the Incarnation and Atonement of Christ. This may be all the truer with respect to the sin that precipitated the Fall, since it was done in a state of purity.

Why, then, would God not have miraculously instilled original righteousness into the children of the first humans, since those children were not responsible for their parents' sins? Because, if Christ's Atonement was *both* demanded by the Fall *and* sufficient to save both those who precipitated it and their descendants, this further miracle would be needless. Furthermore, if the first humans fell despite possessing the concreated virtues, how likely is it that each subsequent generation would avoid the same fate, particularly if raised by sinful parents? If possessing concreated virtues was insufficient for the first humans to achieve union with God, there is reason to suppose that rather than continually restoring these virtues through miraculous intercessions at each new generation, God would turn to a more astonishing way sufficient to save all apart from these virtues – a way that demonstrates His love for us far more powerfully than would have been possible if humans had never fallen.

Second Objection to AC: Premise (6) fails to account for the infinite distance between Creator and creature

In addition to attacking the Protestant view, classical Catholic theologians directly defended their belief that humans could not be naturally ordered to union with God on the grounds that no finite creature could merit such union. This argument amounts to a second objection to AC(6) and can be outlined as follows (argument ANO):

1. God is the infinite Good.
2. If (1) is true, then no finite being could merit being ordered to union with God.
3. Therefore, no finite being could merit being ordered to union with God (1, 2).
4. If (3) is true, then rational creatures are not naturally ordered to union with God.
5. Therefore, rational creatures are not naturally ordered to union with God (3, 4).[34]

The basic idea here is that a being could be ordered to possess an infinite good only if it deserved such a good in light of its infinite worth. As such, only God Himself could be so ordered – or, in terms of Trinitarian doctrine, only the Son and Holy Spirit could be naturally ordered to union with the Father.

We grant that infinite bliss is *absolutely due* only a being of infinite worth, where to be *absolutely* due something entails that: (a) the bestower of the good,

B, owes it to the recipient, R, based on a merit possessed by R; and (b) the merit of R is *not* a good that R possesses *by virtue of B having first bestowed it on R out of sheer grace*. Therefore, in this view, God the Father owes the Son and Holy Spirit union with Him because (i) the Son and Holy Spirit are Persons of infinite worth, and (ii) the Father generated the Son and Holy Spirit by a natural necessity and not out of any gracious act.

However, even if we accept all this, it does not follow, apart from ANO(4), that rational creatures cannot therefore be naturally ordered to union with God. We think ANO(4) is false. First, what is *naturally* due creatures cannot be equivalent to what is *absolutely* due them (in the above sense), since every creature owes its existence and nature to an act of sheer grace. If we equate a creature's natural ends with what is absolutely due it, we end up denying that any creatures have any natural ends.

Surely any such collapse of the distinction misconceives what it means to have a natural end. To have a natural end is to have a nature such that, first, one is directed (through one's powers and capacities and 'design structure') towards the attainment of an end; and second, one is less than fully actualized to the extent that one fails to attain this end. To be naturally due something is to need it in order to be able to exercise one's natural powers and capacities in the pursuit of one's natural ends. Thus, cats are naturally due eyes, since their nature requires eyes in order to exercise the full compliment of their sensitive powers, and this is naturally due them even though they did nothing to earn having eyes.

Similarly, it can be said that rational creatures are naturally ordered to union with God because that is the only thing which, given what they are, will complete them and enable them to flourish. Furthermore, it is only through such union that they can render God the love due Him. This seems true even though rational creatures did nothing to earn union with God, and even though their possession of a nature which orders them to union with God depends on a gracious act.

We think that even more can be said in response to ANO. Specifically, there may be a sense in which rational creatures *do* present to God a sort of infinity which renders union with God fitting. First, the tradition holds that the souls of rational beings, being simple and incorruptible, are naturally ordered to endure forever. Second, and more significantly, they are traditionally taken to have the capacity to infinitely perfect their powers of knowing and loving. Since no upper limit can be placed on these spiritual powers, rational creatures thus contain a kind of *impress* of the infinity of God.

None of this means that it is not *by grace* that rational creatures are ordered to union with God – even if so ordered by nature, their nature is graciously given. They did nothing to deserve it, nor were their natures so perfect that God had to create them in a manner analogous to the way He arguably had to beget the Son and Holy Spirit. The Scholastic Reformed theologian Turretin insisted that humans are ordered to God by grace, but that the gracious act which so orders them is *the very same gracious act* whereby God created them with the nature they possess. Hence, there is no difficulty in being both naturally and graciously ordered to God – the former is an expression of God's grace implanted in one's very nature.[35]

Problems with the Roman Catholic Doctrine of the natural end of humans

We conclude our defence of AC by noting several problems with the Catholic doctrine of the natural end of humans. First, according to this doctrine, God could have legitimately created the first humans without those virtues that Catholics deem supernatural and the Protestants natural (this was sometimes called 'the state of pure nature').[36] However, if God had done so, then on Catholic assumptions the first humans would be characterized by a concupiscence consisting in conflict between animal desires and rational emotions, leading them to overvalue pleasure and undervalue intellectual, moral and spiritual goods – but then it seems God could have created humans initially *in a state of sin.*

Indeed classical Catholic theologians are hard pressed to discern how an Adam and Eve created without the so-called 'supernatural' concreated would have differed from sinful humans who exist now. The best that Joseph Pohle seems able to do, in a rather strained attempt to resolve this problem, is to identify a difference of degree: 'Abstracting from the guilt of sin and the punishment due to it, the state of pure nature may consequently be conceived as somewhat more perfect than the state of original sin.'[37] However, if the difference between the state of pure nature and that of original sin is simply one of degree, we confront further problems. Christ's injunction to 'Be perfect, therefore, as your heavenly Father is perfect' (Matthew 5.48) seems not just a 'council of perfection', but a command of God, or at least a description of what humans ought to be and, in a sense, deeply are. Our sin has the gravity it has for precisely this reason: it so deeply conflicts with what our nature orders us to be.

Advocates of the traditional Catholic doctrine are thus driven towards some unpleasant alternatives. They can reject this high view of human nature, treating Christ's injunction as something that can apply not to humans as they are by nature, but only to those who are supernaturally endowed. The result is that Christ's injunction to be perfect does not show us how far we fall short of where – given what we essentially *are* – we ought to be. The gravity of our sin is thereby minimized. Alternatively, they can take Christ's injunction as a genuine command of God and thus hold that the original nature God imbued humanity with is inadequate to living up to the commands of God – thereby implicating God in the scope and severity of our sinfulness. In short, this doctrine of the moral character of purely natural man must either embrace a very lax notion of sin or endorse the view that God could be the cause of sin.

Furthermore, the classical Catholic theology not only held that Adam's moral and intellectual virtues were supernatural gifts, but that his immunity from sickness and death were *preternatural* gifts.[38] The Protestants (nor surprisingly) took the opposite view. [39] According to Roman Catholic teaching, humans, as composite substances, are by *nature* mortal.[40] Their souls, however, are by nature immortal.[41] Therefore, if God had created humans in a purely natural state, they would have died but their souls would have endured forever, either in a conscious or unconscious state. If unconscious, the soul would seemingly be in an unnatural state and God would be failing to respect the person by withholding what is needed for consciousness. If conscious, the soul would again seem to be in an unnatural state, unless we think the body is not an essential part of humans (something Roman Catholic dogma strongly condemns[42]); and if the soul were in this disembodied but conscious state forever, it seems this would entail a level of suffering vastly greater than that of someone who has lost their limbs or eyesight. Put simply, this view seems to entail that it is part of the nature of rational creatures that they endure forever in an unnatural state – one they could avoid only by being imbued with virtues not natural to them. In fact, it is hard to see how the final – purely natural – state of man in this traditional Catholic doctrine differs substantially from the state of the damned in the Liberal Doctrine of Hell.

5.3 An Argument from God's Love for the Blessed

Our final prima facie argument for DU was first articulated by Friedrich Schleiermacher,[43] and a variant has more recently been defended by Thomas Talbott.[44] It argues that universal salvation is necessary for the blessedness of anyone, and can thus be dubbed the Argument from God's Love for the Blessed (ALB). It runs as follows:

1. Anyone in a state of eternal blessedness possesses both perfect bliss and universal love for all persons.
2. Anyone who possesses universal love for all persons and who is aware that some persons are eternally damned cannot possess perfect bliss.
3. Therefore, anyone who is aware that some persons are eternally damned cannot possess eternal blessedness (1, 2).
4. If anyone is eternally damned, anyone who possesses eternal blessedness would be aware of this.
5. Thus, if anyone is eternally damned, then none possess eternal blessedness (3, 4).
6. God, out of benevolent love for His creatures, confers blessedness *at least* on those who earnestly repent and seek communion with Him.
7. Therfore, God does not eternally damn anyone (5, 6).

What are we to make of this argument? Premise (6) seems uncontroversial – in fact, it seems that to give up on it is to give up entirely on any semblance of Christianity. This leaves (1), (2) and (4).

Consider (1). We have already argued, in defence of AB, that there is a best state for the blessed which God could bring about. Barring the objections we will consider in later chapters, we have also argued that God would will that all enjoy this state. For our present purposes, however, it is enough to note that God would will this *for the blessed*. For reasons already discussed, such a best state would include both of the following: (a) perfect bliss – that is, happiness that is the best *kind* of happiness a person can know, untainted by any dissatisfaction; and (b) moral sanctification, including being perfected in love such that the saved love as God does.[45] The prevailing Christian interpretation of divine love is that it is unconditional, encompassing even the damned.

Nevertheless, some apparently deny that God and the blessed love the damned. Aquinas, for example, claims that the blessed 'rejoice' over the damned's sufferings.[46] Aquinas's view here rests on the idea that the miseries of the damned satisfy divine justice, such that those who have been morally sanctified no longer will the salvation of the damned as an end, and hence do not view their state as something to regret or grieve. As such, an objection to ALB along these lines is based on the same considerations that would inspire objections to AB(5) and AC(5). Since we tackle this kind of objection in Chapter 6, we do not take it up here. In what follows, then, we consider objections to ALB(2) and (4).

First Objection to ALB: Premise (2) wrongly assumes that supreme happiness cannot co-exist with regarding one's state as in some respects unfortunate

Premise (2) seems initially uncontroversial: if we love someone, how could knowledge of their eternal damnation *not* diminish our happiness? Thomas Talbott drives home this point by asking us to imagine that our own child is eternally damned. How could this not affect our happiness?[47]

Nevertheless, Jerry Walls attacks Schleiermacher's argument on precisely this point. Walls argues that *God* can know perfect bliss despite knowing that those He loves are in torment, and if this is possible for God it is possible for the saved. Walls agrees that God would experience 'regret' over the damned's fate, but he thinks God's happiness would be undiminished by this regret because His regret is 'a moral attitude'.[48] Walls apparently assumes here the doctrine of divine impassivity – that is, the view that God has no emotional *responses* to the world, because if He did He would be *dependent* on the world.[49] Apparently Walls thinks *moral* attitudes do not threaten God's independence, presumably because God's moral attitudes are simply the expression of an unchanging (and perfect) moral character. From all eternity, and not based on what creatures do, God has negative moral attitudes towards certain states, including that of eternal damnation. However, if so, we wonder why the same could not be said of emotional attitudes:

from all eternity God is saddened by certain states, including that of the damned. Regardless, Walls thinks these considerations undermine Schleiermacher's argument because 'the blessed may share God's perspective and consequently share God's perfect happiness'.[50]

We find this thinking uncompelling, partly because we reject the doctrine of divine impassivity[51] and partly because we do not think the Christian love ethic can divorce morality from emotions, since Christian love is emotional.[52] Neither point, however, is needed to refute Walls. Either God has emotional responses (as we think) or He does not (as the doctrine of divine impassivity would have it). If He does, these responses would be *part* of his moral perfection in that they would perfectly track his moral judgments – feeling joy at good states of affairs, and so forth.

On this assumption, God's moral regret over the damned's fate *would* diminish His happiness. Emotions clearly have a cognitive dimension, even if we do not take emotions as *nothing but* a species of judgment.[53] As George Pitcher notes, treating emotions as nothing but inner mental states leaves out one of their most important aspects: emotions are *about* something – that is, they have an intentional object, and they involve an *evaluation* of their object.[54] The intentional object of *happiness* is the state in which one finds oneself, and the evaluation involved is a positive one. Persons who are happy *approve* of the state in which they find themselves, and are more or less happy depending on how much they approve and how unmixed their approval is with elements of disapproval.

Of course, different people have broader or narrower conceptions of what constitutes their 'state', depending on how broadly they incorporate the good of others. However, those who are universally loving would identify with *all* persons, and so would be *supremely* happy only if they approved of the state or condition of all. Barring the Thomistic argument taken up in the next chapter, it seems that anyone possessing perfect love would *not* approve of a state in which some of God's beloved creatures are eternally damned. Thus, if God has emotions, then *God* is not happy with such a state.

If, on the other hand, God does *not* have emotions, Walls's argument faces a different problem. Our emotional responsiveness – the fact that we are angered by wickedness and grieved by suffering – seems essential to our human nature. While it may be a flaw that we have emotional responses unfitting to the circumstances, this is overcome by rendering our emotions more fitting, not by their elimination. If we cease to feel fear in the state of blessedness, it is because fear does not fit with the security that fellowship with God involves. However, would we have attained blessedness if we did not *feel* safe in God's bosom, because we had stopped having feelings altogether? While this might qualify as blessedness for, say, Vulcans, it does not sound like *human* blessedness.

In short, if we accept Walls's response to Schleiermacher, eternal blessedness ceases to be the *perfection* of our human nature (as Christians have historically believed), and becomes instead the *swapping out* of our human nature for something else. Seen in this light, Walls's response to Schleiermacher falls short.

James Cain, however, has questioned our understanding of how human happiness relates to judgments about one's state. By implication, he challenges Schleiermacher's view that the damnation of some 'must of necessity be a disturbing element in bliss'.[55] As Cain puts it, 'It is hard for me to see why Y could not love X, recognize that it is unfortunate for X that he or she rejects God, and yet not be emotionally weighed down by X's plight. Y accepts X's having made this choice and is at peace with things.'[56] Cain supports this intuition by invoking an analogous case. Imagine you are attending a party while your friend is 'wilfully and stubbornly sulking' at home. Is it possible for you (assuming you love this friend) to find your friend's state unfortunate but have your enjoyment of the party undiminished by it? Cain thinks so. As he notes, 'recognizing something as a sad state of affairs need not make one sad'.[57] Psychologists warning against co-dependency might say as much.

Cain acknowledges, however, that it does not follow from the fact that 'one can be happy at a party while a friend is sulking … that one can be happy in heaven while a loved one has wilfully rejected God'.[58] Rather, his point is merely that we should question the *universal* principle that a negative judgment about the condition of a loved one necessarily diminishes happiness (or the happiness of those without moral defects).

However, it then remains an open question whether a more circumscribed variant on the principle still applies to the blessed's relation to the damned. There are several features of the party case that *both* distinguish it from the damnation case *and* influence our intuition about the party case. First, a party is a short-term event typically intended to be a chance to set aside worldly cares for awhile; whereas blessedness is not an interlude but a permanent condition. We might suppose that someone could love a suffering person deeply and yet manage, for a time, to set aside the distress caused by that suffering. It is a very different thing to ask whether someone could set aside such distress altogether, enjoying an *eternal existence* unruffled by it, and yet still be said to deeply love the suffering person. Second, a friend may be more or less intimate, and the extent to which their sadness influences us is likewise a matter of degrees; but if the blessed are perfected in love, the degree to which they love the damned will exceed the degree to which we love even our dearest and closest friends. In this regard, Talbott's comparison to parents' love for their children is apt. Third, wilful sulking is not a tragedy; but eternal damnation is not just tragic but (for Christians) the *ultimate* tragedy. It is the very worst thing that could possibly happen to someone. Even if hell is conceived in the mildest terms (as in some variant of NH2) it is still the loss of the beatific vision – the very greatest good and the end for which humans were made; the only thing that could ultimately bring satisfaction.

Furthermore, even if we accept Cain's intuitions concerning the party case, it may not constitute a counter-example even to our general principle that happiness involves a judgment of approval concerning one's state, and that supreme happiness involves a judgment of supreme approval – at least if properly qualified. When the happiness of the blessed is at issue, happiness is meant in the holistic sense as an emotional attitude towards one's life as a whole, as opposed to the more trivial sense in which 'happy' names a passing emotion in response to immediate circumstances which hold one's attention for a time. The happiness of the party-goer is the latter, not the former. Furthermore, there is a difference between temporary and permanent bad states. Perhaps it is possible for happiness to be undiminished by the former – especially if there is an assurance that the bad state will be redeemed. However, it is something else again to suppose that happiness can be undiminished by the latter, especially if there is no hope of redemption. In the former case, the intentional object of one's happiness might be the final state that is ultimately realized. Insofar as this state is worthy of unmitigated approval, supreme happiness might be fitting even given passing evils. What is not compatible with supreme happiness is permanent and ultimate tragedy – for in that case the final state is not one towards which an unmitigated positive judgment is fitting.

Therefore, we might reformulate the key principle underlying ALB(2) as follows: Supreme happiness, understood as an emotional attitude of complete approval with one's state, is incompatible with judging one's *final* state to be characterized by *permanent* tragedies. Is this principle sound? It seems so. Suppose you are a parent of an anorexic child – a daughter who persistently denies herself the very food she needs to survive. That your enjoyment of a party might be unaffected by the wilful sulking of a friend does not imply that your overall happiness with life would be undiminished by the fact that your beloved child is wasting away from anorexia.

However, the blessed, being perfected in love, love the damned every bit as much as good parents love their children; and damnation is a far graver fate than anorexia – for the latter involves being *permanently* deprived of a sustenance far more essential than food. Given DH, this tragedy is final and irredeemable. Hence, the blessed have no basis for holding out *any* hope for the recovery and redemption of those they love more deeply than any parent loves their child; whereas the parents of the anorexic daughter might hope for recovery and so have their unhappiness mitigated. On the assumption that DH is true and the blessed are aware of this, *there is no hope*, and so ALB(2) seems true.

Second Objection to ALB: Premise (4) wrongly assumes that God cannot or will not shield the blessed from awareness of the plight of the damned.

ALB (4) holds that the blessed would be aware of the sufferings of the damned. There are several reasons to think this is so. Schleiermacher offers two: first, that 'so high a degree of bliss is not as such compatible with entire ignorance of others' misery'; second, that the blessed cannot be ignorant of the state of the damned 'if the separation itself [between the saved and the damned] is the result purely of a general judgment, at which both sides were present, which means conscious of each other'.[59]

The second consideration rests on a doctrine held by many defenders of DH; namely, that there is a final judgment at which both the saved and damned are present. Since resolute defenders of DH might deny this, and since Schleiermacher treats this consideration as secondary, we will focus on the first. Here, Schleiermacher holds that ignorance of the damned's fate is *incompatible* with blessedness. His reasons for thinking so become clear if one recalls that blessedness is our final end. Our intellectual faculties are so central to our nature that most philosophers since Aristotle have agreed that our happiness must involve these faculties functioning well. Hence, supreme happiness must involve these faculties functioning perfectly, but it is hard to imagine that these faculties have reached their fullest potential if we remain ignorant of critically important facts that we are able to grasp – such as the fact that, in some human souls, God's redemptive plan is eternally thwarted. This is all the more true given that blessedness involves communion with God. Can creatures defined in part by their capacity for knowledge truly be said to have communion with God if they do not know God well enough to be aware of truths that must be of *monumental* importance to Him – such as the state of the damned?

Furthermore, if some are damned and other saved, there would be some among the damned who are loved ones of the saved. It is hard to see how the saved would not know of their loved ones' dire fate unless God kept this from them.[60] According to most Christians, blessedness involves a heavenly community in which the blessed interact. If this is right, then – barring some sort of deception – how could the blessed fail to notice that some of their loved ones are *absent*? Even if this picture of heaven is mistaken, the special love we have for those closest to us would involve a particular interest in their fate. Unless we want to maintain that blessedness involves a vitiation of some of what is best in humanity, we would therefore have to assume that the blessed would be interested in the fate of their loved ones and would seek to know, if they could, what had become of them; and, presumably, in a state of communion with the omniscient God, they *could* know – unless God prevented it through active deception or misdirection, or through a silence in the face of their inquiries that would be suspicious unless the suspicions were allayed through something amounting to deception.

Despite this positive case, William Lane Craig, in a dispute with Talbott, offers reasons to reject ALB(4).[61] Craig holds that God could 'shield' the blessed from the 'painful knowledge' that some are damned, thereby preserving them in bliss.[62] That God *has the power* to do so is clear; but for Craig's case to succeed he must make two additional claims: (a) that it is morally permissible for God to shield the blessed in this way; and (b) that the resultant state of ignorance would nevertheless be one of blessedness.

Craig holds both (a) and (b), but his reasons are less than compelling. Consider (b): to assess it we must stress, as both Craig and Talbott do, that the happiness of the blessed is not just supreme in the sense of containing no dissatisfaction, but is supremely worthwhile in the sense of being the most valuable kind of happiness that one could possess.[63] If so, Craig must assume that the 'blissful ignorance' he attributes to the saved does not diminish the *worth* of their happiness. While Talbott finds this assumption uncompelling,[64] Craig claims that 'the mere lack of possession of information does not decrease or increase the worthwhileness of the happiness one experiences'.[65]

However, Craig's defence of this claim amounts to nothing but the assertion of his intuition on the matter; and his intuition here contrasts sharply with that of Aquinas, who holds that: 'Were it truly final the attraction of delight would be based on itself. But this is not the case. What matters is the object that gives delight. Consequently delight has its goodness and attraction from elsewhere, and is not the ultimate end but its attendant.'[66] The implication is that the value of delight derives from the object that gives delight. If the object of delight is illusory, then the value of the delight would also be illusory.

Here, Aquinas seems to presuppose the view, sketched out earlier, that emotional attitudes have a cognitive element. In this view, we have argued, *supreme* happiness would be a fitting response only to a state in which none of one's loved ones are damned. As such, the supreme happiness of the blessed (who love everyone) would involve the judgment that every person is indeed united with God in love. According to Craig, such supreme happiness could be supremely worthwhile, even though the judgment constituting its cognitive component is false.

However, can we truly say they are eternally blessed if they are erroneously happy – eternally living a life of bliss that *they* would judge inappropriate if they knew the truth? If you are joyously celebrating your child's college graduation, the truth that your child has actually failed college – even if you are unaware of it – renders the celebration a kind of farce. Craig, in effect, asks us to imagine God presiding over an *eternal* farce. He asks us to believe that this farcical celebration has the same worth as one that responds to a truth worth celebrating – a highly implausible view.

Let us turn, then, to Craig's defence of (a), which holds that it is morally permissible for God to shield the blessed from knowledge of the damned. In support of (a), Craig argues, first, that shielding persons from painful knowledge can be virtuous; second, that God so shielding the blessed is an extension of the kind of love displayed on the cross; and third, that such shielding need not be viewed as *deception* at all.

With regard to the first point, Craig notes that 'we can all think of cases in which we shield persons from knowledge which would be painful for them and

which they do not need to have', and that we regard such shielding as virtuous.[67] However, while it may be appropriate to withhold painful information
from someone in this *imperfect* earthly life – where we must decide which imperfection is worse, ignorance or the pain of knowing – the state of blessedness is
supposed to be a *perfected* state.[68] If God must choose which imperfection to
subject us to, our state falls short of perfect blessedness.[69]

Craig's second point is even weaker. He imagines God keeping the 'terrible
secret' about the damned buried forever in His breast 'in order that He might
bring free creatures into the supreme and unalloyed joy of fellowship with Himself'. Craig takes this to be 'a beautiful extension of Christ's suffering on the
cross'.[70]

But Craig exposes here a key problem with denying ALB(4). He wants to say
that, to facilitate 'the supreme and unalloyed joy of fellowship with Himself',
God eternally withholds from the blessed what must be a very central aspect of
Himself: His grief over the damned's fate. To preserve the joy of the blessed,
God erects a partial wall between Himself and them, rendering their fellowship
with Him something less than full communion. However, surely it is contrary to
Christian assumptions to say that the blessed are rendered more blessed by
limits being placed on their communion with God.

This is perhaps the core intuition underlying Schleiermacher's insistence that
blessedness 'is not as such compatible with entire ignorance of others' misery'.
If the bliss of the blessed hinges on their communion with God, it is hard to
imagine how they could be truly blessed if God withheld an important piece of
Himself from them.[71] The emerging picture is not of a universe in which there
are the blessed, who enjoy communion with God, and the damned, who are
separated from Him. Instead, there are only *degrees of separation*. This is what it
means to say that if some are damned, none can be *truly* saved.

This takes us to Craig's final point: his claim that divine shielding of the saved
does not amount to *deception*. He argues that while it '*would* be deceptive of God
to make the blessed believe that the lost were saved when in fact they are not',
it is not similarly deceptive for God to erase from their minds all memory of the
lost, since the latter does not cause them to hold false beliefs.[72]

There are two problems here – first, the blessed cannot be merely left agnostic concerning the possibility that some are damned. As noted above, the
supreme happiness of those who are universally loving involves the judgment
that *everyone* is enjoying communion with God. Supreme happiness is, for the
blessed, a fitting response only to such a state. Thus, God's act of purging the
minds of the blessed must bring them to believe all are indeed saved. Otherwise, the celebratory joy that only fits such a state would not ensue.

This leads to the second point: even if God has not explicitly deceived the
blessed in stripping away knowledge of the damned, He has even so brought it
about that they adopt an attitude of supreme happiness which they would not
have adopted had they known the truth. This is morally problematic for the

same reasons that deception is. The problem with deception is that it interferes with the capacity to make informed choices. If you are deceived you might choose an act that you think is of type C when it is really of type C*, and thus you perform an act different from what you *chose*. What is true of actions is also true of emotional responses.[73] The blessed are adopting an emotional attitude of supreme happiness based on the judgment that the universe is so ordered that supreme happiness is fitting. Under Craig's assumptions, this judgment is not only false, but the error results because God has stripped them of all knowledge of the damned. *Because* of a divine act, they misperceive reality and therefore make choices they would not otherwise have made. How is this morally different from deception?

Craig offers one final objection that warrants mention. He suggests that perhaps 'the immediate presence of Christ (cf. the beatific vision) will simply drive from the minds of His redeemed any awareness of the lost in hell … the redeemed will still have such knowledge, but they would never be conscious of it and so never pained by it.'[74] In other words, mere knowledge that the damned suffer is not enough to diminish happiness. Conscious awareness of it is also required; and the beatific vision would so captivate the blessed's attention that there would be no place for such awareness.

There are numerous problems here. First, if one's happiness depended on a lack of *awareness* of facts that, were one aware of them, would lead one to judge one's happiness unfitting, then the same considerations raised earlier with respect to lack of knowledge of the damned apply to lack of conscious awareness: the happiness in question seems a false happiness. Second, as Talbott argues, Craig essentially treats the beatific vision as a kind of ecstasy-inducing drug that 'fixes one's attention on oneself and upon the quality of one's own experience', rather than as a sanctifying experience that fills us with love for God and His creation. If the blessed know about the damned but are so overwhelmed by the beatific vision that they lose all awareness of others' misery, it seems the beatific vision has rendered them *less* loving rather than more.[75]

Underlying Talbott's response here is the idea, expressed by Simone Weil, that one cannot love someone if one does not *attend* to them.[76] Attention is a fundamental expression of love for the other – perhaps the *most* fundamental. Luther expresses this idea when he says that to love one's neighbour is to '"put on" his neighbour, and so conduct himself toward him as if he himself were in the other's place … A Christian lives not in himself but in Christ and his neighbour. Otherwise, he is not a Christian.'[77] In other words, you cannot truly love your neighbour as yourself if you do not put yourself in your neighbour's position, and, in effect, understand what the world looks like through your neighbour's eyes. This is something that you can hardly do if you fail to pay attention to your neighbour. If Craig's account of the effects of the beatific vision is correct, the beatific vision has the effect of *diminishing* our love of our neighbour by driving out our ability to attend to our neighbour's plight.

In response to this line of argument, Craig says that someone would be less loving and more callous 'only if he fails to love all those persons of whom he is aware; but it would be fatuous to so describe someone for failing to love a person of whose existence he is completely unaware'.[78] However, this response misses the point, which is that to know that someone is suffering terribly and yet remain blissfully unaware of their plight is to fail to love to them. If we love others, then their suffering *demands our attention*. The fact that we sometimes become so absorbed with other things that we have no conscious awareness of the sufferings of distant peoples, even if we know that they are suffering, is a clear sign of the *limits* of our love. Surely the beatific vision would expand our capacity to love, not limit it.

5.4 Concluding Remarks

In the previous section we argued that if the moral sanctification of the blessed produces a universal love that extends to the damned, then it is hard to avoid the conclusion that the damnation of some would impede the joy of the blessed. Their happiness could not be supreme and supremely worthwhile if the fate of some human souls is finally and irredeemably tragic. However, God, out of love for the blessed, would wish to bless them with joy that is both supreme and supremely worthwhile – a joy that is supremely great without being a farce. This is something He could accomplish only by saving all.

However, perhaps what all of this ultimately leads to is a final criticism of ALB, one that challenges the apparently uncontroversial premise (6). Perhaps, given that the damned reject God, God has no morally legitimate means of bestowing upon the blessed a joy that is both supreme and supremely worthwhile. Perhaps He can only bestow a kind of second-best blessedness – but this imperfect blessedness might still be worth having.[79] In other words, while God's love for the blessed would lead Him to bestow upon them supreme bliss if He could legitimately do so, He cannot do so. Hence, God does not bestow on the blessed *supreme* blessedness after all.

This means that, in our assessment of ALB, we are left with two contested assumptions: first, the assumption that the moral sanctification of the blessed would produce in them a universal love that would extend to the damned and would cause them to view their damnation negatively; second, the assumption that God has available to Him a morally legitimate means of saving all.

These assumptions are entirely analogous to the premises of arguments AB and AC that we have yet to critically defend – namely, premises (5) and (10) in each. This means that the prima facie arguments offered in this chapter all turn on two questions: first, does moral perfection entail willing the salvation of all as an end? Second, is there available to God a morally legitimate means of achieving this end? If the answer to both of these questions is *yes*, then the arguments for universalism offered in this chapter seem hard to resist; but Christian thinkers have offered negative answers to both. In the next chapter we will consider the chief basis for offering a negative answer to the first – namely, that God's justice demands that the unregenerate be damned.

CHAPTER 6

HELL AND JUSTICE

6.1 Introduction

We begin our critical examination of DH with those species that appeal to retributive justice. Collectively, we will call such species Judicial Doctrines of Hell (JDH). The most important of these is the Classical Doctrine of Hell (CDH), by which we mean any species that affirms CH2 (the notion that God rejects the damned, no longer willing their salvation as an end). That is, CDH names what, in our taxonomy from Chapter 2, we labelled DH1–DH3. Of these variants, DH1 – which combines CH2 with NH1a (the view that God heaps ancillary evils on the damned for retributive reasons) – is the most significant, and is arguably the species maintained by most Western theologians from Augustine until the eighteenth century. Hence, we are inclined to call DH1 'CDH in the strict sense', and regard the other species as falling under CDH only by extension – as moderated variants introduced to address problems with CDH in the strict sense.

Since our focus in this chapter is largely on the strict form of CDH, we will, for ease of reference, simply refer to it as 'CDH' hereafter. If we intend the term in its broader sense, we will specify this explicitly. In any event, we think a careful look at CDH in the strict sense lays the foundation for critiquing not only any version of CDH more broadly conceived, but any version of JDH – including that version we are calling the Retributive Doctrine of Hell (RDH), which is like CDH in the strict sense in affirming NH1a, but pairs it with CH1 (thus holding that God never stops willing the salvation of the damned as an end).

Some might find it strange that we devote a chapter to such 'Judicial Doctrines of Hell' at all, since recent philosophical and theological defenders of DH typically favour variants of the Liberal Doctrine of Hell (LDH), rejecting JDH as unworthy of divine benevolence, or as too beholden to barbaric retributive sentiments that have no place in post-Enlightenment morality. Nevertheless, there are good reasons not to ignore JDH. First, many Christian conservatives still hold to it in some form, especially those (both clergy and laity) in conservative evangelical churches. While intellectuals might be tempted to dismiss such persons as unreflective slaves to tradition, the sincere religious devotion animating many conservative evangelicals must give Christians pause. We need not accept their theology to respect their piety, but neither can we simply dismiss their theology without argument.

Second, while we do not think respect for the Christian theological tradition demands accepting as normative what most earlier theologians have taught, it does require giving due attention to those teachings. At least in the West, many of the greatest Christian thinkers have held to JDH in general, and to CDH in particular.

Third, if we look at scriptural passages that seem to support DH, the most natural reading favours some form of JDH, most typically CDH. Of course, we showed in Chapter 4 that there are scriptural passages supporting DH *and* DU; such that an appeal to Scripture requires straining the most straightforward sense *either* of the universalist passages *or* the damnation ones. However, since the most natural reading of the latter favours JDH, endorsing LDH requires strained readings of *both* universalist *and* damnation passages. While this does not rule out LDH given our approach to Scripture, there is still a sense in which JDH is, scripturally, a more plausible alternative to DU than LDH.

Finally, we think defenders of JDH have internalized an important insight that defenders of DU and LDH have tended to neglect – but they have allowed this insight to degenerate into something we can only describe as morally dangerous. In looking at JDH, we hope to rescue the distinctive moral insight underlying JDH while freeing it from the context that threatens to subvert it.

For contemporary readers, the dangers associated with JDH are probably obvious. The retributive instinct underpinning JDH can easily degenerate into a crude retributivism apt to propagate cycles of violence.[1] While the *considered* retributivist theory developed by the Protestant Orthodox is not of this crude sort, we share Dorner's judgment that – particularly in their writings dealing with hell – they lose sight of this nuanced retributivism and are caught up by the crude form.[2] Consider the following passages from the great Lutheran divine, Quenstedt:

> Death Eternal, or damnation, is that most unhappy state in which, from the just judgment of God, men who remain unbelieving to the end, being excluded from the beatific sight of God, and associated in the infernal prison with the devils, will be tortured eternally … with the most severe and ineffable torments, to the praise of the divine truth, and the glory and exultation of the Godly.[3]

We are, in effect, invited to imagine celebrations in heaven as the saved *exult* in the utter *torment* of fellow creatures. We must confess that for all our respect for the older divines, this teaching strikes us as repellent. We think such retributive sentiments – exemplified so horribly when some death penalty advocates fry bacon outside prison walls as convicted murderers are electrocuted – corrupt Christianity at its heart.

However, the refined version of retributivism developed by the Lutheran Orthodox when focusing on the Atonement is not this appalling species. As we shall argue, however, this refined version cannot support JDH. Only the appalling version can – which, we think, helps explain why retributivism degenerates into its crude form when invoked to defend DH. Thus, we share Talbott's view that the crude retributivism that led the older divines to teach CDH goes hand in hand with the worst corruptions of the Church – Holy Wars, heretic burnings, persecution of Jews and other non-Christians, violence against homosexuals, and so forth.[4] We want to examine JDH in part to expose what is so wrong with this crude retributivism.

However, as repellent as we find *these* retributive sentiments, the moral intuitions underlying JDH do not strike us as entirely wrong. In certain respects we find them *more* Christian than those underlying LDH. Many defenders of LDH hold that God hates sin *solely* because it harms the rational creature, agreeing with those defenders of DU who teach, with Schleiermacher, that wrath is not a divine attribute.[5] On this point, however, we question much liberal theology. Though we reject the idea that God's wrath manifests as a retributivism inflicting non-remedial suffering on the unregenerate, we are drawn to those defenders of JDH who claim that God is not merely pure Himself, but 'demands due purity in creatures'.[6] This demand requires more than that sin cease – it demands that sins already committed be *actively repudiated* and *atoned* for. Sin is so grave a desecration of God's creation that atoning for it requires more than any human could possibly provide or bear – such as a staggeringly monumental act of sacrificial love that only God Himself could perform.

These ideas are too often summarily dismissed by liberal theologians – based, we think, on an underestimation of sin's gravity, the scope of God's wrath against it and the enormity of what God's moral nature requires in response.[7] Defenders of JDH do not underestimate these things, but think that only JDH in some form takes sin and its intolerability seriously enough. We argue, by contrast, that only a species of DU can do so. To see why, we think a careful look at species of JDH will prove invaluable.

6.2 Summary and Examination of a Paradigmatic Account of CDH

For our critical discussion of CDH, it may help to review a detailed treatment we find paradigmatic – namely, J. G. Baier's account from his 1685 masterwork, *Compendium Theologiae Positivae*. This account is particularly useful because it comes at the end of the epoch of Protestant Orthodoxy, the last great theological movement to unequivocally support the strictest form of CDH. As such, it encompasses the outcomes of CDH's development since Augustine's time, capturing its most recurring elements.

Baier begins with a detailed account of what we call NH1a. He holds that damnation consists not only in the lack of beatitude and its attendant goods (i.e. 'the love of God as the highest good, as well as of the joy which results from that'), but in a positive opposition to those goods that includes the most acute evils.[8] The bodies of the damned are, he thinks, hideously deformed, apparently as a sort of overflow of the evil in their souls (the infernal parallel of the heavenly perfection of the bodies of the blessed).[9] Among the ancillary evils (what Baier calls positive evils) that he first mentions are those that afflict them through their intellects. The damned are tormented by an 'abstractive' or non-intuitive knowledge of God – that is, a propositional knowledge divorced from immediate experiential understanding of its truth – which encompasses knowing that God is the Lord of highest majesty whom they have gravely offended, the most just judge who justly punishes them, and the most benign Father (not *to them*, but to the blessed). Baier adds that 'although to know God pertains to the perfection of man, nevertheless to know God as the damned do, is not a perfection, but the most grave misery'.[10]

The damned also suffer various afflictions of the will. They implacably hate God and themselves, envy the joys of the blessed, perpetually grieve on account of the intensity of present evils, and are impatient and desperate because they long to escape their pain but know they never will. Finally, having been deserted by God and refused the grace needed to repent, their wills are determined to evil, so that no matter what they think, say and do, they sin and displease God.[11]

Finally, Baier describes the positive evils that afflict the body. In keeping with tradition he asserts that the 'bodies of the damned will by crucified by a true and non metaphorical (*proprie dicto*) infernal fire which is inextinguishable'. While such burning anguish is the fitting torment for the sense of touch, the other senses will also be tormented in relevant ways. For sight this means constant exposure to hideous ugliness, for smell the most foul stenches and for hearing the most egregious cacophonies.[12]

In addition to this account of NH1a, Baier also offers an account of damnation's causes which encompasses the impelling causes identified in CH2 but goes beyond this to consider other kinds of cause. He begins with efficient causes, noting that the privative evils of hell (loss of the beatific vision and its attendant goods) have no efficient cause, since efficient causes have 'real and positive effects' and not merely privative ones.[13] The evils of intellect and will are caused by the souls of the damned, which have been 'deserted by God'.[14] A will thus deserted 'will determine itself to evil'.[15] The efficient cause of bodily evils consists partly in 'the infernal fire' and partly in the actions 'of bad angels'.[16] However, insofar as 'damnation is considered with respect to punishment', Baier holds that 'the Triune Christian God' is the cause. In an explanatory note, he specifies that God is *not* a cause of the sin that makes a person merit damnation, but rather is the cause of damnation in that He 'designed the place of hell', 'condemns the impious to hell' and 'inflicts the most horrendous pains of hell' on them (if indirectly).[17]

Baier then turns to the impelling causes of damnation. Not surprisingly, he takes the internal one to be God's 'vindicatory justice' and the external one to be the 'non-expiated sins of the damned' (non-expiated because they died without saving faith).[18] Baier notes that, though all sin merits damnation, not all sin is *adequate to it*. He also makes the point that all sins are 'fruits and effects of a lack of faith' (a view which clearly reveals Baier's Lutheranism).[19] In the final part of his chapter on hell, Baier considers the *final* cause of damnation (roughly speaking, its purpose), which he takes to be the 'glory of the divine vindicatory justice, veracity, and power'.[20]

This, then, is Baier's account hell. One feature of it in particular warrants further attention, since it will be an important focus of our critique. Specifically, while he insists (presumably to distinguish the Lutheran position from the Calvinist one) that God does not cause the sins that make a person *deserve* damnation, he does not flinch from asserting that, *by withdrawing grace from the damned, God ensures they will be confirmed in sin forever* – or, put bluntly, that God wills sin as a punishment for sin.[21]

Shocking as this doctrine at first appears, it was explicitly taught by many older divines in their treatments of the doctrines of hell and original sin. Aquinas, for example, insists that 'God, of His own accord, withholds His grace from those in whom He finds an obstacle' and in so doing 'is the cause of spiritual blindness, deafness of ear, and hardness of heart'.[22] He explains that when God hardens hearts, He does so as punishment for prior sin, willing a sinful state as the just penalty for a sinful act. This state, of course, issues in further actual sins unless God again confers grace, which He is not obligated to do. This doctrine was also held by Luther and Calvin.[23]

To be clear, this doctrine does not hold that God *efficiently* causes sin. He does not move rational creatures to sin or counsel them to sin. Rather, for retributive reasons, He *withdraws* the grace that creatures *need* in order to avoid sin. Hollaz sums it up succinctly: 'God does not harden men causally, or effectively, by sending hardness into the hearts of men, but judicially, permissively, and desertively.'[24] Luther makes the same point when he says that we do evil 'because God desists from working within us and permits our natural man to do in arrogance what he desires ... And this nonintervention of God Scripture calls hardening of the heart'. Luther goes on to express the Augustinian view that evil is 'nothing', a lack, and thus 'cannot *occur* ... but comes only when nothing good takes place, or is prevented from happening'.[25] Evil is a privation, and its possibility arises from the original nothingness of the created substance.[26] God's *absence* is its cause; God's presence its remedy.

According to the mainstream of the Western tradition, for created spirits to do good it is not enough that God sustains them in being; He must also activate their powers to do what conforms to their nature.[27] To use a crude analogy, divine grace is to our capacity to do good what electricity is to a light bulb's capacity to shed light. Although bulbs are designed to light up, all they can offer is darkness in the absence of electricity. If the power company shuts off the flow of current to the house, the bulbs therein become incapable of shedding light.

Likewise, if God withholds divine grace He allows the creature not only to sin, but to exist in a sinful state – a state from which the creature cannot free itself unless God again supplies grace.[28] If God hardens hearts as punishment for sin, then (in terms of our analogy) it is as if city officials require that every house turn on its porch lights after dark and penalize any houses that fail to comply by cutting off their power.

6.3 Critique of CDH Insofar as it Holds CH2: The Argument from Willing Sin

We begin our critique of CDH with an argument we will refer to as the Argument from Willing Sin (AWS), which targets CDH insofar as it holds CH2. AWS thus applies to CDH in the broad sense. AWS runs as follows.

1. God is perfectly good.
2. If God is perfectly good, He cannot will sin (in the sense of willing that His creatures sin).
3. Therefore, God cannot will sin (1, 2).
4. If CDH is true, then (given that CDH affirms CH2) God wills sin.
5. Thus, CDH is false (3, 4).

AWS(1) seems utterly uncontroversial, enjoying both enormous scriptural support and essentially unanimous support among Christian theologians. Any who do *not* accept it are invited to view this book as an attempt to spell out what follows for those who do. AWS(2) also enjoys a strong theological pedigree,[29] and it finds support in a rather straightforward argument: anyone who is perfectly good cannot sin, but it is sinful to positively will – as either an end or a means – that another sin. Therefore, anyone who cannot sin cannot *will* that another sin. Hence, if God is perfectly good, He cannot will that any of His creatures sin.

Our initial case for AWS(4) is similarly simple: CH2 holds that God withdraws His grace from the damned as a punishment for sin, and, as such, that God wills that their souls be forever bereft of what is necessary for not sinning; but to will that a person, P, lack what P needs for doing A, is to will that P not do A. (Imagine a teacher who requires that a student write 'I will not talk in class' fifty times on the chalkboard but denies the student any access to chalk or a chalkboard – the incoherence of combining this requirement with this constraint highlights the fact that one cannot coherently will that P do A and that it be impossible for P to do A).However, if God wills that the damned be forever deprived of what they need in order to refrain from sin, then God wills that they not refrain from sin – in other words, that they sin.

Many great theologians, however, have embraced CH2 while fully admitting that it implies that God wills sin (or at least *hardening*, from which sin necessarily follows). As such, these theologians implicitly *deny* AWS(2). Something more in its defence is thus warranted. Specifically, there is a general perspective on morality, which is widely endorsed and refined through Christian history, that entails AWS(2).[30]

The perspective we have in mind rejects both the pure consequentialism of utilitarianism and the deontological perspective (embodied in much of Kant) that takes the essence of morality to consist in respect for universal moral laws. The contrasting Christian perspective takes the fundamental locus of moral concern to be neither overall consequences (although consequences matter) nor respect for duty (although it affirms universally binding moral rules), but rather an appropriate responsiveness to the dignity of beings in accord with their degree of inherent worth – especially *rational* beings (humans, angels and God) who can value things in accord with their intrinsic value and can also be moved by benevolence to do good, even to the unworthy.

From this moral perspective, both the goals we should pursue and the rules constraining how we pursue them are rooted in the inherent value and dignity of God and creatures. Moral norms derive from what this value and dignity requires of us in terms of both inner psychological attitudes and outer behaviour. Both must be *appropriate to* this dignity and value. In effect, we are called to subjectively value beings (*love* them) in accord with their inherent value; and we are called to honour the inherent dignity of beings in all we do – which rules out some behaviours (rape, torture, murder, etc.) regardless of what goods might thereby be achieved. It is also required that we pursue their good (usually understood as what helps to perfect their natures) in permissible ways.

Given this perspective, God's moral perfection consists in His perfect love and respect for Himself, as the most objectively valuable being, as well as in His perfect love and respect for all creatures, especially rational ones, insofar as they are like Him in possessing intrinsic worth. By implication, God hates hatred of both God and creatures, and loves love of them. In short, there are dispositions and principles of acting that God must love and approve of, and others that He must hate. Certain principles and dispositions are loved by God because they accord with the perfection of what He primarily loves: Himself and His creatures.[31] This idea is reflected in Christ's statement, 'The Sabbath was made for man, not man for the Sabbath.' (Mark 2.27)

Based on this moral standpoint – which treats the intrinsic worth of persons as demanding love and respect, giving rise to non-consequentialist obligations towards them – AWS(2) seems unavoidable. Given this moral view, sin is really nothing other than a shortcoming with respect to love and respect for both God and creatures. All failures to abide by the rules of morality – even failures that are directly and immediately failures to value the inherent worth of creatures – are also failures to properly love God, insofar as God prohibits such failures and is the supreme good towards whom we owe perfect obedience. As such, all sin is an affront to God, and the Christian tradition has widely accepted that God's hatred of sin is a necessary outcome of His love for Himself.[32] This is not a selfish love (as noted at length in Chapter 3). To be morally perfect is to value things in accord with their intrinsic value. Therefore, the morally perfect God must love Himself above all things (but not to the exclusion of other things). His moral character thus requires that He be outraged by affronts to His dignity.

How, then, could He will that such affronts occur, even (as is supposed in CH2) as a punishment for sin? We consider how a defensible notion of retributive justice would apply to this question in a later section. For now, we want to highlight the prima facie *incoherence* of asserting that God would will that sin, which is an intolerable outrage, be punished by bringing it about that there are further intolerable outrages. With all due respect to tradition, we cannot conceive of a less coherent idea. If God hates sin primarily as an outrage to His majesty, what He would will is that sin *cease*, and that sinners realize the extent of their wrong. An appropriate view of the Atonement aside, this realization would involve suffering. It is not as if sinners were consumers who, after buying bad detergents, discovered their error and ever after bought good detergents. God is not a detergent, and sin against Him is an *offence*. We think God must will that sinners come to *appreciate* this wrong – not merely in Baier's 'abstractive' sense, but with a full experiential appreciation of it. As creatures with emotions, truly repentant creatures would feel emotions appropriate to that wrong; and since the wrong is enormously grave, the fitting emotion would be soul-wracking guilt. The unrepentant are precisely those who resist such a realization, instead continuing to hate and blaspheme God. That God would will *this* seems incomprehensible. It threatens to render Christian theology incoherent. [33] As such, the case for AWS(2) seems strong.

6.4 The First Objection to AWS: God Wills Sin as a Means Only

Nevertheless, we can think of two significant objections to AWS. The first holds that, assuming CH2, God does not will sin as such, but only as a *means* to a good end; and this, it might be claimed, is *not* incompatible with God's perfect goodness.

Now, saying that god *wills sin as a means* to a good end is not the same as saying He *allows it* for a good end. The Christian tradition has generally held that God might allow sin because of the good consequences that allowing it makes possible. For example, many think that God wills that humans be free to make choices, and that – given human freedom – sin is a possible outcome. However, in this case, while God may *allow* the sin that results from the misuse of freedom, this sin is not a means that God employs to bring about human freedom. It is, rather, an unintended side-effect. Contrast this with the Calvinist idea that God seeks to display the glory of His mercy and justice by saving some sinners and damning others. Displaying His glory in this way requires that there be sinners to save and damn – and so, if God unconditionally wills that the universe be so ordered that He can display both mercy and justice, He must will sin – not as an end, but as a means.[34]

Likewise, some might argue that when God imposes on the damned the evil of being lost to sin forever, the end that God wills is that justice be done, and sin is only willed as a means to this end. The objection we consider here rests on this way of viewing the matter: God does not will sin as an end but only as a means, and it is only the former that is strictly impermissible. The critic of AWS who presses this point would thus hold that AWS(2) should be modified as follows:

2* If God is perfectly good, He cannot will sin as an end, but can will it as a means to a sufficiently good end, such as the glory of displaying His justice.

However, if this is how the premise should read, then AWS(4) needs to be modified as follows:

4* If CDH is true, God either wills sin as an end, or wills sin as a means to an end that is not sufficiently good to justify it.

Let us call this modified argument AWS*. What the critic might say about AWS* is that God wills sin only as a means, *not* as an end; and that the end for which He wills it is sufficiently good to justify it. Hence, (4*) is false and AWS* is unsound.

There are several difficulties here. One has to do with whether the end for which God supposedly wills the sin of the damned as a means – the so-called justice thereby achieved – is sufficiently great to outweigh the evil of sin itself. We set aside this concern here because it will come up again in relation to the next objection, when we consider it at length. For the sake of this objection, we focus on two other replies.

First, the revised premise (2*) smacks of consequentialism, which holds that no kind of act, no matter how evil, is *intrinsically* impermissible and so ruled out in all circumstances. Rape and torture could be justified if they produced sufficiently good outcomes; but consequentialism has not been popular in the Christian tradition. Alan Donagan notes that St. Paul himself condemns it.[35] Critics of consequentialism insist that some acts are intrinsically wrong and so are forbidden regardless of consequences. If anything deserves to be called intrinsically wrong, would willing the eternal moral ruin of a rational creature not qualify? Furthermore, Quenstedt maintains that God's justice is 'the supreme and immutable rectitude of the divine will, demanding from rational creatures that which is right and just'.[36] How, then, could God withhold what is needed for rational creatures to *do* what, by this absolutely immutable will, is demanded of them? Insofar as divine grace is needed, the decision to withdraw it eternally is a decision to eternally prevent rational creatures from doing what God immutably demands of them. As such, this is an act which both wills moral ruin and directly thwarts God's immutable intentions for creatures. Any act that fits under either description alone would seem to be a good candidate for being intrinsically wrong.

Since we will explore similar ideas in relation to the next objection, let us move to another response to this first objection. For this objection to work, we must not only accept the modified (2*) in place of (2) despite its seeming consequential-ism, but we must also agree that the modification to (4) needed in order to pre-serve the argument's validity results in a *false* premise – but is (4*) false?

For (4*) to be true it is sufficient that, given CDH, God wills sin as an end. The critic of our argument has to maintain that this is not true – that in CDH God only wills sin as a means to achieving divine justice. To say *this*, however, damnation would have to be something distinct *from* the divine justice which leads *to* it. However, on the retributivist ethic endorsed by CDH, there is good reason to think that damnation – far from being a means of attaining divine justice – is actually *constitutive of it.*

The kind of retributivist ethic underlying CDH maintains not merely that the wicked deserve to suffer but that their suffering is itself *just.* There may, of course, be further goods which flow from it, but these are secondary. What is most essentially just is *that the wicked be inflicted with the evils they deserve,* and the greatest evil they suffer is precisely God's withdrawal of grace and the attending vitiation of their character.[37] That state is precisely what God, in *hardening the hearts of the damned,* wishes to inflict on them as punishment for sin. If so, then in CDH God wills the sinful state of the damned for its own sake, as intrinsically just, *not* as a means to an end. Hence, even if we accept (2*) as preferable to (2), and so must replace (4) with (4*), we are not thereby led to an unsound argu-ment, since (4*) appears to be true.

6.5 The Second Objection to AWS: The Doctrine of Double Effect

In response, critics might offer a more nuanced argument to the effect that, given CDH, God wills the permanently sinful character of the damned *neither* as a means *nor* as an end – at least not if by 'willed' one means 'intended'. Instead, the sinful character of the damned is simply foreseen and permitted. What is *intended,* the critic might argue, is the permanent withholding of divine grace (and perhaps some other effects of this other than the damned's hardened hearts). Although God knows that a consequence of this will be that sinners are confirmed forever in a sinful state, this is just a foreseen side-effect of what God directly intends; namely, that the damned be punished appropriately by being deprived of grace. However, it is not wrong for God to merely foresee this out-come, given the justice He thereby achieves. The initial plausibility of AWS, the critic might conclude, turns on a rather loose use of 'will', according to which that term means 'intend' in (2) and 'foresees and permits' in (4).

We will set aside, for argument's sake, whether classic defenders of CDH actually meant to say something along these lines. Although we think most of the older divines did think God really wills that the damned be confirmed in sin, the objection here might be viewed as a modification of their view. Let us consider, then, whether this line of objection, with its attendant refinements of CDH, derails our argument.

The crucial thing to notice here is that the objection presupposes a distinction between bad effects that are intended and bad effects that are merely foreseen and allowed. This distinction is central to the venerable Christian moral doctrine of Double Effect – but this doctrine also makes clear (rightly, we think) that not all bad effects are permissible just by virtue of being foreseen rather than intended. Perhaps, then, we can treat the above line of objection as holding, essentially, that premise (2) of AWS should be refined in terms of Double Effect, and that once (4) is correspondingly adjusted, it becomes false. To assess this idea, we first need a clear statement of the doctrine of Double Effect. We think the following captures its essential features well:

> *Double Effect*: For any action A with effects *p* and *q*, where *p* is a good effect the pursuit of which is morally praiseworthy all else being equal, and *q* is a bad effect the pursuit of which is morally blameworthy all else being equal, it is morally permissible for a person to perform A just in case (a) A is not itself morally prohibited by virtue of the kind of act it is, (b) the person intends *p*, while merely foreseeing but not intending *q*, (c) *q* is not the means to achieving *p*, (d) *p* cannot be achieved in a manner that avoids producing *q* or some other effect at least as bad, and (e) the value of *p* outweighs the disvalue of *q*.[38]

This doctrine incorporates consequentialist considerations in requirements (d) and (e), but avoids being *purely* consequentialist by insisting on (a), (b) and (c): (a) allows that some acts may be intrinsically immoral, apart from their consequences, and prohibits such actions; (b) insists that agents must have the right intentions in acting, and must be 'aiming for' the good effect, not the bad one; and (c), which is really an elaboration of (b) insofar as one always intends the means to an end whenever one intends the end, insists that the bad effect must be a side-effect of pursuing the good effect, not something that is intentionally achieved so as to bring about the good effect (for example, killing a homeless person so his kidneys might be used to save a child's life).

When it comes to applying this doctrine to God's withdrawal of grace from the damned – which has the supposedly good effect of meeting the demands of justice but the bad effect of confirming the damned forever in sin – the doctrine faces a unique difficulty that deserves a mention. Usually, Double Effect is invoked when an agent's power is limited, since it is in such cases that (d) is met. If four people are starving and three kill and eat the loyal dog of the fourth, we would suppose that they would rather not have killed it if they could have saved themselves another way. For an omnipotent God, however, situations like this are presumably vanishingly rare. Hence, we should be sceptical when someone says that God *cannot* achieve *p* without producing *q* or another effect at least as bad. Just because we cannot envision *how* God could do it does not mean that a being with infinite resources and creativity *could not* do it.

Later we will argue that the Atonement can be construed in precisely these terms: as a way for God to meet the demands of justice without confirming any creature in sin. For the moment, however, we want to focus on other problems with revising AWS in light of Double Effect. To do so, we should more formally consider how the objection to AWS based on Double Effect would look. First, it would hold that (2) needs to be replaced by a premise that captures the moral requirements embodied in Double Effect. The revised premise might be formulated as follows:

> (2**) If God is perfectly good, He would pursue an act, A, that has the bad effect of confirming another in sin only if: (i) A is intrinsically morally permissible; (ii) A achieves a good that outweighs this bad effect and which cannot be achieved without permitting it (or another effect at least as bad); and (iii) this greater good is what is intended, while the confirmation in sin is merely a foreseen side-effect.

If (2) is replaced with (2**), (4) would likewise need to be replaced with a new premise that looks as follows:

> (4**) If CDH is true, then God pursues an act, A, that has the bad effect of confirming the damned in sin and which is such that either: (i) A is intrinsically morally impermissible; (ii) this bad effect is not outweighed by a greater good that could not have been achieved without permitting this effect or another at least as bad; or (iii) confirmation in sin is not merely a foreseen side-effect of doing A, but is intended either as an end or as a means to the good effect for which A is done.

Let us call the revised argument AWS**. In effect, our critic must maintain that (4**) is false, thereby rendering AWS** unsound.

However, to show that (4**) is false, the critic must show that conditions (i)–(iii) as outlined in (4**) are *all* false. If even one of these conditions is true, (4**) is true, and so AWS** is an effective argument against CDH.[39]

So, is (4**-i) false? On the contrary – we think the reasons in its favour are sufficiently compelling to place the burden of proof on those who would deny it. The act of cutting the damned off from divine grace is an act of removing that which the damned must possess in order to do what God *immutably* wills that *all* rational creatures do; namely, conform to the moral law. Furthermore, the function of divine grace in the life of creatures – the reason God bestows it – is so that they may be perfected according to their natures (especially their moral natures). To cut creatures off from divine grace is therefore to prevent them from doing what God immutably requires by separating them from the very thing God has provided in order to enable to live up to this requirement. Were anyone *other* than God to do such a thing (assuming it were possible), would we not take such an act to be intrinsically wrong, regardless of the overall consequences?

That God is the one who, according to CDH, does this thing only adds a level of incoherence to the act. It would be as if a parent required of her child that she vacuum her room, providing her with a vacuum for that purpose; and when the child refuses, the parent punishes the child by taking away all access to vacuums, though the parent remains sincerely adamant that the child vacuum, insisting the child is still obligated to do so. 'You are absolutely and unconditionally ordered to vacuum your room!' the parent declares. 'I absolutely and permanently bar you from any access to vacuums, but I haven't changed my mind about vacuuming. I order you to do it. Now! It is intolerable that you aren't doing it, but under no condition will I make it possible for you to do it.'

Such a parent would strike most of us as less than sane. If it truly is the case that the child continues to have a moral duty to vacuum, then the parent's withdrawal of the means of fulfilling that duty would directly implicate the parent in the child's failure to fulfil it. Most of us would be inclined to relieve the child of responsibility at this point. While the child might be in the wrong concerning her initial failure to vacuum, she cannot be expected to do what cannot be done, and her parent is being so unreasonable and even psychologically abusive that any parental authority may be compromised, potentially relieving the child of her duty of obedience.

In short, there appear to be two ways to view this situation: either the continued disobedience of the child ceases to speak ill of her and speaks ill *only* of the parent, or her continued disobedience continues to constitute a moral failing on her part, but one in which the parent is implicated. By analogy, it seems that either the continued disobedience of the damned ceases to speak ill of them but speaks ill *only* of God, or God is implicated in their moral failures. Neither alternative is remotely tolerable for theists.

Of course, if a child were given a vacuum in order to clean her room but used it instead to torment the cat, a good parent might take the vacuum away. However, this does not show that God might be justified in removing divine grace from the damned. First of all, a sane and good parent, after taking the vacuum away, would not order the child to vacuum her room and hold her continued failure to do so against her. Instead, if it truly were intolerable for the child not to vacuum her room (as it truly is intolerable for any of God's creatures to sin), the parent would establish conditions under which access to the vacuum would be restored, and would work with the child to bring it about that she met these conditions and – once she had met them – used the vacuum properly. In CDH, however, there are no conditions under which God would restore grace to the damned, let alone any provision for God working with the damned so that grace might eventually be restored.

In any event, divine grace is unlike a vacuum in that it *cannot be misused*. Although the voluntary participation of a creature might be needed for grace to have its transformative effect, all this means is that a creature may fail to receive grace. It does not mean that a creature who genuinely receives divine grace can then use it for wicked purposes (the way a child might misuse a vacuum). As such, no fear of misuse could justify finally and ultimately withholding divine grace; but the necessity of access to it for the sake of what is morally required of creatures would seem to make withholding grace an act of complicity in moral evil.

Suppose, however, that the critic finds a way around these concerns and shows that (4**-i) is, after all, false. Can the critic also show that (4**−ii) is false? To do so, the critic must show both that the benefits of removing grace from the damned outweigh the costs, and that these benefits cannot be achieved by God without incurring the costs. We have already briefly mentioned the latter and expressed our scepticism. For now, then, we focus on the former: do the benefits of withholding grace from the damned *really* outweigh the evil of the damned being permanently confirmed in unrepentant sinfulness against God? If sin is as deep an affront to God and the good as conservative defenders of CDH generally claim it to be, what benefits could outweigh the bad effect of this intolerable evil becoming a *permanent fixture* in God's creation?

By hypothesis, it does the damned no good at all.[40] Thus, if there are good effects, they must be found elsewhere. However, according to defenders of CDH who hold fast to the doctrine of divine impassivity (as it seems they must in order to oppose ALB), God cannot be benefited by anything that happens to creatures; and, even if one leaves aside our arguments in Chapter 5 for the conclusion that the blessed would suffer if any are damned, it seems implausible at first glance to suggest that the blessed, who already enjoy the beatific vision, could have their state improved by the damned *not* doing so. Aquinas, however, holds that 'the elect rejoice' in the punishments of the damned 'when they see God's *justice* in them and realize that they have escaped them'.[41]

One charitable reading of this astonishing assertion is that it is intrinsically just (in the retributive sense) that unrepentant sinners be deprived of God's light. The good effect of withdrawing grace from the damned is nothing other than the realization of this just state – along with the delight that the blessed take in contemplating it. However, how could the withdrawal of grace be a proper expression of retributive justice? Here we need to distinguish between two understandings of retributive justice – alternative visions that will become increasingly important as our discussion of JDH proceeds. First, there is what we have been calling 'crude retributivism', according to which (a) bad things happening to bad people is something to be valued in itself, and (b) the only justification for this positive valuation of evil-for-evil is an immediate intuition of its fittingness (one which may have more to do with the bloodthirsty impulses of our fallen natures than with the image of God).

Second, there is what the Lutheran Orthodox referred to by the term 'vindicatory justice'.[42] Like crude retributivism, vindicatory justice endorses the *lex talionis* principle that punishment should be proportionate in severity to the offence it responds to. However, the intrinsic suitability of proportional punishment is grounded on less suspect intuitions than the bloodthirstiness that seems to underlie crude retributivism. Instead of resting on an implicit appeal to our base desire for vengeance, the concept of vindicatory justice rests on more noble intuitions.[43] Jean Hampton expresses these powerfully in her defence of retributivism. In her view, proportional punishment is the only way to adequately refute the erroneous moral claims implicitly promulgated by wrongful acts.

In this theory, a wrongful act implicitly overvalues the perpetrator and undervalues those against whom the act is directed. As such, Hampton thinks the perpetrator must be subjected to a 'defeat' that expresses the error of the perpetrator's value system.[44] To achieve this, punishment must adequately reflect, in its severity, the *degree of error* implicit in the wrongful act. Proportional punishment is therefore to be valued not for any *external* consequences, but because it affirms the value of what ought to be valued to the degree that it ought to be valued. The intuitions underlying this form of retributivism are these: first, wrongdoing is fundamentally about treating that with inherent value and dignity as if it either lacks such value or has less value that it really does; second, proportional punishment, and only proportional punishment, can vindicate that which has been thus denigrated through wrongdoing; third, such vindication is intrinsically fitting – that is, it is worth pursuing regardless of its further consequences (such as sinners' moral reform).

When the Lutheran Orthodox are being careful in their thinking about retributive justice, *this* is the understanding they invoke. Sin is, at root, a failure to love God and neighbour as one should, and, as such, is a failure to value God and neighbour as highly as their inherent dignity demands. This undervaluing needs to be answered, not merely with a contrary claim, but with *repudiation*. When God is determined by justice to punish any infraction of His Holy Law with proportionate punishment, it is because He wishes to defend and fully manifest the value of something (or, rather, of someone) and so repudiate the evil of failing to recognize and respect that value. God punishes sinners so that His own infinite value, and the value of His creatures, will be affirmed in the face of the sin that actively denies these values.

We will have considerably more to say about both understandings of retributive justice in later sections. For now, however, we want to see whether the only version of retributivism we find tenable – the vindicatory version – might be coherently invoked to support the following idea: withdrawing grace from the damned, although it has the negative effect of confirming the damned in sin, has the greater positive effect of meeting the requirements of vindicatory justice.

The implausibility of this idea should be immediately evident. Vindicatory justice is about vindicating the value of that which has, through sin, been improperly undervalued. Sin is an affront to all that is valuable and good. The sinner, in sinning, implicitly asserts that the neighbour is *not* a creature of boundless inherent dignity, and that God is *not* a being of infinite majesty and worth whose will is perfect and deserving of total submission. This message needs to be repudiated in no uncertain terms. What is at issue here is whether the repudiation of this intolerable message can be achieved through an act that *guarantees that the intolerable message continues to be expressed for all eternity* in the souls of the damned (who eternally fail to appreciate its erroneousness).

Obviously, when we take decisive action to guarantee that some state of affairs, S, continues to be the case forever, we do not succeed in communicating in no uncertain terms that S is utterly intolerable. On the contrary, we would be conveying the very opposite message. Thus, withdrawing grace from the damned does not and cannot meet the demands of vindicatory justice. Hence, a fortiori, the justice achieved by withdrawing grace from the damned does not outweigh the bad effect of the damned being confirmed in sin. If anything, justice would require that God *not* withdraw grace from the damned (especially insofar as it is concerned with vindicating of God's majesty).

As for Aquinas's claim that 'the elect rejoice' in the punishments of the damned, it seems to us that, on the contrary, the elect would weep. Apart from their benevolent love for the damned, the affront to the good that sin represents would, it seems, motivate the blessed to will that sinners repent and sin no more – and so join the ranks of the blessed – because it is only then that all glorify God as they should. Anything short of universal salvation would have to be viewed with regret by anyone who cares about God's glory; and since the saved do care about God's glory, we cannot imagine that they would rejoice in the fact that some continue to forever blaspheme God (and undervalue other creatures).

The *salvation* of the damned – not their continued punishment – would thus be what gives the blessed cause to rejoice. If such universal reconciliation were not possible (perhaps for reasons of creaturely freedom), then this would give the blessed reason to grieve. They would grieve an eternal tragedy, forever saddened by God's ultimate failure to achieve what is best. Even supposing that the 'next best thing' to universal salvation would be sinners who continually pay for their sins, that God *settles* for second best would hardly seem a reason for the blessed to *rejoice*.

However, when Aquinas states that 'the elect rejoice' in the punishments of the damned, he indicates that they rejoice not only in the intrinsic justice of these punishments, but in something else also: the realization 'that they have escaped them'. Perhaps the good effect of withholding grace from the damned is precisely this: the joy that the blessed feel at having escaped a dire fate. However, even if such joy were so great a good as to outweigh the bad effect of withdrawing grace from the damned (which we doubt), there is a deep problem with this thinking: the joy of escaping a dire fate is not contingent on there being others who did not escape.

If a plane crashes and only a few survive, those survivors may feel lucky, but their joy at surviving is likely to be diminished by the thought of all those who perished (in fact, some experience debilitating 'survivors guilt'). Indeed, it seems that only the *wicked* would take extra delight in being the ones who got away while others suffered – but the blessed are not wicked, and so their joy in escaping perdition is not magnified by there being those who did not escape.

Perhaps, however, Aquinas is gesturing towards a different argument, according to which the justice God pursues in damnation is not retributive but *distributive*. Perhaps the reason God does not save the damned is that doing so would be *unfair* to the blessed – who, by their holy lives, have earned heaven. The damned, however, have not, and therefore it is not fair that both should be rewarded with blessedness.

Even setting aside parables of Jesus which directly repudiate this way of thinking, there remain problems with it. First, it seems to prioritize concern for preserving the blessed's sense of having earned their blessedness over concern for the glory of God. However, those who support CDH the loudest are precisely those who most insist on the notion that God is, above all, concerned with His glory. How then could they insist that God would put aside this concern in order to preserve among His creatures the sense that they exist in a meritocracy?

Furthermore, among all God's creatures it is the blessed who will love God the most. Therefore, if God is most glorified by the damned being reformed, that is what the blessed would desire, not that the damned continue to be damned out of 'fairness'.

The problems do not end there. The argument assumes that the blessed merit heaven by their good works while the damned do not; but this supposes that rational creatures might be the authors of their own good works. The weight of the tradition, by contrast, holds that it is God who causes the moral goodness of creatures, and hence it is God who should be praised for it, not the blessed.

A possible response here could be that creatures have the capacity either to *resist* or *not* resist divine grace. A creature that rejects divine grace might then be thought not to deserve heaven in the way the creature that accepts it does – but consider: if a man offers two beggars money (supposing neither has earned it), we would not say that the one who received it *deserved* the food he bought with it while the man who refused it did not. In fact, neither deserved the money or the food. Likewise, if the divine grace needed to do good works is not offered based on desert, then the act of accepting that grace cannot be construed as *conferring* desert; and if the divine grace is conferred based on desert, this prior good would, in terms of traditional teaching, have its root in a still prior act of grace.

Suppose, however, that those who insist that all good comes from God are wrong and that rational creatures could be the authors of their own moral goodness. It still seems apparent that no works the creature could perform would merit heaven. The essential good of heaven is union of God, and God is the supreme infinite good. To *merit* such a good, the works of creatures would need to be of infinite value. However, no finite creature could, by its own powers, produce a work of infinite value. If there is anything that might make rational creatures worthy of an infinite good, it is not their works but their nature (as suggested in Chapter 5); but the damned and blessed share the same nature.

In sum, meeting the demands of distributive justice could not, it seems, serve as the good effect which would justify the evil effect of the damned being confirmed forever in sinfulness. As such, there is good reason to suppose that (4**−i) and (4**−ii) are true. Since only one of (4**i) to (4**−iii) need to be true for (4**) to be true, it follows that even if we modify AWS in light of the moral perspective embodied in Double Effect, the resultant argument against CDH remains compelling.

6.6 Critique of Combining CH2 with NH1a

So far we have only critiqued CDH taken in the broader sense – that is, simply insofar as it holds CH2. Now we turn to a critique of CDH in the strict sense (insofar as it holds NH1a *and* CH2), one inspired by Ritschl. To understand this critique, it may help to recall something Baier says about the 'intellectual evils' that afflict the damned – specifically, the evil associated with the damned's knowledge of God. According to Baier, although the damned have some knowledge of God, it is only an *abstractive* knowledge (knowledge *that* God is such and such), not an *intuitive* knowledge (a direct experiential knowledge *of* God).[45] Abstractive knowledge is propositional knowledge divorced from immediate experiential understanding of its truth – for example, someone may have a 'textbook' knowledge of Niagara Falls being the world's most powerful waterfall without ever having experienced the falls' power first-hand.

One might liken it to a psychopath's 'knowledge' that killing is wrong, even though he regularly kills without remorse. Arguably, the psychopath does not even know that killing is wrong. Maybe all he knows is that *other people* think so – a point which bears on the controversy between internalism and externalism with respect to moral motivation. However, Baier – like all Lutheran Scholastics, and like Aquinas and Suarez – was an internalist, and so he thought the blessed experience overwhelming joy at perceiving God *because* God is the highest good, the genuine perception of which produces joy.[46] In short, Baier thought that while the damned know in an abstractive way *that* God is the highest good, they do not *perceive* this or *understand what it means*. Thus, Baier must hold that the damned, at a deep level, are ignorant about who God is.

Consider also the damned's supposed knowledge that they are responsible for their sins – a knowledge that leads to remorse and self-recrimination. If one assumes CH2, so that the damned are lost to sin and incapable or repentance, it seems that such knowledge and remorse can only be a *false* knowledge and remorse. According to Aquinas, the remorse of the damned is like that of a convicted criminal who regrets committing her crime *because* it led to such an unpleasant outcome.[47] This is not a case of remorse over having *sinned*, but over having done something leading to pain. The damned do not perceive the *wrongness* of their acts, or the fittingness of the punitive hardships. Hence, defenders of CH2 must suppose the damned are gripped by an *ignorance* that keeps them from understanding why they are being punished.

This exposes CDH to a powerful Ritschlian critique. Ritschl observes that older theologians interpreted guilt as 'a merely objective relationship' expressing the fact that sinners are worthy of being punished. Ritschl insists that this objective fact is insufficient to justify punishment; offenders must also have a proper subjective appreciation of their guilt – they need a *conscience*.

Essentially, Ritschl poses a dilemma for defenders of the strictest form of CDH: either the damned still have a conscience or they do not, and neither option is compatible with CDH. As Ritschl puts it, if we follow the 'orthodox' view 'that those who are condemned to eternal punishment recognize its justice, it is inconsistent to deny altogether to the hardened that consciousness of guilt, without which they cannot acknowledge their state of punishment before God.'[48] However, Ritschl argues that, 'a hardening of the sinful will which leaves no prospect of conversion to the good ... is conceivable only if we presuppose that the consciousness of guilt, which as a rule accompanies sin, and under certain circumstances makes conversion possible, is crushed out.'[49] If their conscience is crushed out, it would seem that they should no more be punished than should animals or the insane. Ritschl notes that those incapable of understanding why they are being punished will regard punishments as 'arbitrary acts of violence'.[50]

As such, God would inflict positive evils on the damned (as NH1a asserts He does) only if they can understand why they are being punished, and so can experience real guilt. However, they are capable of the latter only if they are not wholly lost to sin – that is, only if God has not wholly cast them from His presence in the way CH2 posits.[51]

Put simply, if we accept CH2, the damned have been rejected by God and eternally deprived of God's grace; but if this is so, they are incapable of the subjective attitude of guilt which makes the infliction of punitive hardship (posited by NH1a) appropriate. If we embrace NH1a, it will be because the damned can recognize and appreciate the justice of these punishments – which they would be capable of doing only if, contrary to what is posited in CH2, God has not wholly deprived them of grace. It is hard to fathom why God would extend His grace to those whom He has given up on utterly. Thus, given Ritschl's plausible assumption concerning subjective guilt as a prerequisite for legitimate punishment, NH1a and CH2 seem incompatible.

These problems do not merely challenge the coherence of CDH, but also impact RDH with respect to how its defenders should view *how* God knows the damned will never respond to His offer of saving grace. *If* God knows this because the damned have, through their choices, produced in themselves a state of irrevocable hardening, and God, 'to whom all hearts are open and all desires known' is aware of this, then RDH faces the same problems faced by CHD: how could it possibly be just to punish those who are *incapable* of understanding *why* they are being punished?

We think this shows that defenders of RDH should hold that every damned being *could* repent and be reconciled to God – not just in the logical sense, but in the sense of a *real* possibility. The creature's heart, in short, is not irrevocably hardened. Hence, if God knows the damned *never* repent, God will have such knowledge either because He is outside of time *or* because He has middle knowledge; but, as we argue in Chapter 8, maintaining *both* that the damned really could become reconciled to God *and* that they *never will* is deeply problematic.

6.7 *Explication and Critique of Philosophical Arguments for CDH and RDH*

While we have one final argument to direct against all forms of JDH, its basis emerges most clearly when we consider the problems with the chief philosophical arguments *for* JDH. Not all great defenders of JDH believed that it *could* be defended philosophically. Augustine, arguably CDH's author, held that no plausible non-scriptural case for DH could be given.[52] He took it that we believe DH based on Scripture, not reason, and that reason can only answer objections to the doctrine. If our arguments in Chapter 4 are correct, then Augustine (hardly a scriptural literalist) was strangely confused in this point.[53] It was perhaps because they knew Scripture does *not* so clearly teach CDH that later Western defenders of CDH, unlike Augustine, developed philosophical arguments for it. A review of their thinking reveals, we think, two main philosophical arguments for versions of JDH – one for CDH broadly construed, the other for RDH.

The former takes its cue from two retributivist intuitions: first, that the wicked deserve to suffer in direct proportion to the gravity of their offences; second, that the gravity of a sinful act is in part a function of the status of the one the act offends. In Quenstedt's words: 'It was the infinite God that was offended by sin; and because sin is an offense, wrong, and crime against the infinite God, and, so to speak, is Deicide, it has an infinite evil, not indeed formally ... but objectively, and deserves infinite punishments.'[54]

We will call this the Argument from Infinite Guilt (AIG). At least at first glance, AIG gives us reason to think some sins could be so grievous that anyone who performs them deserves to be cast away from God's presence forever. As such, AIG is an argument for CDH, not RDH. In RDH, God still loves the damned and would save them if He could legitimately do so; but if we accept that the damned have incurred an *infinite* guilt, it seems that God could not save them without offending the demands of justice – unless there were an alternate way to meet these demands of which God could avail Himself. However, if that is the case, then AIG could support *neither* CDH *nor* RDH (which, as will become apparent, is precisely our view).

The second argument was adumbrated in the medieval period but is more characteristic of the Enlightenment and finds a strong exponent in Leibniz, who argues that 'one need not, in order to justify the continuation of their sufferings, assume that sin has become of infinite weight through the infinite nature of the object offended' because 'the damned remain wicked' and so 'could not be withdrawn from their misery'.[55] In other words, the damned keep sinning, and so keeping warranting more misery *ad infinitum.*

We will call this the Argument from Everlasting Sin (AES). A moment's reflection reveals that AES could not be used to defend CDH but only RDH. CDH supposes that some persons deserve to be forever deprived of all the grace necessary for them to repent and be converted. It would be circular reasoning, however, to suppose that what could justify a total withdrawal of grace is the everlasting sin *which results necessarily from the withdrawal of grace.* For God to be justified in condemning some persons to a state of moral ruin, some particular sins would have to be *in themselves* so monstrous that retributive justice would demand the most extreme punishment. However, AES does not attempt to show that any *particular* sin could be that wicked. Thus, AES cannot, by itself, support CDH.

RDH, however, is another matter. A retributivist might suppose that if there are persons who forever freely resist God's grace and persist forever in a state of sin, such persons deserve to be everlastingly punished *not* because of past sins, but because each fresh sin demands fresh punishment.

These, then, are the main arguments in support of some version of JDH. Although both have fallen on hard times in recent centuries, they are not quite dead. In the following sections we aim to put the final nails in their coffins.

6.8 General Problems with Crude Retributivism

Before focusing specific attention on AIG and AES, we want to offer some initial critical remarks about the retributive underpinnings of each. Both arguments rely on the retributivist principle that wrongdoing renders the wrongdoer deserving of suffering, so that punishment in proportion to the severity of the wrong is intrinsically fitting and should be pursued for that reason, regardless of whether any further good comes of it. Many defenders of JDH seem to have held this principle to be *per se* evident – that is, as a first principle of morality which can only be known through immediate intuition, as opposed to being derivable from a broader theory of justice.

The natural law systems of both Catholic and Protestant Scholastics permitted such a view, insofar as they held that the first principles of morality are *per se* evident. Jonathan Edwards, in his defence of CDH, clearly treats the retributivist principle as just such a given, simply asserting that: 'The faulty nature of any-thing is the formal ground and reason of its desert of punishment; and the more anything hath of this nature the more punishment it deserves.'[56]

Earlier, we defined 'crude retributivism' as the view that (a) bad things happening to bad people is something to be valued for its own sake, and (b) the only justification for doing so is an immediate intuition. What we are saying here is that many defenders of CDH and RDH seem to have been crude retrib-utivists in this sense.

This label is, admittedly, derogatory. Is our negative judgment justified? One problem with this approach to retributivism is that many intelligent and other-wise morally sensitive people simply *lack* the salient intuition, or are intuitively suspect of it (they have the intuition that it is a false intuition). Why is it intrinsi-cally good for those who have done wrong to be harmed for it? It seems clear that they should try to make amends for what they have done, that they should come to truly repent of it, that they should try not to do it again, and so on; but that they should be positively harmed in any way that does *no one* any good seems puzzling at best.

At one point Aquinas apparently tries to elicit support for this retributivist intuition in the following terms:

> Whenever one thing rises up against another it suffers some detriment therefrom. For we observe in natural things that when one contrary supervenes the other acts with greater energy .... Wherefore, we find that the natural inclination of man is to repress those who rise up against him.[57]

Were Aquinas to be taken here as offering an *argument* for retributivism, it would be a weak one: if an animal is hurt it strikes back – this is natural; hence it is just. However, we see no reason why what is natural *in this sense* should be a reason for accepting the retributivist principle. It is also 'natural,' after all, for us to hate our enemies, love inordinate praise, resent correction, and so on. As such, we think it better to see Aquinas as offering this analogy to nature as an 'intuition pump'; that is, as a way of inspiring his reader to share his own intuition.

We do not deny that Aquinas's intuition is widely shared; but does widespread distribution entail truth? The view that love should be reserved for friends is a widely distributed intuition that Jesus emphatically challenged; and the retribu-tive intuition has some things in common with the intuitive truncation of love to exclude enemies. Why should we trust this intuition, when it is so deeply entan-gled with our more bloodthirsty impulses to exact vengeance on our enemies?

Others, however, have sought to bolster their retributive intuition by relating it to other intuitions about justice, especially the core intuition underlying our concept of distributive justice. The idea here is that these intuitions stand or fall together. If we think that we ought to reward those who deserve to be rewarded, distributing goods at least in part according to some appropriate measure of merit, then how can we deny that we should mete out punitive suffering to those whose demerits warrant it? 'Good for good' goes hand-in-hand with 'bad for bad'. Getting rid of retribution, some might say, demands that we throw out our broader notions of justice altogether, and thereby destroy one of the very roots of our moral system.

To show the weakness of this argument, it is sufficient to offer a plausible portrait of justice which coherently affirms the duty to reward meritorious behaviour without implying a corresponding duty to punish demerits. For this purpose, our own view of justice works well. We regard it as just to treat persons in a way commensurate with certain perfections they have. Some of these perfections are intrinsic to being a person – the *inherent dignity* of persons, if you will. Justice calls us to respect this dignity by not gratuitously harming anyone and by helping them, at least when that involves no inconvenience. Other human perfections, however, are adventitious. If a person performs well at a sporting contest, for example, we regard it as just to recognize this, perhaps with an appropriate reward, and unjust not to. However, it does not follow that if someone lacks an adventitious perfection they ought to be positively harmed. It only follows that we need not bestow upon them those goods (or the kind of respect) we bestow on persons of a higher perfection.

Given this perspective, it follows that wrongdoers might lose the right to be treated as innocent persons. It does *not* follow that wrongdoers should suffer. It certainly does not follow that we should withhold the respect called for by wrongdoers' *inherent* dignity. Consider an analogy: traditional moralists do not think that animals have the right to life, but that does not entail that it is licit to kill them for just any reason. We may legitimately kill or harm animals only if doing so does us some good. Therefore, even *if* the damned have given up certain basic human rights, that would not by itself entail that God should torture them. He should torture them only if by so doing He did Himself or the blessed some good; but, as already seen, there is no compelling non-question-begging basis for holding that the torture of the damned does God or the blessed any good.

In any event, wrongdoers do not lose their essential human perfection and thereby their basic human rights. Wrongdoing vitiates the wrongdoer, producing what is not just a lack of a higher perfection (in the way animals merely lack the reason found in persons), but a *privation* of a good the wrongdoer should, in a sense, possess. The wrongdoer is not an animal but a morally maimed person and should be treated as such. This means that the wrongdoer's humanity must be respected and valued, even in punishment.

6.9 Critique of AIG and AES

Suppose, however, that we accept the retributivist principle on the terms offered by the crude retributivist: it is intrinsically right that punishment should be meted out proportionate to the severity of wrongdoing, and the truth of this is not derivable from some deeper theoretic considerations, but is given by an immediate intuition. Do AIG and AES fare well if we concede this starting point?

We do not think so. Consider AIG, which holds that, since God is an infinitely good being, sin against Him confers infinite guilt and warrants everlasting punishment. It should be clear that one might sin more or less gravely against such a being, and in that case it does not seem intuitively obvious that just any sin against an infinite being would merit an infinite penalty. If all we have to go by is crude retributivism, which tells us to attend to our intuitive retributive sense of the rightness of proportional punishment, how many of us could honestly say that our intuition is in line with the idea that a minor infraction against God's law is as deserving of infinite punishment as a major infraction, simply because the offence is against God, who is infinitely good?[58]

Recall Quenstedt's formulation of this argument. In it, he called sin against God 'deicide', or perhaps we should say 'attempted deicide'. The appellation of sin as 'deicide' is striking, but it points out what is wrong with this line of reasoning: just as not every sin against one's father – not even every serious one – is patricide, so not every sin against God is deicide, or attempted deicide.[59] Do our retributive intuitions *really* tell us that every sin against God calls for infinite punishment, regardless of its relative gravity? This would seem to be at odds with the *lex talionis* intuitions of most, as opposed to being in conformity with them.

Aquinas, of course, thought that only *mortal* sins merit hell. Perhaps he would say these sins constitute attempted deicide; but it seems attempted deicide would need to be a *total* and explicit rejection and hatred of God (and hence of all that is good). The Lutheran tradition, which held that only the sin against the Holy Ghost is unforgivable, described this sin in these terms: a complete rejection of divine grace with full awareness of what is being rejected and of the value of the One offering it.[60]

However, if this is the only thing that warrants damnation given our crude retributive instincts, we confront an important question: could such a total rejection of God take place in a creature that, as *created* by God Himself, is in *essence* good? As Aquinas often insisted, action follows being, so that which is in essence good must always have some goodness in its action.[61] However, since God is goodness itself, the total rejection of God would seem to imply complete lack of all goodness in one's actions. This appears either to sever all links between essence and action, or to deny goodness to the essence of the damned, thus leading to Manichaeism. In short, the only sin that our crude retributive sense would take to warrant infinite punishment is one whose very *possibility* is dubious (given core Christian assumptions).

Similar problems arise, we think, for AES. In this argument, some creatures are taken to deserve eternal hell not because any past sin is so grave as to call for it, but because the sinner is eternally committed to the rejection of God in such a way that he or she continues to commit grave sins *ad infinitum*, thus continually meriting further punishment. What is hard to fathom here is the possibility of a creature of God continuing to pursue such a recalcitrant pattern *for all time*. We have more to say against the coherence of such choice pattern later, in Chapter 8.

There is one further objection to both AIG and AES when these arguments are put forward in terms of a crude retributivism – an objection related to the importance, for Christian theology, of avoiding any sort of account of our eternal destiny that leaves no room for Christ's Atonement.

There are two problems here: first, crude retributivism offers no theoretic resources for understanding how a vicarious Atonement could satisfy the demands of retributive justice. How could torturing to death an innocent person satisfy the *lex talionis* demand that the guilty suffer in proportion to their offence? Crude retributivism is profoundly *personal* in the following sense: what my retributive intuition tells me when I reflect on, for example, Timothy McVeigh's wrongdoing is not merely that *somebody* suffering in proportion to McVeigh's offence is intrinsically good; it tells me that *McVeigh's* suffering in proportion to McVeigh's offence is intrinsically good. The infliction of suffering on another innocent person does not satisfy our retributive intuition but rather creates another offence in response to which we intuitively seek retributive suffering.

Second, crude retributivism may not take sin seriously enough, insofar as it views the suffering of a human offender (proportionately more severe as the offence increases in magnitude) as somehow sufficient to satisfy the demands of justice. On this point we think AIG, as articulated by Quenstedt and others, comes closer to a key Christian insight about sin than do our retributive intuitions. In a sense, the fact that crude retributivism *does not* support AIG is one of *its* failings: crude retributivism fails to show just how serious our sinfulness is, and, as such, fails to reveal just how incapable we are of meriting God's favour. Crude retributivism lends itself not only to the idea that the damned deserve damnation, but also to the idea that the saved *do not*. After all, if the saved did deserve it, then crude retributivism would call for it.

As such, crude retributivism lends itself to the idea that salvation is, in part, a function of merit. By implication, God's love ceases to be quite as extraordinary as it would be given another hypothesis – namely, that all of us by our sins fall so far short of God's glory that none can rely on good works when standing before God's throne; and yet God's love, because it does not wait on worth, is unflagging and so can manifest in a radical sacrifice on behalf of those who have done nothing to earn it.

Here we cannot resist quoting at some length one of Martin Luther's more passionate outbursts:

> These words, 'The Son of God loved me and gave Himself for me,' are mighty thunderings and lightnings from heaven against the righteousness of the Law and the doctrine of works. So great and so horrible was the wickedness, error, darkness, and ignorance in

my will and understanding that it was impossible for me to be ransomed by any other means than by such an inestimable ransom ... What is the obedience of all the holy angels in comparison with the Son of God, who was delivered, and that most shamefully, to the death of the Cross, so that there was no drop of His most precious blood but it was shed, and that for thy sins? If thou couldst rightly consider this incomparable treasure, thou shouldst surely damn all cowls, shaven pates, all vows, works, merits, before grace and after (*meritum congrui and meritum condigni*), and trample them underfoot, spit upon them and execrate them and cast them into hell. For it is an intolerable and horrible blasphemy to imagine that there is any work whereby thou shouldst presume to reconcile God, since thou seest that there is nothing which can reconcile Him but this inestimable, infinite treasure, even the death and blood of His Son, one drop whereof is more precious than the whole world.[62]

Here, in Luther's words, are found the seeds of a final refutation of any form of JDH. If we are to have a truly Christocentric theology, then Christ's crucifixion must be seen *both* as God's ultimate condemnation of all sin at its root *and*, at the same time, as the greatest expression of divine love for fallen humanity. Crude retributivism does not offer a portrait of sin grave enough to make such an extreme sacrifice necessary, nor does it provide an avenue by which such a sacrifice could actually do for us what the immensity of our sin requires.

6.10 Lutheran Orthodoxy, Divine Justice and the Atonement

In line with Luther's strong Christocentrisim and his rejection of works of righteousness, the Lutheran Orthodox worked out a version of the Anselmian doctrine of the Atonement that relied on a more subtle understanding of retributive justice than what crude retributivism can offer – what they called *vindicatory justice*. In the remainder of this chapter we argue, first, that this conception of justice can provide what crude retributivism cannot: an account of the Atonement in which Christ's vicarious sacrifice for our sins makes sense. However, insofar as vindicatory justice makes a demand in response to sin that only God can meet, it shows that the sufferings of hell are useless from the standpoint of justice; and insofar as the Atonement does meet the demands of vindicatory justice, the sufferings of hell are rendered needless. As such, vindicatory justice cannot justify JDH. If there is a hell, it will not be because justice requires it.

  In developing this case, we begin with the Lutheran Orthodox understanding of God's moral attributes – specifically of divine justice (the divine attribute most relevant to JDH), which the Lutheran Orthodox typically took to come in three forms: dispositive justice, remunerative justice and retributive or vindicatory justice.[63] God's dispositive justice refers to the perfect righteousness with which God governs the universe, and as such encompasses all God's relative moral attributes (those He possesses in relation to His creatures rather than in Himself alone) – including mercy, patience and veracity.[64] The moral law, imprinted on human hearts, is an image of this kind of justice.[65]

God's remunerative and vindicatory justices refer more narrowly to creatures' moral desert. In virtue of the former, God rewards the just; in virtue of the latter, He punishes the wicked. The latter is what bears directly on DH, providing the foundation for the older Lutheran divines for all species of JDH (although remunerative justice may bear on what the Lutheran orthodox called Christ's *active* obedience in atoning for sin).

With respect to God's vindicatory justice, the Lutheran Orthodox generally maintained that God, by virtue of His holiness, is bound to punish all transgressions of His Holy Law[66] (that is, the law demanding that creatures love Him above all things and one another as themselves[67]). Any infraction is an offence against *God* and so carries infinite guilt and a liability to punishment of infinite worth.[68] But at least when they were at their most subtle, the Lutheran Orthodox were not content to justify this idea based simply on a crude retributive intuition. They maintained that what sin does is manifest an undervaluation of God's majesty, and it does so in every case in virtue of sin's essence, which is to operate as if God's worth were less than infinite. The purpose of punishment is to *vindicate* God's majesty – in other words, to reassert God's (and our neighbour's) real worth.

We have already mentioned Jean Hampton's contemporary expression of this view: punishment's function is to repudiate a false valuation of someone. Wrongdoing involves treating someone in ways inconsonant with their worth. Justice demands that we respond not just with a verbal *no*, but with an active response that repudiates the undervaluation in a way that cannot be brushed off, so as to reaffirm the true worth of the one who has been undervalued. For Hampton, this is exactly what proportional punishment does, and hence what makes it just: by imposing on wrongdoers a 'defeat' comparable to what they inflicted on their victims, we say, in a way that wrongdoers *cannot* ignore, '*This* is how far off you were in you values. *This* is how valuable your victim truly is.' [69]

To achieve such decisive refutation of wrongdoers' erroneous value judgments, punishment must adequately reflect, in its severity, the *degree of error* implicit in the wrongful act. Proportional punishment is therefore to be valued because it affirms the value of what ought to be valued to the degree it ought to be valued.

However, any human act that falls short of recognizing God's *infinite* value will then attach to God a value that falls *infinitely short* (since the difference between an infinite and finite value is infinite). Thus, the only punishment that would fully vindicate God's majesty would be one of infinite severity.

However, here lies the difficulty: how can the punishment of a finite creature meet the demands of vindicatory justice if the severity of the offence is *infinite*? In keeping with Anselm, the Lutherans generally held that it was not simply *fitting* that Christ become incarnate to save sinners, but that He *had* to.[70] Since creatures, being finite, cannot by their suffering obtain an infinite merit, no punishment of the creature could atone for infinite guilt. Thus, the only way to satisfy God's vindicatory justice is for God to vicariously meet those demands on our behalf. Gerhard clearly asserted this position:

> In order, therefore, that the price of redemption might be proportionate to our debt and infinite guilt, it was necessary that the action or mediation not only of a finite, viz., a human, but also of an infinite, i.e., a divine nature, should concur, and that the suffering and death of Christ should acquire power of infinite price elsewhere, viz., from the most effectual working of the divine nature, and thus that an infinite good might be able to be presented against an infinite evil. [71]

A critic might claim that the punishment of a finite human being could satisfy the demands of justice if it were infinite *in duration*. Some such idea seems to underlie CDH; but while endless suffering may be the closest one can come to satisfying the demands of justice when the one being punished is finite, Anselm and the Lutheran Orthodox insisted that no punishment of a finite creature, even if endless, could fully satisfy the demands of justice.[72] There are at least two reasons. First, there would be no point at which this endlessly endured suffering had been completed, and hence no point at which the demands of justice had been met. Second, punishments that are finite at any given moment cannot be rendered fitting to an infinite offence by being imposed over an infinite duration. While the sinner will feel the sting of punishment every moment forever, the sting is finite and hence minor relative to the offence, and the finite nature of human consciousness entails that the succession of stings will never 'build up' to an infinite sting. Put another way, a punishment that is infinite in duration (and hence, over time, in its quantity of suffering) is not therefore infinitely *severe*.

Consider someone who, as a punishment for murder, has twenty dollars withheld from their income *forever* (assuming this is possible). Would we say that infinite duration has made the punishment fit the crime? No, because in human consciousness suffering is not endlessly cumulative.[73] Nor is the finite human imagination able to fully encompass endless suffering. The experience of horror that is sure to accompany a sentence of endless suffering is nevertheless a finite horror. Thus, the added suffering of facing the prospect of endless anguish will still fall short of infinite punishment.

The implication is that the demands of vindicatory justice simply cannot be met by punishing finite creatures. Only a sacrifice made by the infinite God could possibly carry the infinite significance needed to adequately repudiate sin; but since humans were the offending party, only one who was a true human could make reparations to God on behalf of the guilty. These notions entailed, for the Lutherans as it did for Anselm, that God *had to* (in the moral sense) become incarnate and suffer on behalf of fallen humans in order to appease God's just wrath against sin.[74]

However, the Lutheran Orthodox did not merely repeat Anselm's theory – they went beyond it in several ways. For our purposes here, the most significant way is this: according to Lutheran Orthodoxy, Christ, as He was truly God, could offer up to God a vicarious Atonement of infinite worth. As He was truly man He could do this on behalf of man. These things being so, God's justice demanded that He *recognize* the worth of Christ's sacrifice by *becoming in His heart reconciled to the entire race.*[75] This doctrine came to be known, among the Confessionalist Lutherans of the nineteenth century, as the doctrine of objective justification.[76] Christ so perfectly and infinitely satisfied the law on humanity's behalf that God is now reconciled to the entire race, His wrath wholly put away, and all divine impediments to bestowing the beatific vision on creatures dispelled. In Quenstedt's words, 'The real object for which satisfaction was rendered … comprises (1) all sins whatever, original as well as actual, past as well as future, venial as well as mortal, yea, even the very sin against the Holy Ghost … (2) All the penalties of our sins, temporal as well as eternal.'[77]

The old Norwegian Lutheran Synod stated the doctrine powerfully by declaring that 'with the general atonement that took place in Christ for the world, also for Judas, the whole world, including Judas, was justified and received forgiveness of sin and therefore became a child of God and an heir of heaven'.[78] In short, God is reconciled to *all* humans and there is nothing sinners need do or suffer in order to meet the demands of justice. Later Lutheran theology referred to this aspect of Lutheran Orthodox teaching as 'the objective atonement' of sinners; but for this objective atonement to avail sinners, the Lutheran Orthodox thought sinners must appropriate it through saving faith, thus leading to their 'subjective atonement'. In short, that God is reconciled to us does not mean that we are to Him. Thus, some older Lutherans invoked the metaphor of persons in prison who, upon being told they are pardoned, do not believe the announcement and remain in their cells, chained by their disbelief.[79]

In this metaphor we find some Lutherans moving in the direction of LDH, even if they were not fully conscious of it or consistent about it. In what follows, in fact, we argue that a consequence of the Lutheran doctrine of the Atonement is that any version of JDH must be abandoned. The Lutheran Orthodox at times seemed to realize this, but – perhaps because, as Ritschl noted, it was impossible to work out in so short a time all the ramifications of the 'root principles' of Luther's Reformation – when it came to DH they seemingly forgot their teaching on justification and reconciliation and repeated, more or less exactly, CDH as it had been handed down to them.

In the next section we draw out the implications of the Lutheran doctrine of objective justification so as to show that, whether or not one subscribes to it, the insights the Lutheran Orthodox made use of in fashioning it imply that anyone who accepts the notion that Christ atoned for human sin must reject JDH in any form.

Before doing so, however, a word about the *vicarious* satisfaction of the demands of justice is in order, since the impossibility of such vicarious satisfaction would undermine the Lutheran and Anselmian approach. Recall that, according to the Lutheran Orthodox, retribution against sin is needed to vindicate God's majesty – that is, to repudiate the false value judgment implicit in every sin by expressing in proportionate punishment the enormity of the error. From this standpoint, when it comes to the vicarious Atonement the question is whether God could repudiate the sinner's false judgment by allowing the incarnate infinite God to be *crucified* on account of sin.

While there are difficulties here, the notion of a vicarious Atonement seems more coherent from this vindicatory perspective than from a crude retributive one. While punishing wrongdoers in proportion to their offence is one way to repudiate their error, it may not be the only way. What vindicatory justice demands is that the undervaluing of God and creatures conveyed in sin not be allowed to stand – that it be countered not merely with a verbal denouncement, but with a counterbalancing act that repudiates what was done with 'mighty thunderings and lightnings'.

How might this be achieved, other than by punishing sinners? In fact, if Anselm and his Lutheran followers were right, it *cannot* be done by punishing sinners. If it is to be achieved *at all*, it must be by another way – perhaps by the infinite creator of the universe Himself taking on mortal flesh and dying in agony *explicitly on account of our sin*. Perhaps an act of such staggering enormity can act as a stake that is plunged into reality's heart – a repudiation with infinite resonance: '*This* is what your sin *really* means,' it declares. '*This* is how wrong it is.'

6.11 Objective Justification and JDH

The argument that we have just sketched, although it appeals to Lutheran developments of Anselm, is not just an historical curiosity. Our argument here is that the premises undergirding JDH *demand* something like this version of the Atonement – which in turn undermines JDH.

To see why, consider the following: either God's justice is an essential attribute of Him, or not. If *not*, then His love for creatures (and His desire to see them achieve their end of union with Him) could not be thwarted by the demands of justice. Only if God would be violating some real obligation arising from justice could the demands of justice block His loving will to save all. If justice is not an essential feature of God, then it could not do this. Hence, anyone who wishes to endorse JDH must suppose, with the Lutherans, that God's justice *is* an essential attribute – one determining God to vindicate every sin in a proportionate way. However, the creature's sin is either finite or infinite in severity. If finite, then the demands of justice could not block God's salvific purpose, since only finite punishment would be required.[80] Hence, we find the Lutheran Orthodox asserting that human sin is infinitely serious.

However, on this assumption it would seem that God confronts a problem: no amount of suffering the creature could endure would vindicate its sin. This means – as the Lutheran Orthodox observed – that if God is essentially ordered to vindicate every sin with proportionate repudiation, then *only* something like vicarious Atonement could meet the demands of justice.[81]

Christ's Atonement, however, could not do this if it were *not* of infinite worth; and if it is of infinite worth (as the Lutherans believed), then the demands of justice have been fully met by Christ, and God could no longer be impelled *by justice* to hold anything against creatures. If God is perfectly just, He could not fail to recognize the full value of Christ's Atonement; and He *would* be failing to recognize its value if He did not, in light of it, forgive the *entire* race – what the later Lutherans called the *objective justification* of humanity.

If He limited His forgiveness only to those who *accepted* Christ (as many Christians seem to believe), then He would be failing to attribute to Christ's Atonement its full worth. For if it is the accepting or non-accepting of Christ that ultimately makes Christ's Atonement appease the divine wrath, then it is in virtue of something *we* do, something in us, that His Atonement makes satisfaction for sin. This, however, entails that Christ's Atonement was *not* of infinite worth. If something over and above Christ's redemptive work is needed for God to be reconciled to the sinner – whether it be the sinner's faith or good works – then Christ's Atonement must not have possessed the infinite merit required to expiate sin.[82] However, if Christ's Atonement has only finite merit, then no act of the creature, being finite, could make up the difference – and we are back to the original problem.

A critic might object here that the creature's faith does not *add* to the merit of Christ's Atonement, but simply determines whether that merit will be *attributed* to the creature and so will apply to *their* sin, thereby vindicating it. Perhaps God remains angry at creatures until they *cling in faith* to Christ, whereupon God attributes Christ's merits to them. Those who lack faith are justly condemned even though Christ's merit, being infinite, *would* atone for their sins *were it attributed to them.* [83]

While this objection shares with the Lutheran Orthodox the intuition that Christ's merit must be subjectively appropriated through faith, it distinguishes itself in that it assumes God remains unforgiving until Christ's merits are thus appropriated. The Lutheran Orthodox, by contrast, held that God was fully reconciled to sinners on account of Christ, but that sinners could not enjoy the fruits of this reconciliation without faith.[84] But why follow the Lutherans here? Why *not* say that, even though Christ's sacrifice has infinite merit, God remains wrathful at those who fail to cleave to Christ in faith?

The problem is that this view must make one of two assumptions: either (1) God *can* attribute Christ's merit to the unfaithful sinner but chooses not to, or (2) God cannot attribute Christ's merit to the unfaithful. The former clearly will not work. Given (1), God has the capacity to pay for every human sin and fully meet the demands of justice (by extending Christ's merits to every sinner), but chooses instead to allow the demands of justice to go eternally unmet with respect to some sinners – something He cannot do if, as a retributive theory demands, God is determined by His nature to meet justice's demands. That problem aside, if God has a compelling reason to withhold Christ's merit from those sinners who lack faith, it could not be the demands of justice requiring this – and so one would have to appeal to something else. One would be abandoning JDH in favour, presumably, of LDH.[85]

The second alternative is problematic on many levels. If we assume that a *vicarious* Atonement is possible at all, it is hard to imagine *why* God would be incapable of attributing Christ's merit to the unfaithful. If He can extend the merits of Christ to the faithful, even though they have not earned it, why would He be unable to do so to the unfaithful? If it is logically possible for God to attribute to sinners the merits of Christ, then it would seem logically possible for God to attribute these merits to *unfaithful* sinners. Perhaps one could say that it is not within God's moral power to do so because the unfaithful, due to their lack of faith, do not deserve to have Christ's merits attributed to them. This answer, however, assumes that Christ's Atonement – while it vicariously atones for *most* human sins – does not extend to shortcomings in faith. Faith becomes a good work. However, Luther forcefully argued that shortcomings in faith are the essence of *all* sins.[86] Every sin can be traced to a failure to properly trust and love God. If God's wrath against shortcomings of faith is unappeased by the Atonement, then it is hard to see how *any* sin could be atoned for vicariously through Christ's work; but if *justice* does not demand that God withhold Christ's merits from the unfaithful, then justice is no barrier to God's saving all. If some are not saved, it will be for another reason.

The lesson here is that if we truly want to hold *both* that God is obligated to meet the demands of justice *and* that human sin is infinite in nature (and hence requires infinite punishment), we are forced to accept something like the Lutheran doctrine of objective justification – which says that God, apart from *anything* creatures do, is fully reconciled to them. Their sins have been paid for *in their entirety* by Christ. Thus, justice cannot block God's achieving His redemptive purpose for the world.

It seems the only escape from this argument is to hold that human sin is not infinite, but that some sins (or patterns of sin) merit everlasting (albeit finitely severe) punishment. If this were assumed, then an Atonement of infinite worth would not be needed to pay for sin – humans could pay for it themselves by languishing forever in hell. One would then not be *forced* down the Lutheran path to objective justification, with the concomitant undercutting of the justice-based case for DH.

A strident defender of JDH could then hold that Christ's Atonement was of finite worth (since it did not *need* to be infinite). Of course, to preserve JDH, the defender would have to go even further and say that Christ's Atonement was not even sufficiently valuable to atone for those finite human sins meriting everlasting punishment. Rather, it was just valuable enough so that humans could 'make up the difference' through some act of faith or good works.[87] However, while it is possible to adopt such a view, there are numerous problems that a defender of such a view would have to overcome.

First, this watered-down version of the Atonement seems hard to reconcile with the most natural reading of Scripture, whose most straightforward sense would be that the demands of justice have been fully met in Christ.[88] Although we do not follow the view which imputes divine authority to the plain sense of every text, the texts that speak to Christ's Atonement are part of the very heart of the gospel message in light of which a Christocentric hermeneutic interprets the rest of Scripture. The fact that there is straw in the manger (recalling Luther's metaphor) does not mean we are free to rip out the Christ child's heart and feed it to the sheep.

Second, this view of the Atonement, according to which Christ *almost* pays the penalty for sin, does not seem to leave room for eternal punishment in any event. Since the penalty for sin has been almost paid by Christ, such that an act of faith is all that is needed to make up the difference, surely the alternative to this act of faith is not endless punishment. If the sins deserving endless punishment still deserve endless punishment even after Christ's Atonement, it would seem the Atonement has done no work

Finally, it is hard to imagine any offence that is finite but deserves endless punishment. If the offence is finite, why would the punishment have to endure forever without ever reaching a point at which the price for the offence has been paid? Perhaps an offence that did everlasting damage to a finite creature would be finite (since its victim is finite) but deserve everlasting punishment (as the only punishment comparable to the damage inflicted). The problem here is that no creature *can* inflict everlasting damage on another. Perhaps, then, all that is needed is the *intention* to do so, though this will not work either, for reasons laid out by Marilyn Adams. As Adams notes, an agent's responsibility 'is diminished by his or her unavoidable inability to conceive of the relevant dimensions of the action and its consequences'.[89] A finite mind cannot even begin to comprehend what inflicting everlasting harm would involve. Adams notes that 'lack of experience deprives an agent of the capacity empathetically to enter in to what it would be like to suffer this or that harm, despite more or less detailed abstract descriptive knowledge about such suffering'.[90] However, no human being can even *experience* what everlasting harm is like – even those *undergoing* it, since they will never reach a point at which they have experienced everlasting harm. We cannot really intend what we cannot conceive. While we might *say* we intend everlasting harm, what we are really conceiving of is something less than this.

6.12 Implications of Objective Justification for RDH

Perhaps RDH can escape these problems. In RDH, what warrants everlasting punishment is not any particular sin but an ongoing pattern of sin. In recent literature this version of JDH is vigorously defended by Charles Seymour, whose argument is essentially a subtle development of AES. Seymour asks us to imagine that the eternally damned are those who, in their post-mortem state, perpetually persist in sinning. Each successive sin warrants further finite punishment; but since the former continues indefinitely, so does the latter. Since human sin is here taken to be finite in severity, we are not *forced* into the strong view of the Atonement. But since the pattern of sin continues eternally, the sequence of finite punishments does too.[91]

While this version of JDH may, at first sight, seem consistent with denying the strong doctrine of the Atonement propounded by Lutheran Orthodoxy, we do not think this is the case. In this view, either the punishments imposed by God can 'catch up' with the sins of the creature – such that there is a moment at which the penalty for the creature's sins (up to that moment) has been fully paid – or they cannot. If the former, there is at least a moment at which the penalty for sin has been fully paid. At that moment – since the demands of justice impose no impediment whatever towards saving the creature – if the creature is not saved, the explanation must lie in something other than the demands of justice. At least from the standpoint of justice, there is no reason why God could not in that moment extend efficacious grace and thus save the sinner before he or she has the opportunity to 'sin some more', so to speak.[92]

Of course, a defender of RDH might argue that there is something other than the demands of vindicatory justice preventing God from extending efficacious grace in that moment – perhaps a duty to respect the creature's libertarian freedom. If so, RDH is so akin to LDH that the arguments we direct against LDH in later chapters will apply to RDH as well. The point here is simply that if God's punitive responses to sin can 'catch up' with the creature's sin, then AES fails to meet the challenge posed by our argument based on the Lutheran doctrine of the objective Atonement.

If, on the other hand, God's punishments cannot catch up with the sinner's sin, then the demands of justice can never be fully met by punishing the sinner. The sinner will eternally succeed in 'staying ahead' of God's punitive acts by warranting more punishment before the previous punishments have been completed. If so, punishment again proves unable to meet the demands of justice. At every moment for the rest of eternity there will be sin that has not been expiated, wrongs that have not been vindicated. At no point will the demands of justice have actually been met; and if meeting the demands of justice is not optional for God, we once again find ourselves in a situation where God is compelled to seek alternative satisfaction. Thus, it seems that Seymour cannot escape the need for a vicarious Atonement. We are led along the same path as before: any vicarious Atonement which would satisfy the demands of justice with respect to sinners who keep sinning indefinitely would also remove any impediment to universal salvation based on justice (and justice would not compel God to heap retributive pains on those who, for some different reason, remain unsaved).

It seems that Seymour's only plausible response to this objection is to embrace a variation on Kant's judgment that an 'endless progress from lower to higher stages of moral perfection' becomes, from God's atemporal perspective, 'a whole conformable to the moral law'.[93] The idea that endless movement towards moral perfection counts as moral perfection for God might be extended to the sphere of punishment, such that Seymour could hold that, from God's *eternal* standpoint, the infinite series of finite sins and finite punishments is a completed whole in which the demands of justice are perfectly met. From eternity, in effect, the demands of justice have been met without the need for a vicarious atonement.

This response, however, does not do justice to the force of our objection. Consider the following: in any finite time period, say between T1 and T2, the damned soul is either (a) capable of sinning only a finite number of times, or (b) capable of sinning an infinite number of times. If (a), then God is presumably able to arrange His punitive response so that, at time T2, the demands of justice have been fully met (if only for a moment), and He can thus 'jump in' before the sinner can sin again and grant efficacious grace without justice imposing any impediment. After all, why would an omnipotent God not be able to so combine the intensity and duration of punishments such that the finite punishments incurred between T1 and T2 would be completed by T2? So long as the sinner is only capable of sinning a finite number of times between T1 and T2, God could impose 'concurrent sentences' for the sins committed after T1, regulating the intensity of the suffering involved so as to ensure that every 'sentence' ends at T2. If this is right, then Seymour's defence of hell will work only if we embrace (b) – that is, only if humans are capable of sinning an infinite number of times in any given timeframe, and hence are capable of 'outrunning' God's punitive response by racking up more debt in any given timeframe than God can expiate in the same timeframe. In order for it to be impossible for God to fully meet the demands of justice at *some* time, T, it must be the case that the sinner *continues* to outrun God's punitive capacities *ad infinitum*. As the timeline moves towards infinity, the gap between what the sinner deserves and what the sinner suffers must keep getting larger. If this occurs, then even from God's eternal standpoint it would not be the case that the demands of justice have been met. A vicarious Atonement will be required.

It seems that Seymour's only way out is to claim that there is some upper limit to the amount of suffering that a person can endure at any given moment, so that even if alternative (a) is true, it is not the case that God can simply increase the intensity of concurrent punishments to ensure that all these punishments end at T2. This seems plausible but it does not help Seymour's case. If there *is* an upper limit to the intensity of suffering that a human being can endure at any moment, and if this upper limit is sufficiently low that humans are capable of coming to deserve more punishment in a given timeframe than God is capable of expiating in that timeframe, then human beings are capable of 'outrunning' God's punitive response in the same way that they could if they could sin an infinite number of times in any timeframe. Only if they outran God's punitive response *forever* would God be incapable of fully meeting the demands of justice at some time T; and, as we have seen, such eternal outrunning of God's punitive response amounts to forever widening the gap between what the sinner deserves and what the sinner experiences with respect to punishment. Even from God's eternal vantage point, this cannot be perceived as justice being met.

In short, Seymour's defence of RDH based on AES faces fundamentally the same problem as the defence of CDH based on AIG. Seymour cannot escape the need for a vicarious Atonement in order to meet the demands of justice. We conclude, therefore, that any successful defence of DH cannot be found in the appeal to divine justice – at least not in a broadly Christian framework in which something like the vicarious Atonement is recognized as a possibility, and this in turn means that neither CDH nor RDH are plausible *Christian* doctrines of hell.

CHAPTER 7

THE ARGUMENT FROM EFFICACIOUS GRACE

7.1 The Argument from Freedom

In the last two chapters we have done two things. In Chapter 5 we offered three initial arguments for DU in terms of God's benevolent and complacent love. We argued that Christians have good reason to find these arguments convincing, contingent on two presumptions: first, there is nothing in God's character that would conflict with His love so as to impel Him not to will the salvation of the unregenerate as an end; second, there is available to God a morally permissible means of saving all. In Chapter 6 we looked at species of DH that reject the first of these presumptions – namely, 'Judicial' species which hold that for reasons of retributive justice, God does not will the salvation of the unregenerate as an end. We argued that this traditional view is mistaken and that the demands of justice actually provide God with *further* reason, beyond His love, to will the salvation of the unregenerate as an end.

However, this hardly ends the argument. In recent centuries, arguably the most significant theological development concerning DH has been a shift away from defending it in terms of God's justice and towards defending it in terms of God's respect for creaturely freedom – more precisely, towards justifying DH by arguing that God either cannot or will not (for moral reasons) override creaturely freedom on this matter. In short, rather than challenging the first of our presumptions, contemporary defenders of DH are apt to challenge the second.

This is the Liberal Doctrine of Hell (LDH). The argument for it – what we will call the Argument from Freedom (AF) – can be outlined as follows:

1. God can guarantee the salvation of all only by bringing about the salvation of the unregenerate through some means that overrides their freedom.
2. Either such a means is not available to God (it is not possible for God to save the unregenerate by overriding their freedom), or, if it is available, it is morally impermissible for God to make use of it.
3. God will not do what is morally impermissible.
4. Therefore, God either cannot or will not guarantee the salvation of all (1, 2, 3).

If we add that there is no guarantee of universal salvation apart from divine activity, AF has the corollary conclusion that there is no guarantee that all will be saved.

Of course, this conclusion does not rule out universal salvation. A universalist might accept AF but embrace DU out of faith in God's resourcefulness; but such a response is only likely to inspire a stronger version of AF, in which (1) is replaced by the following:

1*. Unless God brings about the salvation of the unregenerate through some means that overrides their freedom, some will never be saved.[1]

When (1*) replaces (1), the conclusion is that some are never saved; but despite the greater force of this modified AF, we focus here on the original version for two reasons. First, premise (2) is the same in both, so any critique of it would apply to both. Second, to show that (1) is dubious we must offer reasons to think that God *can* guarantee universal salvation without overriding anyone's freedom. If God can do this, then both (1) and (1*) are false. Hence, any critique of AF also applies to the stronger version.

We offer just such a critique in the next two chapters. In this chapter we challenge AF in terms of what we call the Argument from Efficacious Grace (AEG). 'Efficacious grace' refers traditionally to that species of grace sufficient by itself to fully convert creatures, such that all who receive it are saved.[2] If there is such grace, and if it is never morally wrong for God to bestow it, then AF fails.

But *how* it fails depends on one's view of freedom. From a broadly Thomistic viewpoint,[3] the exercise of efficacious grace can be construed as a divinely available means of guaranteeing the conversion of the creature that does not violate creaturely freedom. Hence, our defence of its availability as a means of saving all can be construed as challenging AF(1). However, while we pursue this point we do not want our case to rest on the correctness of the Thomistic view of freedom – because we also want the argument to speak to those who favour a stronger libertarian view.

This libertarian view does not, we think, undermine the Thomistic case for thinking efficacious grace is *available* to God. Rather, it implies that God's use of efficacious grace is an instance of overriding creaturely freedom; but (as we argue in the next section) not every case of overriding freedom is morally impermissible. We think there are good reasons to think God *may* morally override creaturely freedom, at least when efficacious grace is the means and the motive is salvation. Thus, in this view of how efficacious grace relates to creaturely freedom, AEG challenges AF(2). More significantly, if AEG succeeds, then – given our earlier conclusion that God would save all if He morally could – the species of universalism we call DU1 follows.

However, even though we find AEG powerful, it assumes either that creaturely freedom is not of a strong libertarian sort or that, if it is, God's obligation to respect it is not absolute. Despite what we say in this chapter, we know many will remain impressed by the idea that creatures *do* have a strong libertarian freedom that God morally must respect. As such, we will not rest our case against

AF (and for DU) on AEG but will, in the next chapter, challenge AF(1) using a different argument – what we call the Argument from Infinite Opportunity (AIO). AIO argues that even if God is morally precluded from extending efficacious grace out of respect for libertarian freedom, He retains a morally permissible means of guaranteeing universal salvation – namely, by preserving creatures indefinitely in a state in which they remain perpetually free to choose communion with God. If we are right that doing so is morally permissible and guarantees salvation, then we are once again led to universalism – in this case, DU2.

One may wonder why, if AIO supports our conclusion with fewer assumptions, we offer AEG at all. Other than for completeness, there are two reasons. First, AIO's support for universalism is probabilistic – it entails that Christians should embrace DU because DU's negation has an *infinitesimally* low probability; but AEG shows that all who accept its assumptions are *logically compelled* to embrace DU. AEG is thus a stronger argument for any who share these assumptions. Second, and more importantly, we think the understanding of efficacious grace provided in the present chapter is correct, and therefore does more to reveal *how* God saves all.

With these preliminary remarks in mind, we turn to our critique of AF.

7.2 'Overriding Freedom' and 'Violating Autonomy'

We begin with a point of clarification with respect to (1) and (2) of AF. Both refer to a means of salvation that overrides the freedom of the unregenerate, but what does it mean to override someone's freedom? Suppose you are a US citizen who voted for Mondale in the 1983 presidential election. In that case, we can meaningfully say your choice was overridden by majority preferences. If, however, you are a Canadian citizen who would have voted for Mondale had you had US voting rights, saying this would not be appropriate. This shows that having one's choice overridden presupposes some kind of legitimate 'say' in a decision – not presumptive control of the outcome, nor a presumption that your rights have been violated if things do not go according to your will, but a *say*. If you are denied your say (if your vote is not counted), then you have been wronged.

Or consider decision making within a hierarchy such as a corporation. As part of your assigned duties you choose from among various ad campaigns for a product, but your boss prefers a different campaign and so goes with it. It makes sense to say that *your* choice was overridden; it makes no sense to say that the mail clerk's choice was overridden (assuming he favours the same campaign as you).

However, neither of you has been wronged; nor is it even prima facie wrong for your boss to override your decision. It would, however, be at *least* prima facie wrong for the mail clerk to deliberately miscommunicate your decision so that your boss ends up going with his preference rather than yours. Having one's choices overridden, in short, presupposes having a claim on one's choices play-ing *some* specifiable role in outcomes. While not every case of overriding one's choices is even prima facie wrong, there is a legitimate scope of authority that has to be presumed in every case of overriding a choice – a scope within which you have a prima facie right to make a choice and expect that choice to play a specifiable role in determining which outcome obtains.

The role might simply be having your choice count as one vote among many, or your choice might play the role of determining the outcome *barring veto from a higher authority*. Whatever the actual role, you have a right to your choice play-ing this role. Therefore, if your choice does play this role, then, even if it *is* overridden, no wrong has been done to you; but if your choice is not permitted to play this role, a wrong *has* been done.

In sum, there is a difference between overriding your freedom in a manner consistent with your choices playing the role they are 'supposed' to play in shap-ing outcomes, and overriding your freedom in a manner inconsistent with your choices playing this role. The latter is not merely a case of freedom being over-ridden, but of what we might plausibly call *a violation of autonomy*.

However, 'autonomy' is not an uncontested concept. The Kantian under-standing, in terms of the exercise of one's capacity for practical rationality, can be contrasted with, for example, Michael Murray's understanding of autonomy as roughly synonymous with what Richard Swinburne calls 'efficacious freedom' – that is, freedom the exercise of which makes a difference for better or worse in the world.[4] The sense of autonomy we propose here might be seen as a *species* of efficacious freedom: one has autonomy to the extent that one's free choices play the role that *one has a legitimate claim on them playing* in the determination of outcomes.

As such, your autonomy has not been violated simply when your freedom has been *bypassed* (as in a case where the university you work for renovates a building near your office without consulting you), or even when it has been *truncated* (as in a case where the university closes a parking lot to give construction work-ers space to store equipment, even though this means you can no longer park there). In cases of bypassing or truncating freedom, you may have no legitimate claim on having your decisions play any role at all in a given outcome – in which case your freedom has not even been overridden.

As we are using the notion, for your autonomy to be violated it is necessary (but not sufficient) that your freedom be overridden. You must have a legiti-mate prima facie claim on having your choices play a given role in determining outcomes. Thus, your autonomy has actually been violated when your choice was not permitted to play this role. Given this sense of autonomy, acts that vio-late autonomy extend over a familiar list, including coercion and deception. There may also be more subtle forms of autonomy violation – for example, when one's choice is caused to play a lesser role than it prima facie ought to play in determining outcomes.

When it comes to God's relation to His creatures, there may be a way that God can violate autonomy which is not possible for others; namely, by intruding directly on our inner psychology so as to erase our capacity for freedom – a kind of 'mind control' in which God dictates what we think and choose, turning us into puppets. If efficacious grace were divine mind control of this sort, then the presumptive case against it would be strong; but, as we argue in what follows, efficacious grace need not be construed in these terms.

Given these preliminary remarks, a few things about AF become clear. First, given that AF is framed in terms of overriding the unregenerate's freedom, granting AF(1) does not, as such, imply that God's available means of saving the unregenerate are even *prima facie* objectionable. To show that, the defender of AF must show that these means do not merely override freedom but violate autonomy. But why not, then, simply frame the argument in terms of autonomy violation in the first place? If we did so, some of our reasons for objecting to AF(2) would simply shift to AF(1). That is, at least some of our reasons for supposing there is nothing wrong with God overriding the freedom of the unregenerate rest on questioning whether these cases rise to the level of prima facie objectionable autonomy violations. As such, it is a matter of indifference how the argument is framed so long as we remain clear about the relevant distinction.

However, there is a more positive reason for framing the argument as we do. Our arguments in the next chapter will target AF(1); and we think these arguments work against more than just the narrow claim that God cannot guarantee the salvation of the unregenerate without violating their autonomy – we think they show that the broader claim, as formulated in AF(1), is false.

7.3 The Argument from Efficacious Grace

What we are calling *the Argument from Efficacious Grace* (AEG) can be outlined as follows:

1. It is always possible for God to extend to the unregenerate efficacious grace; that is, a form of grace sufficient by itself to guarantee their salvation (i.e. sufficient to bring about all that is necessary for salvation, including relevant subjective acts such as sincere repentance and conversion).
2. Making use of efficacious grace to save the unregenerate is morally permissible for God, at least when the recipient would not otherwise have been saved.
3. It is therefore possible and permissible for God to save all through the exercise of efficacious grace (1, 2).
4. If God has a morally permissible means of saving all, then God will save all.
5. Therefore, God will save all (3, 4).

Given the arguments advanced in Chapters 5 and 6, we think AEG(4) needs no further defence. As such, our focus in this chapter will be on defending AEG(1) and (2). In doing so, we simultaneously challenge premises (1) and (2) of AF.

7.4 The Possibility of God Bestowing Efficacious Grace

We begin with AEG(1). That God *can* bestow efficacious grace was assumed to be true by most of the older dogmaticians – Protestant and Catholic – who discussed the matter.[5] However, the Catholics were divided over the nature of efficacious grace. Adherents to the older Thomistic and Augustinian tradition took such grace to differ in kind from so-called 'merely sufficient grace' (which gave sinners all they needed for salvation *other than* the appropriate subjective act of will). Followers of Molina, however, held that efficacious grace does not differ in kind from sufficient grace, but differs only in virtue of the fortuitous situation the creature is placed in when receiving sufficient grace.[6]

While volumes of scholastic theology have been written on this dispute, for our purposes a brief overview is sufficient. According to the Thomists and their Protestant followers,[7] when God grants efficacious grace, He guarantees conversion and regeneration by putting creatures in a state that influences their motives such that they have every reason to respond favourably to the offer of salvation and no reason not to. However, if this is what efficacious grace involves, it raises questions about creaturely freedom. Most significantly, one may wonder if efficacious grace is consistent with *libertarian* freedom – by which we mean, roughly, the power to act or not act on motives that incline but do not determine the will. Freedom in this libertarian sense exists only if, when one makes a choice, *one could have chosen otherwise* – that is, there is some possible world in which one chooses otherwise.

In affirming that God can grant efficacious grace, Aquinas did not mean thereby entirely to deny creatures freedom in something like this sense.[8] Rather, he meant simply to limit its scope. Specifically, the Thomistic view is that what we call libertarian freedom is a coherent understanding of freedom only when the creature confronts *conflicting motives* for action. It does not extend to circumstances in which the creature has every reason to pursue a course of action and no reason not to. Under such circumstances the Thomistic view is that the will of the creature is not merely inclined but is determined to perform the act. The act remains wholly voluntary, but since there is no possible world in which an agent who has *every* motive to do A and *no* motive not to do so nevertheless refrains from doing A, the action is also determined, and so conforms to what is usually labelled 'compatibilist freedom' by contemporary philosophers.[9]

It strikes us, however, that this contemporary language implies something Aquinas did not intend – namely, that there are two kinds of freedom, compatibilist and libertarian. We find it more in tune with his ideas to say that freedom simply *operates differently* under conditions of uniform motives than it does when motives conflict. In the latter case, free choice looks like what we call libertarian freedom; whereas in the former case it looks like what we call compatibilist freedom.

If this is right, then God could guarantee that the unregenerate freely, but inevitably, make the subjective choices necessary for salvation. For Aquinas, this is the essence of how efficacious grace works: it brings all the creature's motives into conformity with the choice of pursuing loving union with God above all things.[10]

The Molinists objected to the Thomistic view of efficacious grace because they took it that freedom has a libertarian character *even under conditions of uniform motives*.[11] Granted this strong notion of libertarian freedom, it would initially seem impossible for God to give efficacious grace *without* first extinguishing freedom. However, the Molinists argued that (i) God has middle knowledge, and (ii) for every rational creature there is a possible world in which he or she would freely (in the strong libertarian sense) respond favourably to God's offer of salvation. That God has middle knowledge means that He knows, for any creature X He might create, what X would freely do in any circumstance God might put X in. Thus, God can give efficacious grace to X by creating that world in which He knows – by middle knowledge – that X would favourably respond to grace.[12]

For several reasons we find this Molinist doctrine unconvincing. First, we are not convinced that divine omniscience entails middle knowledge. In the absence of an actual (libertarian) free choice made under an actual set of circumstances, we doubt there is any *truth of the matter* with respect to what the agent would freely choose in the libertarian sense. Furthermore, as William Lane Craig has shown, supposing that God does have middle knowledge does not, *by itself*, demonstrate that He can give efficacious grace to every rational creature in any world of which it is a member.[13] Hence, we will not defend the Molinist understanding of efficacious grace here. Instead, we argue that God has available to Him a morally permissible means of bringing it about that all of a creature's motives uniformly favour conversion. If so, then – from a Thomistic view of freedom – there is a morally permissible means for God to guarantee that all creatures freely make the choices that are necessary for their salvation.

To make this case, we want first to develop a fuller picture of the Thomistic view of freedom by way of a contemporary philosopher – Thomas Talbott – whose thinking is very close on this matter to Aquinas. Like Aquinas, Talbott insists that one cannot imagine anyone freely choosing what they have no motive to choose and every motive not to choose. Such a choice, for Talbott, is incoherent. If one is in a condition such that all one's motives converge on one choice, Talbott thinks this choice becomes *inevitable*.

In Talbott's view, such a choice could still be free – but only if certain conditions are met. If ignorance or deception entails that one chooses based on *misrepresentations* of the alternatives (such that what one thinks one is choosing is different from what one is actually doing), then one's freedom is impeded; and if controlling affective states entail that an agent is *determined* to choose one option even if informed deliberation would come down in favour of another, then the agent is 'in bondage to desire' and, again, not truly free.[14] However, if someone is 'freed from all ignorance, deception and bondage to desire', the agent's choice is free *even if* all motives converge on a single option, thereby making the choice of that option inevitable.[15]

However, if all this is right, there will be different ways to produce conformity of motives, not all of which should be assessed alike. Consider the following case: suppose Jenny grows up in a dystopian future where children are fed an addictive drug from infancy. They are taught (falsely) to believe that the drug is a medicine they need to stay healthy, while in fact the tyrannical regime uses it to control the people. Given her addiction and beliefs, Jenny's motives converge on the choice to continue taking the drug; but insofar as this choice is governed by deception and addiction, it is not free in Talbott's sense.

However, suppose a resistance group reveals to Jenny the truth. She now knows the drug is harmful but remains addicted. Hence, she has reason-based motives to stop taking the drug, but these are impotent due to her addiction. Now suppose the resistance gives her a counter-drug that weakens but does not stop her cravings. Whenever she is near the drug she faces an inner struggle. Sometimes, with the right support (and some luck), she resists her craving; but usually she falls prey to it, weeping in shame at her weakness. At this point we might say that she has *some* measure of freedom – but it remains constrained by the hold the drug continues to exert on her.

However, imagine that the resistance finds a way to break her addiction. Now she neither craves the drug nor thinks taking it is a good idea. Let us suppose, furthermore, that she has no other motive to continue taking it but many reasons not to: concern for her health and continued sobriety, gratitude to her liberators, a desire to oppose the unjust regime, and so forth. Suppose, in short, that once freed of her addiction, all her motives converge on the choice not to take the drug. Would we not say that now, at last, her choice is truly free – even if, as Talbott and Aquinas believe, her rejecting the drug is now inevitable?

We think this example shows that the 'libertarian' and 'compatibilist' labels are inadequate for the sense of freedom Talbott champions. Prior to help from the resistance, Jenny's choice to take the drug *would* be free in the compatibilist sense – though not in Talbott's sense. After her final liberation, her choice to refuse the drug *is* free in Talbott's sense – but not in the libertarian sense. What makes the choice free in the one case but not in the other is that reason is no longer impeded from playing the role it ought to play in decision making. Hence, we think the best label for this conception of freedom is 'rational freedom'; and, given Aquinas's emphasis on the will's natural ordering to follow reason, we think such 'rational freedom' best captures the Thomistic view.[16]

Underlying this view of freedom are several presuppositions, which can be summarized as follows: (i) values are objective, such that there are objectively good or best choices and objectively bad ones; (ii) the rational faculty makes judgments in accord with its finite grasp of this objective order of values; (iii) the will can be controlled by non-rational forces (such as addictions or entrenched habits); (iv) the will is naturally ordered to choose in accord with rational judgments such that it inevitably does so in the absence of any non-rational controlling factors.

These presuppositions imply, in brief, that the will is naturally ordered to follow reason (its 'default setting', if you will), and that reason in turn is naturally ordered to discern the objective good. In this view, choices are free to the extent that both reason and will can operate in accord with their nature – that is, there is nothing (such as 'ignorance, deception or bondage to desire') that impedes them from acting on their natural teleology. This, we think, captures the essence of freedom as it is understood both by Aquinas and, more recently, by Talbott.

In any event, what this shows is that one can produce uniform motives in ways that *impede* rational freedom and in ways that do not. If efficacious grace is a divine act producing uniformly salvation-favouring motives, this act may or may not impede freedom in the Thomistic sense – depending on whether this uniformity is produced by inducing false beliefs and/or affective states at odds with reason, or by revealing truth and removing affective barriers to acting on what reason discerns.

Therefore the question is not only whether God can bring about uniformly salvation-favouring motives in the unregenerate, but whether He can do so in a way that promotes rather than impedes rational freedom. In fact, we think an omnipotent being could do both, such that it is within God's power to bestow efficacious grace without violating freedom – at least if 'freedom' is understood in this Thomistic sense. Aquinas and his later followers suggest two ways in which God could do this: first, by presenting the unregenerate with a direct vision of Himself; second, by presenting them with evidence and/or arguments sufficient to demonstrate the value of union with God, while simultaneously liberating them from bondage to contrary affective states.[17]

The case for the former rests on a fuller explication of broadly Thomistic ideas about the nature of rational creatures and their relationship to God and the good – mostly notably in terms of two precepts: (A) every creature is ordered to the good; and (B) God is the perfect good. Claim (A), on a Thomistic reading, holds not merely that all creatures have their own individual good – their own end or telos which is good *for* them – but furthermore, that the attainment of this telos aligns them with the absolute or objective good. The latter seems clear if we accept that the individual good of creatures is determined by God, who *is* the ultimate objective good. In other words, given (B), the rich understanding of (A) offered above is appropriate. However, another crucial implication of (B) is that, insofar as every creature is ordered to the good, every creature is ordered to God in the sense of being naturally disposed to *imitate* God insofar as its nature allows.[18]

For rational creatures, this ordering to the good and to God takes a special form. Rational creatures, by definition, can choose based on reasons – that is, they are motivated to act not merely by instinct or appetite, but by the recognition that certain apprehended truths (reasons) entail that a course of action is good to do. Saying that *rational* creatures are ordered to the good means two things: first, when they directly and clearly encounter the perfect good in unclouded experience, they will recognize it as the perfect good; and second, the perfect good (which, by definition, is the standard according to which all other goods are measured) would, under conditions of immediate and unclouded apprehension, present itself as overridingly worthy of love. Creatures' subjective values will thus spontaneously fall into harmony with the objective good, with all choices reflecting this proper valuation.[19]

Put another way, immediate awareness of the perfect good will so sing to the natural inclinations of the soul that love for the good will swamp all potentially contrary affective states. One would have every reason to conform one's will to the perfect good and no reason not to. This latter point gains further strength from the Christian notion that what is prudentially good for rational creatures (what promotes their welfare) does not ultimately conflict with what is morally good – both are realized through union with God. Unclouded apprehension of the perfect good will thus harmonize prudential and moral motives such that every rational creature presented with a clear vision of God would have every reason to love God and no reason to reject Him.

From all of this it follows that God could guarantee uniform salvation-inducing motives in rational creatures simply by presenting an unclouded vision of Himself. God's doing this certainly seems *metaphysically* possible, and hence within God's power; and if (as Aquinas maintained) free acts are not random but motivated, it follows that any rational creature presented with the vision of God will freely but inevitably respond affirmatively to the promise of loving union.

If this is what efficacious grace involves, then the alignment of motives that results from bestowing efficacious grace is more like what happens to Jenny when the resistance liberates her from deception and addiction than it is like the conformity of motives produced by the tyrannical regime. Efficacious grace in this sense, rather than interfering with rational freedom, appears to be its culmination.

There is, however, a second basis for thinking that efficacious grace is possible, rooted in an alternative means of conferring it, one explicitly defended by Aquinas and – more recently – by Talbott. Aquinas believed that God could grant efficacious grace to rational creatures, even without bestowing a clear vision of Himself, by first granting a person the 'gift of wisdom and council [such] that his reason should in no way err regarding [either] the end [God] or the means [to the end] in particular'.[20]

Were one an intellectual determinist, holding with Socrates that one always does what one thinks best, this would end the matter: show people the truth and all will turn to God. But Aquinas, with Aristotle, believed that passions can become so disordered that creatures cannot do what they have every intellectual reason to do. In that case, however, would it not be in God's power to eliminate such disordered passions? Aquinas thought so, arguing that God could counter the disordered passions of a person by 1) granting 'infused virtues' so that 'his will is more firmly inclined to God', and 2) divinely inspiring his 'mind to resist sin' whenever an 'occasion for it presents itself'.[21]

7.5 Objections to the Possibility of God Bestowing Efficacious Grace

So far, we have considered two ways God might bring creatures into a state in which – granted the Thomistic or rational view of freedom – they would infallibly but freely choose God. However, both of these ways of bestowing efficacious grace might be challenged, even by those who accept the Thomistic view of freedom. In this section we consider several such challenges, beginning with two reasons why critics might think God could not bestow on the unregenerate an unclouded vision of Himself. First, critics might argue that to see God at all a person needs a certain type of character. Perhaps, because of bad habits, vicious people cannot see God (just as they cannot see that justice is good). Second, critics might take their cue from the Eastern Fathers and argue that *no* finite creature can 'see' God, since God is infinite and nothing finite can see what is infinite.[22]

As to the first objection, it certainly seems that if God can create creatures *ex nihilo*, He could reform their characters so as to remove vicious traits blocking their ability to see Him. There seems to be no metaphysical impossibility here. Consider that if certain traits really block a creature from seeing God, it seems this would be because either (a) the trait causes him or her to irresistibly look away, as in when we reflexively look away from the sun, or (b) the trait somehow diminishes his or her perceptual powers so that he or she is incapable of seeing God even if they attempt to look. Given (b), then – at least assuming it falls within the scope of human nature to have perceptual powers adequate to seeing God – there cannot be any metaphysical impossibility of the creature seeing God, and hence no impossibility in removing what would amount to a defect.

If, on the other hand, we suppose that (a) is true, then the creature is somehow in the grip of controlling affective states – states which either (i) determined them to look away regardless of what they believe, such that they could not see God even if they knew the value of doing so, or (ii) determined them to look away *given* certain false beliefs about God; that is, beliefs which portray God (falsely) as an appropriate object of aversion. If either of these is the case, it would seem that God could turn to the second means of bestowing efficacious grace that we discussed (as endorsed by Aquinas and Talbott) as a way of making the creature ready to experience the beatific vision. Hence, the force of this objection piggybacks on the critic's ability to mount a successful objection to the second means of bestowing efficacious grace outlined above: the critic must show that God cannot liberate the creature from ignorance, deception and bondage to controlling affective states.

Of course, there remain worries we have yet to address about the *morality* of a God who produces virtuous character traits in creatures apart from them freely *asking* God to reform them in these ways. These worries we will take up in the next section. The question at hand is whether God *can* bestow efficacious grace, not whether He morally *may*; and it certainly appears to fall within God's omnipotent power to reveal truths to the unregenerate and liberate them from controlling affective states – even if this is done without their voluntary cooperation.

Even if we can decide to block the vision of God by, as it were, deliberately averting our gaze, the notion of the creature as ordered to God, coupled with God's infinite causal power, seems to entail that it is within God's power to override such resistance. After all, environmental conditions outside our control routinely cause us to acknowledge truths we might not want to see (we go to our wine cabinet, certain the special bottle of Pinot Noir we've been saving for our anniversary is there, but after searching frantically are forced to conclude that it is not). Likewise, such conditions can produce character traits entirely apart from our voluntary cooperation: brain injuries can turn us from being even-tempered to being short-tempered; traumatic childhood abuse can make us irresistibly untrusting in relationships. If the physical environment can do these things, then a fortiori so can an omnipotent God.

Nevertheless, some will not be convinced – and others, despite what we say in the next section, will think such an exercise of divine power is ruled out for moral reasons. Since such persons will not be convinced by AEG, we direct them to the argument in the next chapter, AIO.

What about the second main objection to the possibility of God employing the beatific vision to convert the unregenerate, based on the view of the Eastern Fathers that no finite creature can see an infinite being? Based partly on Scripture,[23] the Western tradition has rejected this view, holding instead that seeing God is the creature's ultimate subjective end. However, in holding this position, the Western tradition does not mean that creatures can fully *comprehend* God. Seeing an infinite thing does not entail fully comprehending what is seen.[24]

This is true even for finite things. Consider a person gazing at *The Night Watch* in the Rex museum in Amsterdam. The person sees the painting, but does not fully *grasp* it. The point is that while the Eastern Fathers may be right that a finite being cannot comprehend an infinite God, it does not follow that it is impossible for a finite being to directly encounter the infinite God in experience – which is what 'seeing' God really means.

However, this response engenders a modified objection. If no finite being can fully comprehend God, what guarantee is there that a finite being who sees God will comprehend that they are encountering the *summum bonum* infinitely worthy of love and devotion? We have two answers: first, if we assume we are ordered to the good, it seems God's goodness would be the one thing that would blaze most vividly in our consciousness when faced with the beatific vision. Second, could an all-powerful God not reveal Himself *in such a way* that, even if we could not grasp God in His entirety, we would 'see' that God is perfect goodness, the being most worthy of love?

Again, the analogy of the person gazing at *The Night Watch* is instructive: a talented tour guide could, during a brief viewing, call attention to its salient features in such a way that the person viewing it could not help but notice them. Likewise, God could call attention to those aspects of His nature that would, once perceived, guarantee a response of loving devotion.

However, even if one holds to the Eastern view that no one can 'see' God, the Eastern Fathers embraced an analogue to the beatific vision that arguably does the same work. They held that the saved become 'divinized' (an end for which every rational creature was created). Instead of this divinization occurring through a direct vision of God, they adopted a theory of divine energies, which they took to be uncreated aspects of God – truly divine, even if not the divine essence – by which He exerts Himself to creatures. Gregory Palamas thought of the divine energies as a kind of celestial light which could be seen and experienced by holy persons.[25] Someone filled with this light would be so filled with divine holiness, joy and blessedness that they could not sin.

It seems to us that any notion of salvation as union with God requires something along these lines – if not the beatific vision, then something like these divine energies. What is essential is that the creature be able to experience the divine in a manner suitable to the creature's nature and sufficient to produce an unambiguous appreciation of the reality of God as the highest good. Whatever the divisions within the Christian tradition, that *this* is possible seems a point of unanimous agreement.[26]

There is, however, one more objection to the possibility of God bestowing efficacious grace – an objection that extends to both means of bestowing efficacious grace discussed above. The objection, articulated by Andrew Martin Fairbairn, essentially holds that reordering an unregenerate person's motives sufficiently to ensure salvation would involve *replacing* the unregenerate person with a different person altogether. As such, efficacious grace cannot save the unregenerate person, since it does away with that person.[27]

This objection is seriously flawed. Not only does it raise troubling questions about infant baptism (and should thus be considered cautiously by those who endorse such baptism), but it confuses *persons* with their *personalities*.

A person, in Boethius's definition, is an individual substance of a rational nature – not a set of beliefs, attitudes, memories, habits, affective states, and so on. All these are things the person *has* – they are not what the person *is*. A personality, by contrast, is something a person has. A person can change their personality, without in the strict sense ceasing to be the person they were before. They remain the same individual substance of a rational nature, but with an altered personality.[28]

If this is right, then a transformation *destroys* a person only if it removes something essential to *being* a person – such as the person's rational faculty. A transformation in *personality* does not do this. This is especially true in the case of efficacious grace, where the transformation involves removing only those states *contrary* to a person's rational nature. Efficacious grace is analogous to what the resistance does for Jenny in our earlier example. To say that their activities do not save Jenny because they cause the drug-addicted, benighted individual to cease to exist makes little sense. Likewise, it is hard to see how doing away with the ignorance and bondage to sin that afflict an unregenerate person would entail destroying them.

Even if there were a metaphorical sense in which such a transformation might be called destruction of the 'old' person, there would remain a continuing substance who would be the *beneficiary* of that destruction. In fact, we think much biblical language invoked to support DH (or DA) might be understood in these terms – referring to the metaphorical destruction of the old self by efficacious grace, a destruction that salvages the creature's essential core from sin's ruinous effects. In fact, if the biblical language of destruction is conceived in this way, it may help to reconcile some of the more troubling hell texts with God's benevolence. The vessel of wrath then becomes the false self – the sinful personality destroyed through the divine act of bestowing efficacious grace. The vessel of mercy becomes the person's true essence – the enduring beneficiary of grace.

Still, there are lingering concerns here relating to respect for autonomy. We suspect this is Fairbairn's real worry: our status as *independent and autonomous* selves requires retaining an instrumental role in our self-development. In short, freedom must play a key role in character development. If God simply erases the character formed by our free choices, then God has not merely overridden our freedom, but has ignored our prima facie claim on having our free choices determine what kind of people we become. In the language introduced earlier in this chapter, God has *violated our autonomy*.

While the unregenerate would not cease to exist in this view, they would cease to be independent selves whose character is what it is because of their own choices; but if this is what lies at the root of Fairbairn's objection to efficacious grace, his argument is not that God *cannot* save the unregenerate through efficacious grace, but that doing so intrudes on the domain within which creatures' choices have a moral claim on dictating outcomes. In short, efficacious grace is immoral. This, then, is the issue we turn to next.

7.6 The Morality of Bestowing Efficacious Grace: Talbott's Case

In order to respond to the charge that God's bestowing efficacious grace would be morally wrong because it would violate autonomy, we want to briefly recall the second way Aquinas held that efficacious grace might be granted. In his view, it is within God's power to (a) clearly reveal to the unregenerate that union with God really is the *summum bonum*, thereby eliminating any reasons they might have for rejected God rooted in false beliefs; and (b) eliminate controlling affective states which would prevent creatures from acting on their judgments concerning what is best. Employing both methods, God could guarantee that all of a creature's motives converge on accepting God's offer of loving union with Himself. Thus, given a Thomistic view of freedom, God could guarantee that all creatures freely respond affirmatively to God's love.

However, Aquinas, in spite of believing that some ignorance or disordered affection is always involved in a creature's rejection of God,[29] was driven by his desire to preserve God's justice in damning some to insist that creatures who reject God because they were not given the grace to do otherwise nevertheless make voluntary (and hence truly free) choices. In other words, in order to maintain God's justice in damning some, he held that the choice to reject God is free, if only in the compatibilist sense.[30]

Talbott, however, questions whether any such choice could actually be *free*. As already noted, Talbott thinks that in order for a choice to qualify as truly free, the person making it needs, first, freedom from 'all ignorance and deception'; and second, freedom from any 'bondage to desire'. However, anyone who understands the options and is free from bondage to desire would have no motive to resist God's grace and every motive not to. As Talbott puts it: 'no one rational enough to qualify as a free moral agent could possibly prefer an objective horror – the outer darkness, for example – to eternal bliss, nor could any such person both experience the horror of separation from God and continue to regard it as a desirable state.'[31]

Those who resist God's grace would either do so because they do not know that such resistance commits them to the outer darkness and deprives them of eternal bliss, or because they are in bondage to controlling affective states that make it impossible for them to act otherwise. If Talbott is right about this, then any creatures that resisted divine grace would not be free on this matter. As such, it would make no sense for God to withhold His grace out of respect for their freedom. They *lack* freedom, and to provide it God would need to do precisely what Talbott holds to be sufficient for salvation: remove all ignorance, deception and bondage to desire. In doing this, God would, in fact, be ensuring that the conditions *necessary for free choice are in place.*

In Talbott's view, then, a free decision about union with God is unlike other free choices in a crucial respect: the conditions which make free choice on this matter possible are also the conditions *under which choosing union is guaranteed.* Unlike, for example, choosing between equally appealing menu options, the nature of the choice between union with and alienation from God is such that no truly free agent would have any motive for choosing the latter.

Hence, God can save all simply by eliminating barriers to free choice and so guaranteeing that all are in fact free on this matter.[32] In short, what Aquinas took as a means of bestowing efficacious grace, Talbott takes as a means of bestowing *the conditions necessary for freely choosing God.* If this is right, then what is arguably the chief challenge to the moral permissibility of bestowing efficacious grace – that doing so would violate autonomy – is overcome. As argued earlier, a necessary condition for the violation of autonomy is that one's freedom has been overridden; but if efficacious grace involves *establishing the conditions for free choice,* then, a fortiori, it cannot override free choice.

7.7 Walls' Critique of Talbott

Jerry Walls, however, has proposed an ingenious two-pronged response to Talbott.[33] His strategy is first to concede Talbott's central claim – that those who choose damnation (or choose to resist the grace needed for salvation) are not making a free choice. What Walls rejects is the claim that God could therefore save the damned without overriding their freedom. In brief, Walls looks in turn at both ignorance/deception and bondage to desire and argues that both states could be freely chosen by the damned. Hence, if the damned are those who freely choose one or both of these states, God could save them only by overriding their freedom.

If Walls is right about this, then even those who accept Talbott's basic understanding of freedom – Thomistic or 'rational' freedom – may still have grounds for thinking that bestowing efficacious grace threatens freedom in a problematic way. Suppose Talbott is right that anyone freed from ignorance, deception and bondage to desire (hereafter 'salvation inhibitors') would freely but infallibly choose union with God. Walls suggests, in effect, that these salvation inhibitors have not just been freely chosen, but have been chosen by rational creatures with a prima facie right to have their choices play a decisive role in determining whether they possess them. Removing them thus violates autonomy.

In the first part of his response to Talbott, Walls concedes that those who fully understand the choice would never freely choose damnation.[34] This choice is possible only if they are relevantly ignorant. However, Walls thinks their ignorance might be *wilful,* resulting from freely chosen self-deception.[35] Thus, even though their choice might not be free in itself (due to ignorance or deception), freedom is still ultimately responsible for the choice because the ignorance or deception was freely chosen. To save the damned, God would have to override their free choice to remain ignorant,[36] which would presumably intrude on their freedom at a point where they have a legitimate claim on their free choices determining relevant outcomes.[37]

In the second part of his response, Walls considers whether God could liberate sinners from 'bondage to desire' without overriding their freedom. Those in bondage to desire have developed bad habits so entrenched that they can no longer resist them. They are 'in bondage to sin'; but while we can explain why damnation is chosen given such bondage, it is hard to see how anyone could call the choice free. Talbott thinks that if God were to liberate the damned from their bondage He would not be interfering with their freedom precisely because liberation from this state is necessary for making a free choice. He likens such divine liberation to the act of a doctor who, without a patient's consent, cures the patient of a heroin addiction. This act does not violate the patient's freedom precisely because being addicted to heroine interferes with the patient's ability to make free choices. Liberating the patient from this addiction is therefore a precondition for the patient being able to freely consent to anything. [38]

Walls, however, asks us to consider a case in which the patient freely chooses addiction, making friends and family aware of this choice before the heroin robs him of his freedom.[39] In this case, it is not so clear that the doctor has not violated the patient's freedom. Likewise, we can imagine that someone freely chooses to become a slave to sinful desires 'because he did not want to exercise the discipline necessary to impose order on his desires'.[40] If God liberated this person from bondage to sin, Walls thinks the person 'might resent' being forced anew to choose 'either to impose order on his desires, as Swinburne put it, or allow his desires to impose their order on him'. [41] Preferring the latter 'in a settled way', God's refusal to permit the latter would violate the person's autonomy.

Like the first part of his proposed solution to Talbott's problem, Walls essentially agrees that the choice to be damned is not itself free, but then argues that it is based on a prior choice that *is*: in this case, the choice to become a slave to sinful desires.

7.8 The Failure of Walls' Critique

Ultimately, however, Walls' response to Talbott fails. The first problem is this: in order for self-deception to result in *eternal* damnation, it must endure forever – but is it really possible to cling *forever* to the relevant false beliefs? Talbott says no. He thinks that as the damned persist in their false beliefs and in the choices that follow upon them, the increasingly painful reality of sinfulness will eventually shatter their illusions.[42] Just as alcoholics who 'hit bottom' can no longer tell themselves that alcohol improves their lives, neither can sinners who come face to face with the anguish of alienation from God continue believing that such alienation is preferable to God's loving embrace.

While Walls tries to resolve this problem, his solution falls short. He agrees that sinners confronted with mounting suffering would eventually break down and cast aside their illusions, but he does not think their doing so would be free. Walls claims that if God were to cause those who reject him to become increasingly miserable until their illusions are finally shattered, this would be *coercion*. God would be like the legal authorities in England centuries ago who, to convince accused criminals to enter a guilty plea, would press them under increasingly heavy iron weights.[43]

However, this analogy misses an important point. If Christianity is true, then everything that is good comes from God, and without God there is only misery. Thus, we need not claim that God *imposes* escalating suffering on the damned. He needs merely to permit the damned to face the *natural* consequences of their choices. What 'forces' them to change their beliefs is not torture under God's hand, but the experience of having what they chose. They discover that their belief is false because, in trying to get by without God, they experience what that is really like.[44]

Walls might well insist that the 'truth' they confront is eventually so over-whelming that they are no longer free to deceive themselves; but to claim that this is a *violation* of freedom would be like claiming that one's freedom is violated by having clear eyesight. Because one sees clearly, one is not free to adopt the false belief that the rangy mutt sitting on the lawn is a water buffalo. Does such clarity of vision really violate one's freedom?

The point is this: even if we admit that our freedom to deceive ourselves is limited in the face of reality, it does not follow that God is *overriding* our free-dom (let alone violating autonomy) when He simply *allows* us to face the reality that exposes our self-deception as a lie. As already noted, there is an important distinction between our freedom being truncated and its being overridden. That encountering reality limits what we may freely believe may be the former, but it is hardly the latter.

Furthermore, in order for the damned to persist forever in self-deception, God would presumably have to *shield* them from reality and so *aid* their self-deception – but it seems that a God who hides from creatures the truth about their state is actually interfering with their autonomy by concealing knowledge necessary to make an informed choice. Furthermore, we may ask whether it is really loving to help others perpetuate a profoundly damaging self-deception, simply to 'protect' their freedom to deceive themselves. Would that not mean that God actively participates in their damnation? Given the weight of argu-ments already mounted, it is clear God would do no such thing.

However, even if all of this is true, Walls still has his argument that bondage to desire may be freely chosen. Unfortunately for Walls, there are problems here as well. First, Christian orthodoxy teaches that *all* of us 'are in bondage to sin and cannot free ourselves'. Hence, divine intervention is essential for any to be saved.[45] What Walls claims, however, is that some of us *freely choose* our bond-age – and for those of us who do, God cannot intervene to break that bondage without violating our freedom.

This answer is problematic, first, because it seems unlikely that anyone actually *chooses* – freely or otherwise – to be in bondage to desire. What seems more likely is that such a state 'sneaks up' on us: we routinely act on the desires we have, failing to pursue opportunities to develop the discipline to resist sinful desires. Eventually we find ourselves simply unable to resist them. While our choices play a role in becoming slaves to sin, we never actually choose such a state. Rather, we make a series of bad choices that have the cumulative effect of depriving us of free choice.[46] Thus, in eliminating such bondage, God would be removing an unintended *effect* of our choices, not anything chosen for itself. And insofar as this unchosen state interferes with our capacity for free choice, how can its elimination *override* our freedom? In cases of overriding freedom, we choose something in a context where we have some claim on our choice playing a role in the outcome, but then do not get what we chose. However, insofar as states of character are not chosen at all, getting something other than the states we have cannot override out choice.

This problem, however, is not decisive. Walls could argue that even if people do not choose *initially* to make themselves slaves to sin, they can do so after the fact, thus *endorsing* who they have become. The damned may be those who have not merely stumbled into bondage but have chosen to embrace this aspect of themselves in defiance of God, thereby rebuffing the grace necessary to eliminate such bondage. This seems to be what Walls has in mind when he refers to those who have made a 'decisive choice for evil'. They are like the addict who wants to stay addicted, embracing their bondage.[47]

Whether the choice to be a slave to sinful desires is made in advance of developing that character, or after the fact, we may still ask why anyone would make such a choice. And here lies the deeper problem with Walls' argument: he does not sufficiently consider the conditions under which choosing bondage to desire is possible.

This leads us to a general problem that applies to both parts of Walls' reply to Talbott. With respect *both* to the choice of ignorance *and* to the choice of embracing bondage to desire, the perplexity Talbott expresses about freely choosing damnation seems equally appropriate. Why would anyone with full freedom to choose, and a complete understanding of what the choice involves, freely choose ignorance or bondage to sinful desires? According to Walls' own hypothesis, these choices (if sustained) produce *eternal damnation*. Possessing full and accurate information about God is not only in our interests, but of ultimate importance to our eternal destiny, and likewise for freedom from bondage to sin. Thus, those who choose ignorance or bondage to desire are choosing something that is not only morally objectionable but, in all conceivable respects, immensely harmful to them. In other words, anyone who knew what this choice involved and was free from controlling affective states would have every motive not to make this choice and no motive to make it. Assuming rational or Thomistic freedom, it follows that anyone who chooses ignorance or bondage to desire must do so based on some pre-existent ignorance or bondage. They may choose to remain ignorant, for example, because they do not understand what such ignorance entails. Hence, the choice is not free, and God would not be violating autonomy by eliminating the ignorance.

If Walls tried to move the free choice back another step (arguing that the choice to be ignorant or in bondage to desire is based on some previous ignorance or bondage to desire that was freely chosen), he would trap himself in an infinite regress. Either the choice to be in one of these states is always based on a previous choice to be in one of these states, ad infinitum, such that we never arrive at a truly free choice; or there is some initial ignorance or bondage to desire that is not chosen based on any prior similar state, and hence could not be the result of a free choice. Either way, God could eliminate the ignorance or bondage that blocks His salvific intentions without violating freedom.

It seems, then, that the choice to deceive oneself or put oneself in bondage to desire could not itself be made unless one were either ignorant or in bondage to desire, and hence not free. Thus, Walls' response to Talbott fails.

The only way we can see for Walls to avoid this outcome is to back away from his admission that, in the face of full and adequate understanding of the nature of the choice, no one would freely reject communion with God. In other words, he would need to adopt the view that freedom has a libertarian character even in cases of completely uniform motives. This is the possibility we explore in the next chapter. Before turning to that issue, however, we want to consider two final points in relation to efficacious grace.

7.9 Overriding Freedom without Violating Autonomy

So far, we have argued that – at least assuming a Thomistic view of freedom – God has available to him a means of bestowing efficacious grace that does not override creaturely freedom. Hence, a fortiori, it does not violate autonomy; but suppose that we are wrong about this. Suppose that, despite our arguments so far, a critic remains convinced that if God wipes away a creature's salvation inhibitors without their voluntary cooperation, He has overridden their free choices. It does not follow from this that God has therefore done anything morally troubling, because instances of overriding free choice need not be instances of violating autonomy. Recall the earlier case of someone who, as part of their job, chooses among ad campaigns for a product. The person's boss, however, prefers a different campaign and so exercises her veto privileges. While the boss has thus overridden her employee's choice, she has not thereby violated the employee's autonomy. The reason is because the framework within which the employee makes his choice is one in which that choice is given a specifiable role in determining outcomes – and even though the outcome that he chose is not the outcome that resulted, his choice was still allowed to play the role he had a presumptive right for it to play. Since, in the context in which the choice was made, the boss held legitimate veto power, that she vetoed the employee's choice does not amount to a wrongful violation of his autonomy.

The decision to respond affirmatively to God's offer of salvation is a species of a broader class of decisions that ordinarily fall within the scope of human choice. Specifically, salvation consists, among other things, in participation in the beloved community and moral sanctification. Understood in these terms, salvation has implications for one's *relationships* and one's *character*. Are these not matters about which our choices should (prima facie) play some determining role?

They clearly *do* play this role in circumstances less grave than our final destiny. Whether we have a relationship of a given type is, of course, never entirely up to us; but absent relevant choices of ours, a relationship of any given type *is* ruled out. A mutually loving relationship never arises in ordinary affairs without our choosing to contribute our part to it. That is, it ordinarily falls within the scope of our choice to *reject* the establishment of such a relationship. Character seems to be shaped not only by matters independent of our control such as who parented us and what traumas we have endured, but also by our choices about such things as who to spend time with and what activities to participate in. In fact, while negative character traits are something we tend to stumble into, positive ones are more often a matter of deliberate cultivation. When it comes to virtues, we have them because we have chosen to strive to become people of a certain type.

Let us suppose that not only is this the way our choices ordinarily function, but the way they presumptively should function – at least in ordinary circumstances. If so, then in ordinary human affairs we have a prima facie right to expect that we will not find ourselves in a mutual loving relationship without having chosen to be in one; and we have a prima facie right to expect that we will not have a positive character trait that we have not sought to cultivate.

But that we have these rights in ordinary circumstances does not entail a presumptive claim on being free from divine 'veto' when it comes to our eternal destinies. A business may grant an employee the authority to make unsupervised decisions when it comes to purchases under a certain budgetary threshold, but require that these decisions be reviewed by a higher authority possessing veto power when the purchases are above this threshold. Given God's status as our creator, there is reason to suppose that, with respect to very many outcomes in which our decisions play a role, the legitimate scope of that role is constrained by God's will. Therefore, if God has available to Him a means of saving the unregenerate which overrides their freedom, then we cannot simply assume that this means of saving them is a morally problematic violation of autonomy.

There are, in fact, reasons to suppose it is not. Consider the following: a one-year-old has developed some capacity for choice, expressed in their preference for certain toys, foods and activities. Caring parents typically afford their children some room to exercise this budding capacity, but if the child chooses to insert a knitting needle into an electrical outlet, the parents intervene. Similarly, when it is time to strap the child into its car seat and drive it to a well-baby check-up, the child is not consulted – the parents simply scoop the child up and go.

Now it may be that this is not even an instance of overriding the child's freedom; that the parents have simply made a choice for the child that *bypasses* its freedom. However, even if we assume that the parents have overridden the child's freedom, it hardly follows that the child's autonomy has been violated. Even if the child has some rudimentary right to make choices within a certain range, and we expect them to play a role in determining outcomes, when it comes to the child's health the parents retain a kind of veto power.

There is reason to think that when it comes to our ultimate destinies we are like infants, and God therefore legitimately reserves this kind of parental veto power should we make poor use of our nascent capacity for choice. Marilyn Adams, in *'The Problem of Hell'*, reminds us of the conditions under which we develop our capacity to make choices. We start out ignorant and helpless and only gradually develop a picture of the world, influenced by others who are as imperfect as we. From early on we are 'confronted with problems that we cannot adequately grasp or fully cope with, and in response to which we mount (without fully conscious calculation) inefficient adaptational strategies'.[48] These strategies eventually become entrenched in our adult personalities. 'Having thus begun *immature*, we arrive at adulthood in a state of *impaired freedom*, as our childhood adaptational strategies continue to distort our perceptions and behaviors.'[49]

While we might imagine someone who develops under these conditions wilfully rejecting God, it does not follow that such rejection is truly free; but even if we concede that in some sense it is free, it hardly follows that God should refuse to interfere with such choices out of respect for freedom. As Adams points out, given our broken state we are no more competent to be entrusted with our eternal destinies than a toddler is to be entrusted with life-and-death decisions.[50] On the matter of our eternal destiny we are as infants – and just as parents retain veto power when it comes to the more serious choices children make, God might retain such power when it comes to our eternal fate. If so, then even if efficacious grace overrides freedom, it does not violate autonomy.

7.10 The Impossibility of Avoiding Autonomy Violations

Let us suppose that none of this is compelling, and that were God to save the unregenerate using one of the species of efficacious grace outlined in this chapter, He would violate their autonomy. Nevertheless, there may be conditions under which such prima facie impermissible autonomy violations are justified.

One reason to suppose it might be permissible to violate the autonomy of the unregenerate is because eternal damnation is just too horrible to permit. In previous chapters we argued that not only is damnation bad for the damned and the blessed, but the continuing sinfulness of the damned is an affront to divine majesty. While we have argued that divine justice cannot coherently justify damnation, insofar as doing so would involve responding to the intolerable affront of sin by ensuring that this affront persists eternally, divine justice may warrant stripping away the usual rights to have one's choices play a certain role in determining outcomes. Just as we think criminals forfeit the right to freedom because of their misuse of it, we might suppose the unregenerate forfeit this right and may be justly punished by having their freedom taken away. In short, justice demands that sin cease, and this demand gives God the authority to destroy the false self that clings to sin – a destruction which (temporarily) produces 'wailing and gnashing of teeth'.

However, rather than rest our case on this argument, we want to close this chapter with a slightly different point – namely, that if bestowing efficacious grace *does* violate autonomy, and if some would be damned but for the bestowal of efficacious grace, it follows that it would be impossible for God to bestow genuine blessedness on *any* of his creatures without violating their autonomy. To make this point, we want to recall argument ALB from Chapter 5. ALB holds that the blessed would, by virtue of their perfected moral character, regard unalloyed bliss as an unfitting response to a reality in which some rational creatures are eternally damned. As such, were the blessed aware of the damned's plight, their joy would be diminished – and so they would not, in fact, possess the supremely worthwhile happiness that Christians usually think constitutes blessedness.

In discussing ALB, we critically assessed William Lane Craig's strategy for solving this problem – namely, by proposing that God might shield the blessed from any awareness of the damned. We argued that such shielding would amount to *a violation of their autonomy*; since perfect joy would not be something they would regard as fitting given the way the world is (assuming some are damned). Therefore, by shielding the blessed from awareness of the damned, God would be deliberately bringing it about that they have a false belief, which in turn leads them to make a choice they would not have made had they known the truth.

When first presenting ALB, we regarded this as a significant problem with Craig's proposal. However, now we are positioned to see that ALB gives rise to an even deeper problem for defenders of DH who reject universalism on the grounds that it would require God to violate creaturely autonomy – because if any are damned in this view, securing the perfect blessedness of the saved would require that God violate *their* autonomy.

The problem can be formulated as follows: defenders of LDH must explain why God could not just interfere with the autonomy of the unregenerate to secure universal salvation. Two answers are possible: (a) it is morally objectionable for God to violate His creatures' autonomy, even for the sake of securing their blessedness; (b) a state of eternal blessedness cannot be attained in ways that violate autonomy. In short, one must suppose that it is either *immoral* or *impossible* for God to secure blessedness through autonomy violations.

However, if either (a) or (b) is embraced, then it seems that God cannot legitimately shield the blessed from the painful awareness of the sufferings of the damned, and so cannot secure genuine blessedness for *anyone*. The only escape from this problem, it seems, would be for defenders of LDH to distinguish different kinds of autonomy violations, with the kind involved in securing ignorance among the blessed (what we will call 'Craigian autonomy violations') being either morally permissible or logically compatible with blessedness in a way that those needed to secure the blessedness of all are not. In other words, either (a) or (b) would need to be modified so as not to extend to Craigian autonomy violations.

Modifying (b) in the way needed is problematic. Craigian autonomy violations are *constitutive* of blessedness in that being deceived about the truth is an ongoing requirement for the saved to continue in bliss. If *all* are saved, then *no* creature will need to be secured eternally in false beliefs in order to enjoy supreme happiness. Thus, if all are saved, Craigian autonomy violations (which are *constitutive* of the blessed's state) will not be necessary in order to secure anyone's salvation. Instead, what would be required (if anything) is an autonomy violation that is *causally* related to *achieving* the state of blessedness (such as a full revelation of God that irresistibly transforms the creature's character). Since these means of achieving blessedness are not constitutive of that state, it is hard to see why they would be logically incompatible with being *in* that state. Craigian autonomy violations, however, *could* be incompatible with being in the state of blessedness, since they are, by definition, an ongoing feature *of* that state. We think that some of the concerns about the farcical nature of the joys of the blessed, discussed in Chapter 5, offer formidable reasons to think Craigian autonomy violations *are* incompatible with authentic blessedness. Hence, to modify (b) in the way needed would require that defenders of LDH show that the sorts of autonomy violations that appear to be compatible with the state of blessedness are really incompatible, whereas those that appear to be incompatible are really compatible.

With respect to modifying (a), defenders of LDH face several challenges. First, as already argued, there is good reason to think that all that is needed to secure the salvation of any creature would be an unalloyed vision of God. If the unregenerate not only saw but *experienced* the truth about God and their own relation to Him, they could no longer reject Him. Even if we make the contestable concession that such a full revelation of God violates creaturely autonomy, defenders of LDH find themselves in the unenviable position of explaining why an autonomy violation that *reveals* the truth is more objectionable than one that *conceals* it.

Second, there clearly *is* something prima facie wrong about Craigian autonomy violations. Presumably, defenders of LDH would have to hold that Craigian autonomy violations are morally justified because perfecting the happiness of those in (partial) communion with God outweighs the prima facie case against such violations. Now this claim has some plausibility; but if it is plausible to say this, then is it not also plausible to say that God's revealing Himself to the unregenerate to secure their repentance would be justified because the end of lifting creatures out of damnation and into supreme bliss outweighs whatever prima facie case there is against this kind of revelation? If the former kind of autonomy violations are justified by the improvement in the state of those violated, it is hard to see why the latter kind *cannot* be justified, even though the improvement in the state of those violated is *incalculably greater*. Also, if we want to say that a deontological moral constraint renders the latter sort of autonomy violation impermissible regardless of how good its consequences are, it becomes hard to see why the same moral constraint would not apply to the former sort.

In short, there seems to be no plausible way to modify (a) or (b) so that they prohibit God's bestowing efficacious grace but not His shielding the blessed in the manner Craig proposes. Hence, those who wish to defend LDH by appealing to God's duty to respect autonomy are driven to conclude that the saved never enjoy unalloyed blessedness. They *could* hold that salvation brings something less than supreme happiness – that what Christianity promises is an *imperfect* final end, marred forever by dissatisfaction with the state of the world; or they could hold that blessedness does not include perfect sanctification – maintaining that the blessed, despite being in communion with God, remain out of touch with God's love for the damned. However, neither alternative is appealing – both seem to involve an adulteration of the spirit of Christian theism.

Thus, the view that some are damned because God cannot save all without violating creaturely autonomy, which is impermissible for God, is a view with a surprisingly high cost; but as we have argued in this chapter, this is not a cost that those who embrace a Thomistic view of freedom need to bear. Given the 'rational' view of freedom, God *can* save the unregenerate without overriding their freedom, let alone violating their autonomy. But what about those who ascribe to a more strongly libertarian view of freedom, such as the Molinist one? Is this a price *they* have to pay? We think not, and in the next chapter we explain why.

CHAPTER 8

FREELY CHOSEN UNIVERSAL SALVATION

8.1 Introduction

In the previous chapter we argued that it is possible and permissible for God to extend efficacious grace to those who reject Him, and that He therefore would do so. We noted that the most significant worry about this way of defending DU (which endorses DU1) is the fear that extending efficacious grace to the unregenerate overrides their freedom in impermissible ways.

In response, we argued three things: first, that from a Thomistic view of freedom God can extend efficacious grace without overriding creaturely freedom; second, that even if this sort of efficacious grace is assumed to override freedom, there is reason to think it does not violate autonomy and hence is not a prima facie impermissible case of overriding freedom; third, that even if this form of efficacious grace is taken to violate autonomy, there is good reason to suppose it is a justified case of violating autonomy.

In relation to AF (the primary argument for LDH), our thinking so far might be summarized as follows: there are numerous reasons to suppose that, given a Thomistic view of freedom ('rational freedom'), AF1 – which holds that God cannot guarantee the salvation of all without overriding the unregenerate's freedom – should be rejected. There are also reasons to suppose that, even if AF1 is accepted, AF2 (which holds that it is either impossible or impermissible for God to override creaturely freedom even for the sake of their salvation) should be set aside. We will not pursue the latter any further, instead assuming for argument's sake that securing a creature's salvation by overriding their freedom is impermissible, and hence that AF2 is true. We will also assume that our readers are unconvinced by the account of freedom upon which we have so far based our criticisms of AF1. We will grant, in short, that the freedom of the unregenerate is of a more strongly libertarian sort than we have so far supposed. In this chapter we argue that, even given these assumptions, there is a version of DU that is more compelling that DH, namely DU2.

Since AF1 will be our focus in what follows, it may help to state it more precisely. It seems that AF1 is essentially what Eleanore Stump has in mind when she says: 'It is not within God's power to ensure that all human beings will be in heaven, because it is not within the power even of an omnipotent entity to *make* a person freely will anything.'[1] In other words, given the nature of free choice, what an agent freely chooses cannot be *determined* by another. Hence,

God cannot *bring about* a creature's free choice (even in Plantinga's weak sense), and so cannot guarantee that all are saved in a manner that respects freedom. AF1 might thus be reformulated as follows:

> It is not within God's power to bring it about (weakly) that both (i) every person who is saved freely chooses to be saved, and (ii) all are saved.

Let us call this the 'No Guarantee Doctrine', or NG. What we essentially did in Chapter 7 was argue that, assuming a Thomistic view of freedom, God *can* bring about both (i) and (ii) for anyone simply by guaranteeing that the conditions of free choice are obtained. At first glance, then, it seems that defenders of NG must reject Thomistic or 'rational' freedom, perhaps in favour of a Molinist alternative – but appearances can be deceptive. In fact, we think that there are *two* ways to reject the implications for NG which we have drawn from the Thomistic view of freedom. The first, of course, is to reject this view of freedom, holding instead (in the spirit of Duns Scotus, Molina and others) that human freedom is essentially and *radically* libertarian: we can choose what we have no motive to choose and every motive not to choose, such that even if all salvation inhibitors are removed and we are left with uniformly God-choosing motives, we might still reject God.

We think, however, that there is a second response which rejects neither the Thomistic view of freedom nor Talbott's claim that genuine freedom with respect to the choice of salvation guarantees salvation. Rather, the response holds that true freedom in relation to the choice of salvation – choice unimpeded by ignorance, deception and bondage to desire – is only available *to the saved*. What Talbott describes – the state in which creatures are liberated from *all* ignorance, deception and bondage to desire – is nothing other than the state of salvation itself.

The idea here is that the objective order of values is never perfectly available to the unsaved, so that choices *about* salvation simply *cannot* be free in the rational sense. As such, there is only one way that God can liberate the unsaved from all salvation inhibitors and thereby produce uniformly God-choosing motives: by saving them. This means that if creatures' choices are to play any role in whether or not they are saved, the choices must be characterized by *imperfect* freedom.

Given the inevitable ignorance that precedes salvation, choices made in this state exhibit an indeterminacy characteristic of what we typically associate with libertarian freedom: whatever one chooses, one might have chosen otherwise. While this indeterminacy may be regrettable, genuine rational freedom – and its guarantee of choosing God – is possible only for the saved.

There are reasons to be critical of this second approach to defending NG. One might wonder why it is so important for God to respect the *second-best* freedom of the unsaved. If, due to inevitable ignorance, a creature is subject to an uncertainty that leads it to decide against communion with God – not really understanding fully what it is deciding against – why would it be morally impermissible for God to step in and reveal the truth (even if this amounts to saving them)? In other words, defending AF1 in this way raises questions about the defensibility of AF2.

However, we will set aside those concerns, assuming that God is morally compelled to respect a freedom that is inevitably indeterminate in its outcomes – either because it has the radically libertarian character endorsed by Scotus and others, or because it is inevitably imperfect due to the inescapable ignorance that clouds the judgment of the unsaved. Our argument is that, *even so*, NG is false.

In making this case, we make two assumptions. First, for the sake of simplicity we assume that what is necessary for salvation is a single free choice to accept (or not resist) God's grace, rather than a series of choices. This is really just a procedural assumption to simplify discussion. Our argument will work even if salvation is reached through an ongoing sequence of choices that are free in the libertarian sense.

Suppose, for example, we follow the Lutheran Orthodox view that once we make the choice not to resist God's grace, we in effect allow God to 'flood' into us and do whatever is necessary to secure our blessedness, including transforming our character or *sanctifying* us. This sanctification process is conceived as occurring over time and occurring with the *concurrence of the reformed will*; but at this stage in the process the will is freely concurring with God in only a compatibilist sense. The only libertarian choice in the process is the choice not to resist God's grace.[2] But this libertarian choice can readily be understood, not as a single choice, but as an ongoing sequence of decisions not to 'unplug' oneself from the divine grace that drives the sanctification process. As such, there may be – throughout the process that culminates in eternal beatitude – a sequence of free choices (in the libertarian sense) not to reject grace.

For simplicity's sake, however, we develop our argument *as if* what is at issue is a single choice. Once we have made the argument in these terms, we show that it makes no difference if what is at stake is a single choice or a sequence of choices.

Our second assumption is more substantive. Specifically, we assume that once we come to enjoy the beatific vision we are confirmed in this state. That is, once we are in heaven we will never tumble into hell. This assumption is, we suspect, nearly universally embraced by Christians. How could the blessed truly be 'saved' from damnation if their status is precarious and they could at any time fall into the outer darkness? How this assumption relates to human freedom depends on one's view of freedom. If one adopts the Thomistic view, any indeterminacy that characterizes freedom prior to salvation disappears once salvation is achieved.[3] If one adopts the Molinist view, one might think that freedom has served its purpose once one has attained the beatific vision – and so can be suspended without any violation of the person.[4] Both alternatives will be considered again when we consider objections to our argument.

8.2 *Arbitrariness in Human Choices*

As noted above, defenders of NG must insist that the choices of the unsaved are subject to indeterminacy in one of two ways. In this section, we argue that either approach makes the choices of the unsaved partly arbitrary, which in turn renders them subject to the probabilistic laws governing events that are wholly or partly random.

First, we consider the approach that presupposes a radically libertarian freedom according to which it is possible for those not in bondage to a non-rational affective state *both* to judge (correctly, on Christian assumptions) that communion with God is infinitely preferable to alienation from God *and* to choose alienation.

Typical accounts of this sort of radically free choice betray an implicit confusion by appealing to motivations such as 'pride' to explain the choice. This is confused because an implication of the judgment that communion with God is infinitely preferable to alienation is the judgment that satisfying one's 'pride' is infinitely inferior in value to achieving communion with God. Since we are assuming the person is not in bondage to a non-rational affective state, we are assuming the person is not *determined* to act out of pride. Thus, this supposed 'explanation' turns out to have the following form: a person, not in bondage to prideful feelings, who recognizes pride to be utterly unworthy of choice, chooses to act on pride. 'Pride' can hardly explain one's choice here, since one is free not to act on prideful feelings and has no reason to choose pride.

In fact, any explanation for choosing to act contrary to one's settled best judgment, when one is not in bondage to a non-rational affective state, amounts to this kind of empty explanation. If no ignorance, deception or bondage to desire explains the choice to reject God, then such a choice *must* remain inexplicable, because there cannot be any reasons for making it.

The result is that we can only account for this sort of radical view of freedom by insisting that human beings can make choices *for no reason at all* – that is, *arbitrarily* or at random – even when they have good reasons that might guide them.[5] Thus understood, the damned are precisely those who (1) ignore all reasons for making a choice; (2) choose at random; and (3) randomly choose alienation from God. It is as if they have made their decision by flipping a coin; and, unfortunately, the coin lands 'rejection-side-up'.

We should note that arbitrariness and reason can be simultaneously at work in decision making. Consider, as an analogy, a many-sided die, each face of which is painted one of two colours: red or blue. When rolled, random forces decide which side lands face up; but there may be some *reason* why eighteen of twenty sides are red. Likewise, one may have reasons why one chooses in such a way that it is far more likely that one will randomly choose communion with God over alienation. We might suppose that if one has excellent reasons to favour the former option and none favouring the latter, one would 'roll a die' heavily weighted to the former. If the agent nevertheless chooses alienation, it is because the agent's choice is partly random.

Someone might think to avoid this picture of what radical libertarianism entails by holding that removing all salvation inhibitors does not mean removing all non-rational motives for action. Even if we are no longer in *bondage* to such motives, they might persist. Perhaps we can choose to reject God because we retain the power to act on irrational desires – desires that would motivate us to reject God – even after we are freed from *bondage* to them. The idea here is that libertarian freedom involves the power to select among motives, and even once all salvation inhibitors are removed there may remain motives that would lead us to reject God *were* we to choose them.

However, this response supposes that freedom involves *choosing* among motives, and so we can ask why we would choose one motive over another. What motivates the choice of motives? Is it nothing? If so, our choices turn out to be arbitrary; but if there is something influencing our choice of motives, what would that be? Is it some second-order motive? If we are freed from all salvation inhibitors, what second-order motive could inspire us to choose a first-order God-rejecting motive? We would, by hypothesis, know the second-order motive to be unworthy of choice and be free from bondage to it. Hence, either our selection of motive is arbitrary or is explained by the fact that we have *chosen* to have our choice of second-order motives determined by an irrational third-order motive; but then *this* choice needs explaining. To escape an infinite regress, we must hold that at some point we choose arbitrarily.

This line of thought leads to a more devastating problem with the radical libertarian view. For those freed from all salvation inhibitors, there can be no motive to choose to let arbitrariness – in whole or in part – determine their eternal destinies. At any level of choice – the choice of motive, the choice of what will determine one's choice of motive, and so on – the choice to be arbitrary on this matter is utterly irrational.

When I look at a menu and cannot decide from among the entrées, I may decide to choose at random – but underlying that choice is the more basic choice to 'let chance decide', and this choice is *not* random, but is based on the reasoned judgment that, since my preferences do not lean me towards one entrée over another, and since I must choose if I am to eat, it makes sense for me to make the choice at random. However, it makes no sense to do this when it comes to accepting or rejecting God's grace, at least not if I am freed from all salvation inhibitors. To let chance decide between the very best conceivable thing and the very worst is to leave to chance the very last thing any remotely rational beings would leave to chance if they could help it. Thus, if chance does influence this decision, it is because it *cannot* be helped. There simply *is* a random element operating in human choice – one that, in a crucial sense, falls outside the person's control.

This is a deep problem. Defenders of libertarian freedom ultimately want to make *agents* responsible for their choices. Even if agents choose *at* random, it is still the *agents* who choose – not their motives, and not the operation of random forces. Choosing at random is not the same as one's choice being a random event. Consider this point in relation to a dominant libertarian theory of freedom – namely, the theory of agent causation.[6] This theory holds that agents cause their choices and so initiate a subsequent causal chain of events culminating in a human act; but this initiation of a causal sequence – undetermined by prior causes outside the agent – is not therefore unrelated to *reasons* for action. It will *either* be based on such reasons *or* not. If not, then it is being made *at* random. It will, however, still be the agent making the choice for no reason, as opposed to the choice just being an event that happens for no reason.

This distinction, however, breaks down if randomness in one's choices results from the operation of a random element that falls *outside* the agent's control. According to the radical libertarian view of freedom, the agent – who by virtue of being freed from all salvation inhibitors is as *perfectly sane* as it is possible to be – might still choose something that is, in effect, the single most insane choice conceivable. Since there cannot be any motive for such a choice, it must be random; and since the agent has no motive to choose *at* random and, on the contrary, the most compelling and unambiguous reasons not to do so, the randomness itself can only be explained as an ineradicable random element in human choice that imposes itself on agents regardless of what they will.

If any are damned in this view, then they are damned by bad luck, not because of anything they can be held responsible for. This implication is sufficient in itself to warrant rejecting a defence of NG based on such a radical understanding of libertarian freedom. Our arguments in the next section, however, will show that even if this implausible view of human freedom is embraced, universal salvation can be guaranteed.

Before turning to that argument, however, we need to consider the second way of defending NG, which argues that the freedom of the unsaved is necessarily imperfect. Here, the idea is that salvation is a *condition* for full rational freedom, because it is only once we enjoy the beatific vision that all deception and ignorance are gone. Rational freedom thus cannot be what we are talking about when considering the choices of the unsaved. Of course, one conclusion to draw from this is that NG is trivially true but not an impediment to God's saving of all. This follows if we hold that rational freedom is the only kind of freedom that there is. In that case there would be no freedom prior to salvation, such that no one could freely choose union with God. It would be trivially true that it is not within God's power to guarantee that everyone makes such a choice; but in that case, no good God would make such a choice a prerequisite for salvation. Hence, any argument for LDH relying on NG would collapse.

Thus, the defender of LDH has to say that there exists a kind of freedom which is not rational freedom but is nevertheless a freedom worth having, and which God is called upon to respect. But what would this 'next-best freedom' look like? Clearly, much of what Talbott says about choices made in the grip of ignorance, deception or bondage to desire is indisputable: those who are misled into doing X (thinking they are doing Y) are not freely doing X. Likewise, those who are controlled by affective states that they cannot override cannot reasonably be called free; and surely God can liberate us from such obvious impediments to free choice, even without displaying the full glory of the beatific vision.

If NG is to be taken as referring to a 'next-best freedom', then it would need to be understood as the freedom that exists when all salvation inhibitors have been removed *except those that cannot be removed short of experiencing the beatific vision*. If there is anything that God cannot do *prior* to saving us, it is to free us from *all ignorance*. Our existence prior to salvation features an ineradicable uncertainty about what is truly best – and uncertainty about the relative value of our choices is enough to generate an indeterminacy in decision making.

However, to say that our decision making prior to salvation is inevitably subject to the indeterminacy that flows from uncertainty about the relative value of our choices is simply to say that, in this pre-saved state, there is inevitably some arbitrariness in our decision making. This is most obvious when faced with the need to choose when we have *no* reason to regard one alternative as being preferable to another. Reason cannot decide the matter for us. We must decide, and so we choose – at random. In cases of complete uncertainty, our choice *must* be arbitrary.

The same is true if, among the available alternatives, we confront equally strong (or weak) reasons in favour of (and/or against) each. In this case we lack any reason to prefer one alternative (A) over another (B). When we choose (A), we might share the reasons that speak in (A)'s favour when asked, but those reasons would not explain why we did (A), since we had equally compelling reasons to choose (B). No reason *could* explain our choice; but that we choose even so may be rationally defended as an alternative to paralysis. This power to choose among reasons for action that are equally compelling is nothing other than the power to avoid paralysis when choices must be made but reason cannot decide on them.

As such, the arbitrariness here is not the wholly irrational arbitrariness we confronted in the radically libertarian view of freedom. In that case, arbitrariness was clearly contrary to the decisive reasoned judgment of the agent, and hence could be explained only by positing in human freedom an inextricably random element indifferent to reason and beyond the agent's control. However, in the face of unavoidable uncertainty about what is best, arbitrariness in one's choices may in fact be *rationally defensible* as the only alternative to paralysis.

In many cases, of course, one alternative stands out as having the strongest considerations in its favour, in which case, while we have reasons for choosing the favoured alternative, we cannot have reasons for choosing the *less* favoured one. The choice relating to communion with God seems to be like this: the reasons *for* choosing God far outweigh the reasons *against* choosing God (at least when we have 'next-best freedom'). If we choose against communion, it will not be on the basis of reasons, and so would have to be because there is an element of arbitrariness in our choice.

However, under conditions that characterize 'next-best freedom', there may be some justification for preserving a dimension of arbitrariness even when the weight of reason favours one alternative – at least given that the arbitrary dimension of the choice may be progressively less influential as the weight of reason becomes more lopsided (recall the example of the many-sided die with one of two possible colours on each face). Such arbitrariness may be the agent's way of reflecting the ineradicable uncertainty that persists in the pre-saved state. For example, an agent may intuit that he or she has a chance, however small, of reasoning incorrectly about the matter at hand, and may (unconsciously) counterbalance this chance by introducing into their decision making a similarly small chance of randomly choosing contrary to their reasoned judgment. Since choosing in a given way often reveals knowledge otherwise obscured, an error in one's judgment that a choice is unworthy might permanently deprive one of the evidence necessary to refute that judgment – unless one retains a measure of arbitrariness in one's decision making (perhaps proportionate to one's perceived risk of error).

The most plausible way to reject this conclusion, it seems, is to argue that our choice of the less reasonable alternative is explained not by arbitrariness, but by the wilful decision to attend to reasons in a distorted way. The decision to reject God could then be explained in terms of a capacity to attend to some (but not all) of the evidence, and hence allow the less compelling evidence to move us. The problem with this explanation is that it posits a choice that itself needs explaining; namely, the choice to attend disproportionately to the less compelling evidence. Why choose that? The weight of reason could not speak in favour of it, so this choice would have to be made either based on a prior choice to attend to reasons in a distorted way, or arbitrarily. To avoid an infinite regress of choices, we must ultimately appeal to arbitrariness.

Advocates of libertarian freedom may be unhappy with this perspective because they want to hold that when someone is acting freely, it is the *person* – *not* their motives and *not* random chance – that is responsible for the choice. We do not deny this. We are not saying that random forces *determine* choices; rather, we are saying that at some point in the many-levelled choice-making process, agents reflect the uncertainty of the state prior to salvation by being (at least somewhat) arbitrary *in* their choices. While the agent chooses *at* random, it is still the agent – and not random forces – that ultimately makes the choice.

Unlike the case of radical libertarianism, the arbitrariness here can be explained by the agent's deliberative processes. Hence, agents can be said to be responsible for their arbitrariness in a way that cannot be said in the case of radical libertarianism. In that case, the choice simply could not originate in the agent's deliberative processes, because absolutely *nothing* in that deliberative process, at any level, could favour arbitrariness.

However, given ineradicable uncertainty, arbitrariness may be justified both as an alternative to paralysis and as a guard against error. As such, saying that an agent chooses *at* random does not force us to say that it is randomness, rather than the agent, that chooses. Unlike coin flips, in which random forces determine the outcome, the decisions of an arbitrary agent are mediated by the concurrence of the agent's will: randomness would not determine the outcome but for the agent's *willing* that it does. The agent thus remains the efficient cause of the choice.

However, when agents choose arbitrarily, their choice pattern exactly resembles what we would observe had the choices been determined by random forces. In effect, agents are allowing or permitting a kind of mechanistic randomness to guide their will. Therefore, as is the case with truly random events, arbitrary choices are subject to the laws of probability – a fact which affords God an avenue for guaranteeing the salvation of all.

8.3 Libertarian Freedom and the Infinite Opportunity Argument

Given the premise that agents (at least prior to salvation) can and do choose contrary to the weight of reason – what we will call the broadly libertarian view – does it follow that an omnipotent God cannot guarantee that all will freely choose salvation? We argue here that it does not. Given our initial assumptions, which imply that once creatures choose communion with God they are confirmed in bliss, it follows that God can save all even assuming this broadly libertarian view. The only things God must do to ensure universal salvation are (a) strip away all the salvation inhibitors that He can strip away prior to salvation;[7] (b) sustain all persons in a *temporal* existence, at least until they choose communion with God;[8] and (c) leave the choice of communion with God an 'open choice' such that every person is free to choose it at any time.

The argument for this conclusion, which we call the Argument from Infinite Opportunity (AIO), runs as follows:

1. It is in God's power to bring about (a) to (c)
2. In bringing about (a) to (c), God would not be doing anything morally impermissible
3. If God brings about (a) to (c), then all persons will freely choose salvation.
4. Therefore, it is in God's power to bring it about that all persons will freely choose salvation without doing anything morally impermissible (1, 2, 3).

Since (4) implies the negation of NG, AIO's success undermines NG. Claim (1) seems uncontroversial. If God is omnipotent in the sense of having the power to do whatever is logically possible, then surely God can accomplish (a) to (c), since neither collectively nor individually do they imply a contradiction. What about (2) and (3)? We will consider (2) in a later section. For now, we focus on (3). Why think that bringing about (a) to (c) will guarantee that all freely choose to be saved?

To see why (a) to (c) would ensure universal salvation, consider the following. We have already argued that if (a) is met, a free person will more likely than not choose communion with God over alienation, even assuming a broadly libertarian freedom. For the sake of argument, however, let us suppose the odds are even.[9] If God brings about (b) and (c), then the choice whether to embrace communion with God is not made once, but is confronted *every moment* of an existence of potentially infinite duration. At each moment of this indefinite existence, there is an even chance that this person will choose communion with God – at which point the person is saved. Under these conditions, the person's salvation becomes a mathematical certainty.

The certainty of this outcome can be usefully depicted using the language of possible worlds. To do so, it will help to introduce some terminology. Let us call a complete possible state of affairs at any particular moment a 'possible moment'. A 'possible world' is a totality of temporally successive possible moments. A 'possible world segment' is a totality of temporally successive possible moments up to a particular time. A 'possible world tree' is a collection of possible worlds sharing the same possible world segment up to time T (the 'trunk' of the tree), after which they diverge. An 'indeterminacy' in a possible world segment is some random factor operative at T such that after T there is more than one possible world sharing the same world segment up to T. At any moment, there are a finite number of possible world segments in a possible world tree. However, as the timeline moves towards infinity, so long as there are indeterminacies remaining within any possible world segment, the number of possible world segments within a tree expands without bounds.

With this terminology in mind, consider the claim that universal salvation is guaranteed under conditions (a) to (c). Imagine a possible world segment P1 in which the only thing that offers any indeterminacy is Fred, who at T1 has yet to choose communion with God. Suppose further, for simplicity, that the only choice open to Fred – and thus the only source of indeterminacy in P1 – is whether to accept communion with God. By hypothesis, given Fred's 'next-best freedom', there is an even chance Fred will choose communion with God. We can assume that even though any segment of time is infinitely divisible, practically speaking, humans can only make a finite number of choices in any time interval. We will call each such discrete choice-making opportunity a 'moment'. With this in mind, at T2, the moment immediately following T1, we have two possible world segments in the possible world tree that shares P as its 'trunk'. In one of these possible world segments (P2saved), Fred chooses communion with God. In the other, P2unsaved, he persists in rejecting God. At T2, P2saved lacks any indeterminacy: since Fred has chosen communion with God, and since that choice confirms Fred in salvation, the possible world extending into the future from P2saved is a possible world in which Fred is saved at every subsequent moment. In P2unsaved, however, Fred is confronted at T2 with the same choice he faced at T1. Thus, at the subsequent moment, T3, we have three possible world segments: P2saved-ext (the extension of P2saved up to T3), P3saved and P3unsaved. This process continues indefinitely. As the timeline progresses, the number of possible worlds in which Fred remains unsaved becomes a progressively smaller percentage of the possible world segments in the possible world tree branching from P1. As the timeline approaches infinity, within this tree the percentage of world segments in which Fred remains unsaved approaches zero. In other words, given infinite time, it is mathematically certain that Fred is saved.

In effect, we can liken Fred to a penny that starts out heads-side up in a box and has crazy-glue on its heads-side. Even if there is an even chance at any shaking of the box that the penny will remain head-side up, we would expect that in a few shakings it would get 'stuck' heads-side down. If we are willing to rattle the box indefinitely, we are guaranteed that the penny will eventually stick in the heads-side down position, because the percentage of possible world segments (in the relevant tree) in which the penny remains head-side up approaches zero as the timeline approaches infinity.

Obviously, the number of pennies in the box makes no difference, since the same analysis can be applied to each penny. Likewise, if we have a world with twelve billion people rather than just Fred, the outcome will be the same. In short, by bringing about (a) to (c), God can ensure that all are saved. Lengthening the intervals between decision moments changes nothing, since there would still be infinite decision opportunities given infinite time; but what if we abandon our procedural assumption that salvation is based on a single choice, holding instead that it is based on a series of choices? Again, it makes no difference. Imagine that for the penny to stick heads-side down in the box, it must land heads-side down on twelve successive occasions. The probability of this happening in any given sequence of twelve coin flips is very low. Hence, we would expect it to take a long time for the penny to get stuck heads-side down. However, if we had infinite patience and kept rattling forever, we would eventually achieve the desired result. The reason is the same as before: the percentage of possible worlds in which the requisite sequence of outcomes has not yet appeared becomes progressively smaller as the timeline moves forward, approaching zero as the timeline approaches infinity.

8.4   Objections to AIO(3)

One objection to our defence of AIO(3) challenges our appeal to an infinite timeline to guarantee Fred's salvation. Many believe that, since one never reaches the end of an infinite sequence, no *actual* sequence is infinite. Hence, in any *actual* timeline it is possible that Fred remains unsaved. Put another way, at any time T the probability that Fred has yet to choose communion with God is a real probability greater than zero.

Even granted this point, two responses are possible. First, those who claim that some person – say Fred – is *forever* damned are making a claim *about an infinite timeline.* They are not merely asserting that Fred is alienated from God up to some time T, but that Fred is damned *at every time T.* Insofar as this claim is about an infinite timeline, the mathematics of infinity applies. Of course, someone who takes seriously the idea that we never reach the end of an infinite timeline might be prepared to abandon any claims about persons being forever damned, embracing the more modest view that, for *any* time T, it remains possible that there are persons who remain alienated from God. Thus, at no time T do we have a guarantee that all are saved.

But if God allows our temporal existence to continue *until* we choose salvation, and if the likelihood of our remaining unsaved becomes increasingly remote as the timeline progresses, is there not still a sense in which our salvation is guaranteed? Given an indefinite (if not infinite) timeline, the question becomes whether we will eventually reach some time T at which we choose communion with God. This is akin to asking whether, given the ability and willingness to flip a fair coin *indefinitely* (even if that should take a trillion tries), we will eventually toss a coin that lands heads-up. The answer to the question above is such a resounding yes that we have what *amounts to* a guarantee. Certainly, under these conditions it is not merely reasonable to believe that the coin will eventually land heads-up – it would be madness to think otherwise. Likewise, it would be madness to think LDH is true.

However, this assumes Fred's choice to reject God at T1 will not impact the probability of Fred continuing to reject God at T2. A critic might argue that, on the contrary, it is a fact of human psychology that our choices produce habits which dispose us to make similar future choices. God might be motivated to create us with this psychological feature because it enables us to choose to become a certain kind of person. We can choose our *character*, not merely isolated acts. Defenders of DH routinely appeal to this fact of human psychology, arguing that we can become so confirmed in God-rejecting habits that can no longer accept divine grace.[10] Were God to intervene in this process, He would be interfering with our freedom to choose the kind of people we become.[11]

Following this line of thought, our critic might say that if Fred is freed from all salvation inhibitors (or at least those that can be eliminated prior to salvation) he might yet choose to reject God, which might initiate a process of character formation that would, if Fred is sufficiently unlucky, culminate in a fixed God-rejecting character. The more often he rejects God, the more he hardens his heart against God; and God could not interfere with this process without also interfering with Fred's freedom to choose who he is to become. As such, it is not in God's power to ensure that Fred is saved without interfering with Fred's freedom. Hence, NG is true after all.

This line of objection might presuppose a radically libertarian view of freedom, or it might presuppose that our freedom is imperfect prior to salvation. If the former, the objection falls prey to the core problem noted earlier: the damned are consigned to hell because of random bad luck. Put simply, if there really is a random element operating in human freedom, it is hard to see why God would feel constrained to respect it, even to the point of letting persons be damned by it. But if we insist that God does feel so constrained and so adopts a policy of non-interference, we might be able to reconcile this with God's goodness if we supposed God so structured human psychology that only deliberate choices – not those resulting from the random element – had the effect of fixing character. However, the following conjunction cannot, it seems, be reconciled with God's goodness: the random element in human freedom has the capacity to fix character, and God refuses to interfere with this random process or its consequences even when the process results in a person's eternal damnation.

But what about if we couch the objection in the idea that, prior to salvation, all choices are based on a next-best freedom that is inevitably made under conditions of ignorance? Could hardening of heart explain damnation in that case? The chief problem here is that, from this view, if Fred chooses to reject God, the reason is not any special aversion to union with God but the fact that, out of deference to his uncertainty, Fred allows a bit of arbitrariness to guide his decisions. Thus, it would seem that what would become habituated by such a choice is *arbitrariness*, not an aversion to choosing God; but our argument here is undermined only if the arbitrary person (Fred), rather than becoming habitually arbitrary, instead becomes habituated to the most frequent *outcomes* of his arbitrary choices.

On this picture of things, Fred *is not* getting the character he chooses. If the justification for the habit-forming character of human choice is that we get to choose the kinds of people we will become, then Fred, by habitually choosing arbitrarily, should have *that* tendency habituated, not the tendency to reject God. Hence, it seems we must reject the idea that Fred's arbitrary choice to reject God creates a habit of rejecting God – if anything, it creates the habit of making this decision at random; but if it is the latter of these, then God can guarantee that Fred freely chooses salvation by bringing about (a) to (c), and our original argument stands.

Here, however, a critic might argue that one who is habitually arbitrary could not experience salvation because they would bring that arbitrariness with them into heaven, and thus could fall away from blessedness at any time. However, this assumes such habits could survive the irresistible appeal of the beatific vision, which seems dubious; though if we suppose they could, then this arbitrariness would be a negative affective state that interferes with the exercise of the agent's rational freedom. The agent, now in possession of the beatific vision, would have a rational desire not to be controlled by any arbitrariness that would take that vision away. Hence, God could eliminate this disposition without violating the agent's rational freedom. To those inclined to say that, by eliminating this habit of arbitrariness, God is not permitting one to choose to become an arbitrary person, we have two replies. First, it seems that those who – under conditions of next-best freedom – choose arbitrariness, do so not because they desire to become arbitrary people. Rather, they do so because arbitrariness is a reasonable decision-making tool *in the state of uncertainty*. Second, even if an agent did choose to become an arbitrary person while ignorant of the truth and hence operating under conditions of next-best freedom, no one who experiences the beatific vision would have any desire to remain an arbitrary person – and thus would choose to be freed of any arbitrariness once in this state.

However, this final response to the 'hardening of heart' objection gives rise to another. The guarantee of universal salvation defended here depends upon our assumption that, once a person has made the choice (or sequence of choices) that brings about communion with God, that person is confirmed in bliss and there is no longer any possibility of them becoming alienated from God; but a critic might wonder whether, given this assumption, we can meaningfully claim that anyone *freely* chooses communion with God.[12]

To see the worry here, consider the following case. Imagine a universe in which a supremely powerful devil can confirm in damnation anyone who chooses to commit a particular sin, S. Suppose, as before, that there is a random element operative in human choice. All it takes for damnation is *one* unfortunate random choice. We will assume, furthermore, that those who persist in resisting S do not become confirmed in that choice. They do not become 'S-resistant', but remain equally likely to choose S at some time in the future. We might imagine that, as before, the random element in choice is affected by rational judgments, so that those who judge S to be a foolish choice are *unlikely* to randomly choose it (and hence damnation), but still have some possibility of doing so. In such a case, it is guaranteed, given an infinite timeline, that even these wise persons who consistently resist S over time will be damned, because given infinite time it is mathematically certain that there will be at least one unlucky roll of the dice. Thus, universal damnation would be guaranteed. But would we want to say that, in such a universe, *all* the damned *freely choose to be damned?* Surely not. Hence, our critic will argue, it is likewise implausible to claim that the saved freely choose salvation given DU2.

This criticism, however, assumes parity between the cases that does not hold. The claim that the damned in the analogous case freely choose their state is implausible for reasons that do not apply to the claim that the saved freely choose *their* fate when they finally choose communion with God. The disanalogy between the cases rests on *why* the damned in the analogous case would be confirmed in damnation.

In the introduction to this chapter, we sketched out two possible accounts of how human freedom might be related to the assumption that the saved are confirmed in bliss once they have made the choice (or sequence of choices) that brings about communion with God: either human freedom is such that once one experiences loving communion with God there is no possible world in which even a free person turns away from it; or freedom has served its purpose once one has achieved this ultimate good, and hence can be suspended without any violation of the person. The first alternative assumes the broadly Thomistic view that when clearly confronted with the ultimate good (God), one loses all uncertainty about what is best and so is left with only God-choosing motives. The second alternative assumes that freedom has a *telos* in the created order which can reasonably be said to have been achieved once communion with God is realized, such that the freedom can be revoked at that point without any violation of the person.

Neither alternative can be plausibly invoked in the case of someone confirmed in damnation. Given the first alternative (which we find more plausible), prior to salvation, we necessarily lack complete knowledge of the ultimate good. In the absence of such knowledge, there remains room for arbitrariness in our choices; but once we have achieved communion with God we have the complete knowledge we had lacked. With this knowledge our rational freedom can operate unimpeded by ignorance (or arbitrariness), and so will inevitably choose what is best: that is, union with God.

In this picture, it should be obvious *both* that confirmation in blessedness is no violation of human freedom (but rather the perfection of it) *and* that there can be no confirmation in damnation that has a parallel explanation rendering it similarly compatible with human freedom. On the contrary – for someone to be confirmed in the choice of damnation the person must be in the grip of significant deception or bondage to desire – both of which impede freedom. Put simply, the only way to confirm someone in alienation from God is to *thwart* the exercise of freedom, whereas all that is needed to confirm someone in blessedness is to bring it about that all impediments to freedom are finally removed.

The critic of our argument fares no better by opting for the second account of the relationship between human freedom and confirmation in blessedness. In this account, the reason why the blessed cannot fall away is because their freedom has achieved its purpose and hence it need not be sustained. This account is best understood in terms of the radically libertarian idea that even when one has entirely uniform motives to choose A over not-A, one might still choose not-A because one is in the grip of a randomness beyond one's will or control. It is admittedly hard to fathom what purpose such freedom would serve in the created order. It is hard to fathom why someone would regard such freedom as valuable at all, let alone the most valuable kind of freedom.

But let us assume for the sake of argument that there is something *intrinsically* valuable about this kind of radical libertarian freedom. If we make the further assumption, as defenders of LDH do, that freely chosen salvation is superior to salvation that is not so chosen, then the purpose of this kind of freedom – its *telos* in the natural order – would presumably be to achieve this superior outcome. However, freedom of this kind, if possessed by the saved, *would compromise their salvation* by rendering it subject to arbitrary loss – and a salvation that can be lost by an unlucky roll of the dice is no salvation at all. Hence, if we construe freedom in this radical way, it *must* be revoked for salvation to exist; and if freedom's purpose is to make possible freely chosen *salvation*, then it can only serve its purpose if it is revoked once union with God is chosen. Such revocation would not violate the *telos* of freedom but would be required by it, and hence could not be construed as a morally objectionable violation of freedom. However, revoking it when a creature has chosen damnation would violate freedom – thus explaining our intuitive judgment in the analogous case.

To avoid this outcome, our critic would need to assume a different purpose for human freedom. Perhaps there is something intrinsically desirable about a universe in which the final destiny of every person is freely chosen, and the purpose of human freedom is to bring about such a desirable state. However, if freedom is understood to involve an inexplicably random element, this would amount to saying there is something intrinsically desirable about a universe in which the final destiny of every person is determined by chance. As hard as it is to make sense of the claim that radical libertarian freedom is intrinsically valuable and that salvation freely chosen in this sense is preferable to salvation not so chosen, it is even more difficult to make sense of the claim that there is something intrinsically desirable about a universe in which at least some are damned by, in effect, bad luck. Surely, given the Christian understanding of God, we could not think that *God* would judge such a universe intrinsically desirable.

What all this shows is that there is something fundamentally misguided about the view that radical libertarian freedom is intrinsically valuable and preferable to the kind of rational freedom that the Thomists and Talbott endorse. Hence, those who want to defend NG (and reject AIO2) are better served by accepting the Thomistic view of freedom but arguing that prior to salvation it can only operate imperfectly. If, however, this is accepted, it is plain why we can plausibly maintain that the damned in the analogous case did not freely choose their state while the saved, given conditions (a) through (c), did.

8.5 The Mystery of Freedom

One final objection to this part of our argument deserves attention. This objection is both more ambiguous and, we think, more important than the others. It runs as follows: throughout the development of AIO, we have assumed that human choices are explained either by reference to the agent's existing motives or by arbitrariness – that is, either the agent chooses on the basis of some reason or for no reason at all – and we have assumed that this is true not only for first-order choices, but also for higher-order choices among motives (or between being motivated or arbitrary). While it is hard to deny that humans choose either for some reason of for none – to deny this would seem to violate the law of excluded middle – assuming this is true renders the agent's motives or randomness (or some combination of the two) the explanation for every human choice. However, if agents' choices, at every level, are determined either by their motives or by randomness, how can they be held morally responsible for their choices? While it is hard to offer an account of free choice that does not render chance and existing motives the ultimate explanation of every action, this only shows that human freedom is profoundly mysterious, perhaps even ineffable. To preserve morality, we must hold that freedom is such that *agents* – not their motives and not arbitrariness – bear ultimate responsibility for choices. Even if we cannot give an account of freedom that does this job, the need to affirm moral responsibility requires that we say of human choice that its ultimate efficient cause lies in the agent as such. Insofar as our efforts to understand freedom fail to do this, AIO rests on false views of freedom.[13]

Even though this objection offers no alternative to the accounts of freedom we have suggested, it still raises a significant issue warranting a response – of which we have several. First, while we agree that the radical libertarian understanding of freedom renders every choice causally determined by extant motives or chance, we are not convinced that this is true of Thomistic rational freedom, even in its 'next-best' form. As has already been noted, there is a difference between saying that randomness determines our choices and saying that we choose *at* random. Likewise, there is a difference between saying that our motives cause us to act and saying that we choose to act based on motives. Even if we admit that whenever we make a choice we must either have a motive or not, *we* are still the ones who are choosing based on some motive or none at all; but for the will's activity, which concurs with the dictates of reasons or chance, neither chance nor reasons would generate choice or action.

This cannot be said in the case of radically libertarian freedom, since the possibility of rejecting God when all salvation inhibitors are removed can only be explained by the existence of a random force that operates *on* the will *in spite of the agent*. But in the cases of rational freedom and 'next-best' freedom, the uncompelled concurrence of the will with the dictates of reasons or chance is coherent. Hence, we can say, under these notions of freedom, that when we choose – based on reasons or arbitrarily – *we* are doing the choosing, not those reasons or random chance.

While we find this reply significant, it may not be entirely satisfying. Critics might argue that, for the sake of moral responsibility, it must be possible for Fred to decide, without being controlled by an affective state he is not responsible for, to prioritize his own hedonistic gratification over neighbourly love. However, in the 'next-best freedom' account, Fred would do so because he is legitimately uncertain which is better, and therefore he allows arbitrariness to play a role in his choice. How, then, can we blame Fred for his choice? It seems we can blame Fred only if he *knows* that neighbourly love *should* be prioritized and yet makes a *non-arbitrary* decision (uncontrolled by any affective state) to prioritize his own hedonistic gratification. It may be impossible to offer an account of human freedom that makes sense of such a prioritization, but that just means human freedom is fundamentally mysterious.[14]

In fact, we are drawn to the idea that freedom is mysterious. Ultimately, however, we do not need a full account of human freedom (of the sort provided above) to ground AIO. While such an account is helpful for understanding the argument's power and appreciating its merits, the argument works even in its absence. All we need to support AIO is the minimal understanding that is common to all more developed views of libertarian freedom: namely, that whenever one freely does X, it must be the case that one could have done otherwise. We might call this the core doctrine of libertarian freedom.

If this core doctrine is embraced, then whenever Fred freely chooses alienation from God there will be some possible world in which Fred chooses communion with God. If this is to be a *real* possibility (and it seems that genuine libertarian freedom would require a real possibility), the percentage of possible worlds in which Fred chooses communion with God must be a real number. In short, for Fred's choice to be free, the probability that Fred will choose communion with God at any time T must be a real one. Whether that probability comes from arbitrariness or some other mysterious operation of the will we do not and cannot understand, there must *be* such a probability in order to make sense of the core doctrine of libertarian freedom. Hence, anyone who is committed to the core doctrine of libertarian freedom is forced to accept AIO2 and so reject NG.

However, while we think this is correct, a resolute critic has a significant response. Specifically, if freedom really is *mysterious*, perhaps it defies probabilistic laws in some ineffable way, such that the possibility of choosing otherwise does *not* entail that this possibility can be subjected to analysis in terms of probabilistic laws. But this move is philosophically weak: since what is invoked is the *mystery* of freedom, the critic cannot explain how or why the possibility of choosing otherwise does not entail a real possibility of choosing otherwise which can be assessed in terms of probabilistic laws. It is an ad hoc assertion of an unlikely sounding claim, warranted by nothing more than the fact that the mystery of freedom *might*, for all we know given its mysteriousness, entail just the improbable truth needed to shut down our argument.

Despite its weakness, however, this response may be seen as highlighting a weak point in our argument where, if certain speculations about the nature of freedom could be substantiated, our comparative defence of DU might collapse – but we think this weak point is only apparent. Even if a theory of freedom could be offered that exempts libertarian free choices from the laws of probability, we still think God could guarantee that all freely choose salvation by preserving the unregenerate indefinitely in being while leaving the choice of union with God open.

Why? First, we think there is ample reason to reject *radically* libertarian conceptions of freedom, wherein persons who are in full possession of complete and immediate understanding of the choice-worthiness of union with God (and free from contrary affective states) might still reject God. As such, we think the best reason to think God cannot guarantee that all freely choose salvation is that complete and immediate understanding of God's choice-worthiness is only available to those who experience the beatific vision, and hence are already saved. Prior to salvation, there remains uncertainty about what is best, and hence there is room for libertarian freedom.

However, uncertainty can be erased in more than one way. Let us grant, for the sake of argument, that God cannot demonstrate beyond all uncertainty the choice-worthiness of union with God without providing the immediate experiential encounter with God that is constitutive of salvation. Does this mean there is no way, short of saving the creature, for God to eliminate all uncertainty with respect to this choice? No – because God can let them have an immediate experiential encounter with the *alternative* to union with God. If one has a choice between A and not-A, and there is uncertainty about which choice is better, there are two ways to erase such uncertainty. If a demonstration of A's choice-worthiness is unavailable, it may still be possible to demonstrate the supreme unworthiness of choosing not-A. That is, God may not be able to bestow the beatific vision prior to salvation, but that does not mean He cannot let them have the alienation they choose, and so experience fully what it means to exist apart from the source of all that is genuinely valuable. Perhaps a full experiential understanding of the unworthiness of this choice does not become immediately apparent. Perhaps the unregenerate can, for a time, offset their misery by hoping that a range of illusory goods will satisfy them; but if so, God can let those illusory hopes be fulfilled one by one, thereby shattering them. Therefore, by preserving the unregenerate in being and leaving communion with God an open choice, God can ensure that eventually the damned will have every last illusion shattered, and so have an immediate experiential understanding of what it means to reject God, an understanding in which no doubt or uncertainty lingers. They will come know, wholly and completely, that what they have chosen is utterly without worth, utterly empty;[15] and God's hand will remain extended to them for as long as it takes.

8.6 The Hellist's Last Way Out: Challenging AIO(2)

Staunch critics of AIO might still challenge premise AIO(2). That is, they might hold that there is something *morally* objectionable about performing (a) to (c).

If it would be morally wrong to perform (a) to (c), then a morally perfect God would not do so even for the sake of saving all. While it would be in God's *metaphysical* power to save all, it would not be in His *moral* power. In effect, someone might embrace the following variant of NG, which we will call the 'No Permissible Guarantee Doctrine', or NPG:

> (NPG): There is nothing that God can do *and* is morally permitted to do which is such that, were God to do it, He would bring it about (weakly) that both (i) every person who is saved freely chooses to be saved, and (ii) all are saved.

Since we have shown that God can bring it about that all freely choose salvation by bringing about (a) to (c), NPG amounts to the claim that it would be morally impermissible for God to bring about one or all of (a) to (c). In 'Three Versions of Universalism', Michael Murray defends precisely this claim. His attack focuses on Talbott's version of universalism, which he takes to be a variant of DU2. Murray's basic strategy has already been touched on in Section 8.4, when we considered the argument that the habit-forming character of human choices might prevent a person from choosing communion with God even given an infinite sequence of decision opportunities. At that point, we focused on a version of the objection holding that it is *impossible* for God to circumvent this habit-forming character without violating human freedom. However, Murray's way of framing the objection suggests a different version of it, one which focuses on the *moral impermissibility* of extending to a person an infinite sequence of decision opportunities.

More precisely, Murray challenges the moral permissibility of accomplishing (b) and (c); that is, sustaining every person in a temporal existence at least until they choose communion with God, and leaving the choice of communion with God an 'open choice' such that every person is free to choose it at any time.

Murray calls this version of DU 'Sophisticated Universalism 1', but in the terminology of this book it would be DU2. Hence, we refer to it as such hereafter.[16] Murray, in effect, raises two objections to DU2. The first amounts to an affirmation of NG, and hence falls before the arguments offered earlier this chapter; but the second line of objection is best understood as an attack on the moral permissibility of providing persons with an infinite sequence of decision moments in which they can choose to accept or reject God.

In essence, Murray argues that even if, in this way, God can guarantee that all freely choose to be saved, this strategy of saving all would violate creaturely *autonomy* (which, presumably, God is morally prohibited from doing). To understand this argument, we first need to know what Murray means by autonomy. For Murray, it involves a free choosing *'that is expressed in actions that influence the course of events in the world'*.[17] In his view, '[A] world with "autonomous" creatures is a world where creatures are not only allowed to make evil *choices*, but choices which issue in evil *acts* and have evil *consequences*.'[18]

Murray notes that one kind of consequence our actions can have is on our states of character. What we do can strengthen or weaken our habituated dispositions.[19] The value and significance of this fact about human psychology ultimately becomes an important part of Murray's argument.

Murray's argument rests on the idea that continuing to offer the opportunity for salvation to those who have rejected it by the end of their earthly lives violates their autonomy because their choice to reject God is not being accepted. They are not permitted to *have* what they have chosen – namely alienation from God. Although free to choose alienation, their choice has no ultimate consequences because they are forced to keep on choosing until they change their mind.

He argues for this perspective in terms of an analogy involving a fast-food drive-through which includes both healthy and rotten hamburgers on its menu. Those who order rotten burgers receive what they ordered and get sick. We can expect that this ill experience might lead the rotten-burger-eaters to reconsider their choice, but Murray asks us to imagine someone who has cultivated a taste for rotten burgers through repeatedly choosing them. They continue to choose rotten burgers every time they get into line out of a fixed state of character. Murray tells us that DU2 involves, in effect, repeatedly *forcing* rotten-burger-eaters to order again and again until they start choosing healthy burgers (communion with God) and their former state of character begins to break down. In this sense their preference for rotten burgers is not being respected. They are not permitted to be rotten-burger-lovers, because they are required to keep returning to the queue until they start choosing healthy burgers and their habits start to change.[20]

In unpacking this analogy, the choice between the healthy burger and the rotten one can be understood in two ways. On the one hand, it might represent the choice, at any time T, between communion with God and alienation from God. On the other hand, it might represent the choice between *eternal* communion with God and *eternal* alienation from Him. We think Murray fails to adequately distinguish these alternatives.

Suppose Murray takes the healthy burger to represent *eternal* communion with God, and the rotten burger to represent *eternal* alienation. In this view, if, at some time, T1, someone chooses eternal alienation, God refuses to accept that choice and 'sends the person back in line' to choose again. If at T2 the choice is the same, once again it is rejected. This continues until at some time, Tn, the person chooses eternal communion, at which point the person joins God in blissful communion for eternity.

If this is what the advocate of DU2 is committed to, then DU2 may well involve autonomy violation in Murray's sense. Even though the person who ultimately chooses eternal communion with God does so of their own will, it is only because the alternative choice has been consistently denied them each time they *tried* to choose it in the past. The person has no real freedom to choose eternal alienation.

Notice, however, that this way of setting up the choice is itself an *autonomy minimizing* strategy. According to this approach, at time T1 I am to choose between communion with God at *all* times and alienation from God at *all* times. This means the choice is set up at T1 so that, if my choice is accepted at T1, I am deprived of all future choice on the matter. Only if my choice is rejected at T1 (and my autonomy is therefore directly violated) do I still have a choice on the matter at T2. Set up in this way, there is an inevitable restriction of autonomy whether my choice is accepted or not.

In other words, if the choice is conceived in this way the advocate of DH is little better than the universalist when it comes to autonomy violations. In effect, God is saying at T1, 'choose now and forever'. Even if God respects one's choice at T1, the way in which the choice is set up places restrictions on one's autonomy by denying one the possibility of ever changing one's mind; but it is precisely this 'choose now and forever' approach that DU2 denies.[21]

Put simply, if the choice is conceived in this way, then it is not clear that God has any moral obligation to respect the autonomy of those who choose eternal alienation (by giving them what they have chosen). It is hard to imagine that anyone could really choose *eternal* alienation, since it is hard to imagine that anyone who thought they were choosing such a thing would really understand what they were choosing. However, even if they could, to give them what they chose at T would be to decisively cut off their capacity for future choice. It would be to let a foolish choice at one moment deprive the agent at every future moment of both freedom and, a fortiori, of autonomy. While Murray is certainly right to think that human beings need autonomy and not merely freedom, it hardly follows from this that we need *all* of our free choices to have significant consequences. Insofar as greater freedom – and hence greater opportunity for autonomous choice – is preserved by refusing to give those who choose eternal alienation at T what they have chosen, it seems implausible to claim that God is morally obligated to give them what they have chosen out of respect for their autonomy.

Thus, we think DU2 is better represented if the choice at any time T is between communion with and alienation from God *at T*. Understood in these terms, DU2 holds that people always get exactly what they choose with respect to their relationship with God at any time T. All are saved, in this view, because everyone will eventually, given enough time, choose the 'healthy burgers' and so learn that they are infinitely more satisfying than the rotten ones, leading them to consistently choose them from then on.

However, Murray might still insist that this arrangement violates autonomy, because even if people 'get what they order' at any time T, their choice for the 'rotten burger' is not respected if they are 'forced' to get back in line and order again. In fact, Murray says precisely this;[22] but in saying this, we think he only reveals a limitation of his analogy. The reason why all are 'forced' to choose again and again at all times is simply because God offers communion with Himself as a kind of 'standing offer', one which is never withdrawn and so *remains* an option at any time T.

A better analogy than Murray's, which captures this idea of a 'standing offer', would be to imagine that Joe offers everyone in town the chance to live in his home for as long as they desire. If this offer is never withdrawn, you are 'forced' to choose at every moment whether to accept it. Suppose, furthermore, that Joe's home is so wonderful that it is intrinsically preferable to all others (and is so spacious it can comfortably accommodate the town's population). Anyone who takes Joe up on his offer finds it so rewarding that they stay forever; and so long as a person is not in the grip of false beliefs about Joe's offer or trapped by bad habits, given an infinite sequence of opportunities to 'check out his house', it is mathematically certain that those who stay there will eventually do so.

The fact that standing offers 'force' us at all times either to accept or reject them in no way thwarts our autonomy. On the contrary, 'limited-time offers' pose a greater threat to autonomy, as can be attested by anyone faced with high-pressure sales tactics. When a choice must be made *now* or (as Murray holds) *by the moment of death*, one's choices are *restricted* in a way they are not if one is free to choose at any time. Hence, contrary to Murray's claim, his version of DH places greater restrictions on autonomy than does DU2.

So far, however, we have left out an important dimension to Murray's analysis. Specifically, Murray holds that one crucial thing denied us under DU2 is the autonomy to become *people of a certain type*, that is, people with a certain character – namely, a God-rejecting one.[23] A person with a God-rejecting character has a fixed disposition to reject God, and will therefore continue to do so ad infinitum unless stripped of this disposition. Even given a standing offer to choose God and unlimited time to take God up on that offer, a person with a firm God-rejecting *character* will remain forever alienated unless subjected to pressures that strip away that character. Universalism is guaranteed under DU2, then, only if God is prepared to strip away such God-rejecting dispositions, thereby allowing creatures to 'start from scratch' and develop their character anew – and to keep doing so until they develop a God-choosing character.

Here, Murray's argument moves away from conditions (b) and (c) and focuses on the moral permissibility of God bringing about (a) – that is, of stripping away salvation inhibitors that impede the exercise of libertarian freedom. Murray's complaint about (a), in effect, is that were God to do (a) He would make it impossible for persons to get what they have chosen if they choose to become God-rejecting people.

We have already offered one response to this line of concern. Specifically, any choice to reject God made under the 'next-best' freedom attainable prior to salvation would have to be made arbitrarily. As such, what would be habituated is not a God-rejecting character, but an arbitrary one – which is not an impediment to salvation.

Perhaps Murray's concern here has to do with bringing creatures into this state of 'next-best' freedom in the first place. Such freedom may arguably be attainable (at least in some cases) only if God strips away character dispositions chosen by the agent. Perhaps Murray thinks that stripping away the salvation inhibitors that can be stripped away prior to salvation – thereby bringing about the closest approximation of rational freedom attainable this side of salvation – is impermissible because it prevents those who choose God-rejecting dispositions to get what they choose.

However, can the choice of such dispositions be rightly called free in any worthwhile sense if they were chosen prior to achieving even the 'next-best' freedom that is possible short of salvation? Everything we have said so far suggests not, but let us suppose for argument's sake that it can: someone still in the grip of ignorance, deception and bondage to desire can still freely choose a God-rejecting state of character. The question remains whether God would do anything morally wrong in stripping away this state.

In considering this question, we should point out that Murray is wrong to say that, under DU2, we are simply not free to become God-rejecting people. Under DU2 we *are* free to become God-rejecting people. What is not possible is to hold onto such a state of character *for all eternity*. Eventually these states will be 'stripped away' – and not necessarily through a miraculous transformation, since God might subject the unregenerate to remedial punishments which are, given sufficient time, always successful in inspiring the unregenerate to shake off their bad habits; however it is done, in DU2 God does not permit anyone to cling to a God-rejecting character forever. Is this sufficient to justify Murray's claim that DU2 violates autonomy?

Murray asks us to consider a hypothetical person who, if allowed to go through the process of forming a fixed character and being stripped of it ten times, would develop a God-embracing character on only the sixth and ninth occasions. If we assume DU2, then, as Murray rightly notes, the process of stripping away character dispositions would be stopped on the sixth occasion, and the person would thereafter enjoy communion with God. However, Murray asserts that stopping the process at this point would be 'arbitrary',[24] apparently because, if a person would develop a God-rejecting character eighty per cent of the time, then it makes more sense to stop the process at a God-rejecting cycle or not at all.

Clearly, however, stopping the process on a God-embracing cycle is *not* arbitrary, for only then will the person enjoy the beatific vision. A perfectly loving God would presumably end the process at a point which would be most beneficial to the person; but given the context within which Murray makes his remarks, we might take it that his real objection to ending the process at a God-embracing cycle is not that doing so is arbitrary, but rather that doing so fails to respect the creature's autonomy. Perhaps Murray thinks that since the creature *would* choose a God-rejecting character eighty per cent of the time, the creature is 'voting' in favour of a God-rejecting character by the frequency with which they choose it, and that by ending the process on a God-embracing cycle, God is failing to respect this 'vote'.

Murray considers one possible response to this argument; namely, the view that once one has cultivated a God-embracing character, one would continue to do so in future cycles. Murray sees no reason to think this is true, since 'the dispositions constitutive of one's character are, on this picture, completely purged after each cycle'. What Murray neglects is that this 'purging' is a stripping away only of the *habituated* dispositions, not of dispositions *intrinsic to human nature* (such as the natural ordering of the will towards the good), nor of the knowledge of what it was like to be confirmed in a given character-state. Given the hypothesis that the chief human good is communion with God, there is no surer way to become acquainted with this good than to experience it by developing a God-embracing character. If God should strip away the habit of choosing God from someone who has cultivated it, there is every reason to think that in the absence of any *habituated* disposition, but with a *natural* ordering towards the good and full knowledge that God is the greatest good, the person would quickly develop a God-embracing character anew.

A second problem with Murray's argument based on character-choice is his assumption that we *choose* our states of character (and so are being denied the fruits of our choices if God strips us of them). In some cases this is true, but in other cases it is not. Computer solitaire addicts do not usually choose that state. Rather, they choose to play solitaire many times, and the bad habit just creeps up on them. *It* is not what was chosen. This seems to be also characteristic of bad states of character.

Thus, there are both chosen and unchosen states of character. With respect to the former, we presumably choose to cultivate a given state of character because we believe it is the best character to have – a belief that can be either true or false. If false, we are making our choice with a mistaken understanding of the state we are choosing, and hence cannot rightly be said to have autonomously chosen what we got. Thus, stripping it away would not violate our autonomy; and, of course, belief that a God-rejecting character is the best one to have *is* false in Christian assumptions. In short, if someone did develop such a character, it would either be an unchosen consequence of repeated bad choices, or it would be chosen on the basis of misinformation. In either case, no denial of autonomy results from stripping it away.

However, when someone develops a God-embracing character, stripping away such a state of character *would* be autonomy violating, for reasons that should be clear. Either a God-embracing character is directly chosen – in the sense of being consciously cultivated on the basis of the judgment that having such a state of character would be for the best – or it emerges as a result of successively choosing, not the character-state as such, but the activity of embracing God. If it is directly chosen, then it is chosen based on the belief that embracing God is best – that is, on correct information. To strip away a state of character that is chosen based on accurate information *is* autonomy violating. If the state of character was not directly chosen but emerged from successively choosing to embrace God, it nevertheless seems that anyone developing such character would *endorse* it, or choose it after the fact, once given full information. After all, such a state of character would inspire them to continually choose their chief good. To strip away a state of character endorsed on the basis of accurate information would also be autonomy violating.

Thus, when Murray claims that ending the 'process of character-making and purging' at a God-embracing cycle is autonomy violating, he is mistaken – because respect for autonomy *requires* ending the process at a God-embracing cycle.

8.7 *Concluding Remarks*

We have argued that God could ensure that all freely choose salvation by (a) stripping away all those salvation inhibitors He can strip away prior to salvation, (b) sustaining everyone in a *temporal* existence at least until they choose communion with God, and (c) leaving the choice of communion with God an 'open choice', such that every person is free to choose it at any time. Since (a) to (c) guarantees the salvation of all, at least given core assumptions that Christians should be loathe to abandon, it is difficult to maintain the 'No Guarantee Doctrine'; and while Murray offers reasons to think that God's bringing about (a) to (c) would be morally impermissible, these reasons collapse under careful scrutiny – leaving little reason to believe the 'No Permissible Guarantee Doctrine'. It appears, therefore, that even if we assume that freedom prior to salvation has a libertarian character, it is both possible and morally permissible for God to bring it about (weakly) that all freely choose to be saved. The supposed impediment to universal salvation created by God's duty to respect freedom proves to be no impediment at all.

As such, even if one thinks freedom so important that it would be morally better for some to be damned than for their freedom to be violated, there is no compelling basis to favour DH over DU on such grounds. More generally, there are no philosophical difficulties with DU that can compare to the philosophical problems faced by DH. It seems, then, that our comparative defence of DU is essentially complete: there is no rational basis to prefer DH to DU, and there are compelling reasons to prefer DU. Given Scripture's ambiguity on the matter, Christians ought to be, on philosophical grounds, universalists.

CHAPTER 9

FINAL CONCERNS

9.1 Summary of Our Argument

Our aim in this work has been to systematically argue that, within an essentially conservative Christian context, DU is more defensible than DH. In making this case we began by noting that the plain sense of the most directly relevant scriptural texts provide, at best, an ambiguous guide when it comes to choosing between DU and DH, and that it is in any event preferable to extend authority, not to isolated texts, but to the lessons that emerge when the Christian community engages with Scripture holistically as a means of encountering Christ, and then brings the insights from that encounter to bear on the interpretation of Scripture in an evolving, respectful, but critical discussion across generations.

With this in mind, we turned out attention to several prima facie arguments for DU based on theological principles emerging from just this sort of historic engagement with the Christian Scriptures – principles pertaining to God's benevolent love for creatures, His complacent love for them and His love for the blessed. These arguments, however, all assume there is no compelling divine motive that would override His motive for willing the salvation of all as an end, and that it is within God's power to achieve His will without doing anything morally impermissible.

The oldest and most pervasive version of DH in the West – the Classical Doctrine of Hell (CDH), which takes it that some are damned for retributive reasons – denies the first of these assumptions. Thus, we turned to CDH to see if the arguments for it could undermine the prima facie arguments for DU. We found two reasons why they could not. First, CDH needs to suppose that sin is an intolerable affront against God, His creatures and the good. However, given that the Christian tradition has held that the sanctification which comes through the beatific vision is the only means of fully purging rational creatures of sin, and given that all versions of DH agree that the damned are denied the beatific vision, it follows that damning any creatures ensures that they remain eternally mired in sin. God would be responding to the intolerable affront of sin by making sure that this intolerable affront continues unabated for eternity.

Second, we argued that any account of sin and retributive justice which could call for *eternal* damnation as a punishment for sin would call for more than that: it would also demand a strong version of vicarious Atonement of the sort embraced in much of the Christian tradition. However, any such understanding of Christ's Atonement would sweep away any impediments to God's willing the salvation of all rooted in the demands of retributive justice, thereby also sweeping away the case for CDH.

Next, we turned to the version of DH that arguably prevails among theologians and philosophers of religion today – namely, the Liberal Doctrine of Hell (LDH), which holds that some creatures may freely choose eternal alienation from God, and when they do, God either cannot or morally may not save them. We offered a disjunctive response to the main argument for LDH, based on whether or not one thinks that God can and morally may extend efficacious grace to creatures. In fact, we argued that God both can and morally may extend efficacious grace, because God can and morally may present creatures with a full understanding of what union with Him involves while removing any affective impediments to acting on this understanding – moves which, assuming a Thomistic view of freedom, would guarantee the conversion of any creature. As such, in this Thomistic view, DU1 (which holds that God saves all by employing efficacious grace) is more plausible than LDH. However, what if one adopts a more Molinist account of freedom, in which the choice of union with God is essentially undetermined by the totality of motives (at least in the case of those who are not yet saved)? In that case, we argued that God could achieve a mathematical guarantee of universal salvation by leaving creatures indefinitely free to choose union with God at any time – and God would be doing nothing morally wrong were He to do so. In other words, from a Molinist view, DU2 (which holds that God saves all by preserving them in a state where they remain perpetually free to choose communion with God) is more plausible than LDH.

Therefore, we conclude that some version of DU is more plausible than any version of DH. Our comparative defence of DU is thus essentially complete.

However, some lingering worries remain. In this final chapter, we take up what we suspect are the five most significant of these.

9.2 Annihilationism and Soteriological Agnosticism

Even if our arguments have shown that some version of DU is more plausible than any version of DH, a critic could rightly point out that DU and DH are not the only alternatives. At least two others have had adherents in Christian history: the doctrine of annihilation (DA), and what we call the doctrine of soteriological agnosticism (DSA).

The former of these holds that, rather than preserving the unregenerate in hell, God extinguishes their existence altogether. What should we make of this alternative? That depends on why we think God would annihilate some creatures. One reason parallels LDH: God wishes to save them, but they freely reject Him – a free rejection that God (somehow) foreknows will continue eternally. Rather than allow them to eternally suffer the effects of such alienation, God 'puts them out of their misery', thereby annihilating them as an act of mercy.

It should be clear, however, that in this case our arguments in Chapters 7 and 8 apply to DA as well as to LDH. If these arguments succeed in showing that creaturely freedom is no impediment to God saving all from eternal alienation, then they also succeed in showing that God need not annihilate them in order to spare them the grim consequences of freely chosen alienation from Him. Perhaps the annihilationist thinks that God might annihilate creatures who *would* eventually be saved were He to sustain them in being – but why would God make such a choice? To spare them the suffering that they would endure prior to their salvation? This seems implausible, since finite suffering followed by infinite bliss has infinite positive value (the suffering is swamped by the good that follows). It is no act of mercy to deprive a creature of *eternal joy in union with God* for the sake of avoiding merely finite suffering brought on by temporally finite choices.

Perhaps, then, DA is better seen as an alternative to CDH. In other words, perhaps God annihilates some creatures as retributive punishment for sin. Positing annihilation as the punishment for sin avoids *one* problem with CDH – namely, that God brings about perpetual sinfulness as a penalty for the intolerable wrong of sinfulness; but problems relating to the Atonement remain. If annihilation is motivated by the demands of retributive justice, then what would motivate annihilation if these demands have been met on the cross? And if retributive justice demands something less severe than eternal damnation – such as annihilation – would it not follow that the demands of justice do not require an infinite penalty for sin? And if the demands of justice do not require an infinite penalty for sin, then meeting the demands of justice could not serve as an impediment to God saving all. Rather than annihilating the unregenerate, He could impose a different finite penalty that enabled them to experience salvation once the penalty was paid.

Perhaps, however, the argument is that annihilation is actually more *serious* than eternal damnation, because non-being is objectively worse than existence in a state of even the most total torment. The defender of DA might, on those grounds, argue that while the demands of justice cannot be met by damnation – since the suffering of a finite being is of finite severity even if it endures forever – these demands can be met through the creature's annihilation, thereby removing the need for a vicarious Atonement.

But even if we grant the implausible assumption that annihilation is worse that eternal torment because the former is truly infinite in gravity while the latter is not, what follows – that is, what follows if we assume that a vicarious Atonement is unneeded since God could meet the demands of justice by *annihilating* His beloved creatures instead of by becoming incarnate and dying for their sakes? Does it follow that God would choose the option which expresses His justice but *not* His love (annihilation), rather than the option which makes it possible *also* to express His love (vicarious Atonement)? Hardly. And so it seems that, within a broadly Christian context, DU is preferable not only to DH, but also to DA.

What, then, of DSA? Many are drawn to DSA because of the apparent humility of adopting an agnostic posture towards what God might do in response to unrepentant sin. In itself this humility seems praiseworthy; but our case against CDH did not merely support an agnostic position on whether God would eternally reject any of His creatures. More strongly, we argued that a God anything like the God of traditional Christianity *would not do so*. Our case against LDH systematically challenges argument AF, whose conclusion is that God either cannot, or will not, *guarantee* the salvation of all. We argued, on the contrary, that God *can* and *morally may* (and so will, given our previous arguments) guarantee the salvation of all. If this is right, then our arguments do more than just undercut reasons for embracing LDH by appeal to human freedom. They also undercut comparable reasons for embracing DSA. In short, if neither respect for freedom nor the demands of justice impose an impediment to God's saving all, then – given the strong prima facie basis for thinking that God would save all barring impediments to doing so – the proper conclusion is not agnosticism but DU.

9.3 Pragmatic Concerns

Many critics of DU worry that if hell is not a possibility – if our salvation is guaranteed – this would erode our motive to be morally good. As Marilyn McCord Adams puts it, 'many religiously serious people reject the doctrine of universal salvation, on the pragmatic ground that it leads to moral and religious laxity. Withdraw the threat, and they doubt whether others – perhaps even they themselves – would sustain the motivation for moral diligence and religious observance'.[1]

This concern is problematic on many fronts. First, it assumes that there are no compelling reasons to be moral beyond extrinsic rewards and punishments – but there clearly are reasons to be moral apart from such extrinsic considerations. Most obviously, there is the fact that being moral is an intrinsically good thing to be. Furthermore, as Kant would note, anyone who is motivated by fear of extrinsic consequences to behave in outwardly moral ways is not being moral in any real sense in any event. Behaviour control is not the same as morality.

Furthermore, DU does *not* hold that one can be saved while continuing to sin. Rather, it holds that everyone will eventually cease sinning, because everyone will come to see the intrinsic preferability of opening themselves up to the sanctifying power of divine grace. Until they acknowledge this preferability, however, they will remain in the intrinsically inferior state of being a sinner – a state that in itself is a source, ultimately, of nothing but dissatisfaction and misery. DU does nothing to deny or negate the claim that sin is bad *for* sinners. The version of DU we affirm emphatically insists on this point. Hence, there is excellent reason to avoid sin and seek moral sanctification, since the former is in all conceivable ways bad (including bad *for sinners*) and the latter is in all conceivable ways good.

Furthermore, Adams notes that her pastoral experience teaches her that 'the disproportionate threat of hell ... produces despair that masquerades as scepticism, rebellion, and unbelief. If your father threatens to kill you if you disobey him, you may cower in terrorized submission, but you may also (reasonably) run away from home'.[2]

Beyond this point, we think there are deeper pragmatic harms flowing from belief in DH. Any version of DH draws as sharp a line between human beings as it is possible to draw: human souls are divided by an unbridgeable gulf – on one side there is the beatific vision; on the other lies the outer darkness. Belief in such a divide cannot help but cast a shadow onto this life. How can we embrace this teaching without seeing in each of our fellow human beings their prospects for damnation or salvation? Given that their eternal destiny has significance in the arc of their existence that is far more profound than anything that might define their mortal life, how can we refrain from seeing them in terms of that destiny?

It seems to us that how we see humanity in this life will inevitably be influenced by the imprint of that eternal gulf. This remains true even if we are reminded of our inability to judge on which side those around us will fall. We cannot say with confidence who will be saved and who will be damned; but that does not stop us from having guesses, and even private certainties. Few of us will be so brazen as Fred Phelps, who, with his congregation of relatives, pickets the funerals of gays and lesbians with signs celebrating that another 'fag' is burning in hell. It may, however, be harder to avoid quieter acts of pigeon-holing, in which we divide those whom we just know are doomed from those that we are sure will join us in paradise.[3]

As we quietly think of *us-the-saved* and *them-the-damned*, and even more quietly locate human beings into one group or the other, it may be difficult to keep this *ultimate* in-group/out-group schism from creating its shadow divisions in this world and this life. In fact, the psychological costs of resisting such terrestrial divisions may be too great for many to bear. If Schleiermacher is right, then compassion for the damned is a recipe for pain. Loving those who suffer requires attention and empathy – and to attend empathetically to the sufferings of the damned is to vicariously experience the ultimate loss. To love the damned is to court empathic suffering.

As such, DH may actually operate as an *impediment* to compassion. To truly love those who are doomed, to love them as a good parent loves his or her child (or as Christ loves us), is to forsake perfect happiness. It is to put one foot deliberately into hell; and thus we create in-groups and out-groups as a form of self-protection, and limit the fullness of our love and compassion to those within our carefully demarcated circle.

The doctrine of hell thus quite naturally gives rise to limitations on the scope of our love. Out of self-protection we are afraid to get too close, to feel too much compassion and empathy, for those who are slated for hell; and the very doctrine of uncertainty that is supposed to guard against this tendency may actually worsen it. Since we cannot know the hearts of our neighbours, and thereby cannot see what fate they court, we are tempted to base our judgment instead on visible markers that we then invest with artificial significance. We protect ourselves from the fear of losing those we love to the abyss by identifying the damned with those who are already outside our circle of loves: the alien, the foreigner, the non-Christian, the person who is divided from us by existing social discrimination and stratification.

Instead of breaking down barriers, instead of creating a world in which there is neither male nor female, rich nor poor, slave nor free, DH threatens to reinforce all the conventional barriers that are already in place. Because of existing social realities that divide us, we grow up in a world where our circle of intimacy leaves out those who are not of our class, race, nationality, ethnicity or religion. It therefore becomes safe to adopt a worldview according to which these *outsiders* are the ones who are damned. After all, if it is those *other* people who are damned – the ones we do not know and love – then we need not worry about our compassion fundamentally compromising our blessedness.

In short, there is reason to fear that DH, from a pragmatic viewpoint, narrows the scope of human love and reinforces artificially narrowed patterns of compassion. If so, then DH is pragmatically at odds with the Christian ethic of love.

9.4 Effects on Evangelism

Others may worry that if we embrace DU, the Christian call to evangelism becomes pointless. If all are saved then the urgency to spread the gospel is lost – but there are several reasons to think this worry misplaced.

First, Christian universalists generally think there are positive life benefits (in terms of life satisfaction and resources for moral improvement) that are possible *in this life* if (and only if) one opens oneself up to the kind of relationship with God that Christianity claims has been made available through Christ's life and work. Desiring that others enjoy these benefits *here and now* would be a motive to evangelize.

Secondly, one might believe that while universal salvation is inevitable, this is not because there is no subjective requirement for salvation but because all will *eventually* meet this requirement. If so, enjoying union with God is only possible for those who have opened themselves up to it – and while it is certain that all will eventually do so, those who do not by the time of their death will exist after death in a state of alienation from God that can only bring increasing misery the longer it lasts. The efforts of human evangelists may be one of God's means for hastening the salvation of all, with Christians called to be God's agents in this way. In the absence of human evangelical efforts, more people might experience the finite 'hell' of alienation from God for longer before realizing their error and turning to God.

Third, Christian universalists might be convinced the Christian worldview makes the most sense of human experience, fitting its elements together into the most coherent whole as well as offering pragmatic resources for living better lives. In other words, one might be convinced Christianity is the worldview most likely to be true. In this case, one might be motivated to share the Christian worldview for the same reason that Richard Dawkins preaches atheism – a belief that one has the truth (or at least the most rational worldview) combined with the belief that it is good in itself if more people believe the truth.

Finally, and we think most significantly, 'evangelist' means 'good messenger' and evangelism is ultimately about sharing good news (the gospel). Understood in this way, evangelism is not primarily about conversion and salvation but about declaring good news as widely as possible. In this sense the motivation for evangelism is, at least in part, the same sort of motivation that would impel someone to call everyone they know as soon as they learn that their child has been cured of leukaemia. They want to share their joy at this wonderful news; but in the case of the Christian gospel, the news also seems to have beneficial pragmatic implications for those it is being shared with. If people are hunkering down in their cellars waiting for enemy planes to fly overhead and drop bombs, the news that the enemy has been defeated will mean that people can come out of their hidey-holes. In such a case, running through the streets shouting out the good news is not merely motivated by a desire to share a personal joy but to let people know that they no longer need to burden themselves in a particular set of ways.

9.5 Butler's Objection to DU

Another concern about DU, nascent in the writings of Joseph Butler, is that it posits a relationship between moral choices and personal welfare that is at odds with what we experience in this life. Assuming that God is the creator of the world, Butler argues that He will presumably respond to continued sin in the afterlife in the same way He responds to it here. But our happiness in this life depends largely on our actions. The violent or intemperate often bring misery on themselves, either through untimely diseases or legal punishment – both of which, Butler holds, should be viewed as appointed by providence. As such, it is part of the nature of the divine government that sin, if not checked after a certain point, carries with it misery.

Furthermore, Butler asserts that the misery which sin breeds is often incurable. Repentance can lead people 'to retrieve their affairs, to recover their health and character' when they have been 'guilty of folly and extravangance *up to a certain degree*', but beyond that degree even 'real reformation' is powerless to save them. The costs of their wrongdoing 'overwhelm them beyond possibility of remedy or escape'.[4]

Butler does not claim to know why God orders the universe such that vice, if unchecked, eventually brings irremediable misery. He claims that 'the whole end, for which God made, and thus governs the world, may be utterly beyond the reach of our faculties'.[5] But the challenge remains: why would God make the world this way if the eternal fate of humanity is so different – as it would be if DU were true?

There are numerous problems with Butler's thinking here. First, Butler seems far too certain that experience reveals a general connection between sin and misery. No doubt certain sorts of sins tend to generate incurable misery in the form of physical sickness, but such sins are hardly the worst kind. It is hard to see a general connection between misery of the sort Butler is talking about and such sins as pride (which the tradition, with some reason, has held to be the worst). It certainly is not part of *our* experience that the pride of the Pharisee draws after it either illness or legal sanctions.

On the other hand, many of the most virtuous suffer from wholly undeserved illness or social persecution, and it really would be very difficult for Butler to prove that the general experience of mankind shows that, in *this* life, vice breeds misery and virtue happiness (at least if we take 'happiness' simply to mean having one's desires fulfilled, whatever those desires happen to be).

Furthermore, much of the rational basis for the higher forms of religion comes from the intuition that virtue and felicity *ought* to correspond *even though* they often fail to do so *in this life*. Kant was, of course, an important philosophical exponent of this idea; but Kant was here expressing a very ancient idea. The first great monotheistic prophet, Zoroaster, saw that the vicious often triumph over the virtuous in this life. He put his hope, therefore, in the redemptive plan of the wise and good creator, resting his faith on the hope that the ultimate course of history would *not* resemble the current state of things.[6]

Zoroaster's eyes were not focused solely on humanity. He also saw all the suffering and cruelty in the non-human world, noting the ways in which innocent animals suffer through predation, starvation, and the like. In fact, Zoroastrian dualism – according to which all evil emanates from an eternal and uncreated spirit of evil – was born in part out of the conviction that the horrors we see in the natural order could not have been instituted by an all powerful and all good God.

If this is right, then much of what we find in the order of nature, rather than serving as an analogy for understanding divine governance, stands in sharp contrast with it. Put another way, because of the corruption of the world, religious faith is often about *denying* an analogy between the governance of things in this world and the divine governance that ultimately will prevail. Much of religious doctrine therefore becomes about explaining why the world is so far removed from what a divine will would judge to be best – in other words, it is about the problem of evil.

In short, the gravity and pervasiveness of terrestrial suffering – and its indifference to the moral worth of those who suffer – reveals a fatal weakness in Butler's case against DU. Ritschl made a similar point when attacking the cogency of the teleological proof for God's existence:

> But if one proceeds with the teleological induction in a statistically precise fashion (others have already shown that one can substantiate innumerable cases where purposeless relationships and purposeful relationships exist side by side), then one reaches no goal at all in this metaphysical view of the world, least of all the safe inference of a supramundane God. The result, rather, like the familiar natural reason of the Buddhists, is that the world which embraces so many purposeless relationships within itself cannot be referred to a rational Source at all but, on the contrary, one can only conclude that it ought not exist at all. But if the opposite seems true (namely, that the world is purposeful), the validity of that truth for us Christians is not based on a more correct metaphysical knowledge, since such knowledge is indemonstrable, but rather on an opposite religious world view.[7]

Of course, one might claim that Ritschl's critique of the teleological proof is beside the point, since Butler is not seeking to prove God's existence here. But our point is this: Butler is claiming that experience does, for the most part, reveal a connection between virtue and happiness and supports the principle that unchecked vice eventually leads to irremediable misery. However, this is, at best, an oversimplification of what experience teaches. If the world of experience is more like what Ritschl takes it to be, then we must either acknowledge on the basis of *a priori* moral principles that God's principles of governance cannot be directly inferred from a study of how things work in the world of experience, or we have to consider what we are to make of the fact that vice does not always lead to misery, and virtue does not always lead to happiness. Is God inconstant – or even capricious – sometimes willing that vice be punished, and sometimes willing that it not be? What are we to make of the fact that the sin of the Pharisee is typically *not* met with punishments in this life, while the ones most often punished by truly natural means are the intemperate? And what implications does this have for the fact that Jesus condemned the sin of the Pharisee most of all? How, exactly, does Butler's analogy work here? It seems to have failed him.

Finally, it is important to look more closely at the class of people whom Butler seems to be pointing to when he makes his case that, beyond a certain point, wickedness leads to *incurable* misery. Consider those who have been sentenced to death row for heinous crimes. Among these, many live out their remaining days in abject misery. Some, however, do not – and those who do not are not differentiated by the gravity of their sin. Rather, what distinguishes those whose final days are characterized by a sense of peace and meaning despite their radically truncated freedom and their impending death is this: *a spirit of grace.*

Or consider those who, after years of unrepentant promiscuity, have contracted HIV. Some fall into bitterness and misery, which becomes compounded by the progress of the disease; but others – even as the illness leaches them of health and energy and eventually life – are lifted up by a spirit of grace and live their final days with a sense of hope and joy.

Somehow, after hitting rock bottom, there are some who realize the futility and emptiness of their lives and turn their eyes to the ultimate good – opening themselves up to it in the midst of their desperation. What conclusion should we reach based on these cases, rare as they might be? That God abandons the unregenerate after a certain point? That some become so far gone that it is just too late for them? Or, rather, that it is never too late for divine grace to exercise its transforming power?

9.6 The Problem of Evil

The final worry we want to consider is probably the most pressing, and it is one that we brushed up against in considering Butler's analogy in the previous section. The worry can be expressed in terms of a question: if all are eventually saved, then why do we not all just *start out that way*? Why endure this life, with its suffering and sin and the certainty of death in all its mystery, if the ultimate fate of all is guaranteed to be a state in which all suffering and sin is done away with in an eternal existence of joyous union with God?

This is an important and difficult question, but it should be clear that it is really a variant of the problem of evil. The question might be restated as follows: how do we reconcile the existence of the evils of this life with belief in a wholly good and almighty creator *who ultimately redeems every one of these evils*? In other words, the question is really just the standard question posed by the problem of evil, but with an additional element; namely, the precept that all the evils of the world – including all sin and suffering – are ultimately redeemed in a blessed state in which all participate. The real question for our purposes here is whether the addition of this element makes the problem of evil more difficult or less difficult to resolve.

The problem of evil is, in simplest terms, the problem of reconciling (a) the existence of a God who is omnipotent, omniscient and wholly good with (b) the existence either of evil as such or of the specific evils we find in the actual world, with their distinctive scope, severity and character (especially their apparent pointlessness from our finite human standpoint). The problem of evil becomes relevant to the dispute between hellists and universalists primarily in terms of whether the inclusion of DH or DU into the set of propositions to be reconciled changes the prospects for developing an adequate theodicy. Primarily, one's allegiance to DU or DH makes a difference in terms of how one conceives of the specific evils that prevail in the world. If one embraces DH, then one holds that some of these evils persist eternally. If one embraces DU, then one holds that none of these evils persist eternally, that all evils are merely finite in scope and severity and are overcome by goods of infinite merit.

The question is which of these views about the nature and scope of evil makes
the problem of evil harder to resolve. The answer seems obvious: DH makes the
problem of evil a *far* more serious problem than it would be were one to assume
DU. This is the insight that motivates Marilyn McCord Adams to pose the 'problem of hell' as a distinctive – and distinctively difficult – version of the problem
of evil for those Christians who believe in hell.[8]

Seen in this light, the challenge to DU based on the puzzle of explaining why
we do not just start out saved seems to be a pseudo-problem for universalism. It
gestures to a problem that *all* theists confront, including universalists. But it is
not *insofar* as universalists embrace DU that the problem arises. In fact, insofar
as they embrace DU, the problem appears to be *lessened*.

Perhaps, however, the concern with DU is not with its initial *prima facie* impact
on the force of the problem of evil, but with its impact on the most powerful
theodicies available to the theist. That is, one might argue that the best theistic
account of evil is unavailable to the universalist. But with respect to at least some
approaches to theodicy, this is clearly not the case. For example, John Hick has
argued powerfully that the Irenaean 'soul-making' theodicy he favours is defensible only on the presumption of universalism. This theodicy holds that the creation of persons is a two-stage process, and the evils of this life provide the
conditions under which the second stage, where creatures participate in their
own self-development, is best achieved. But should the second stage of 'soul-
making' fail for any person, the evils endured by that person have failed to serve
a role in God's providential plan and so are rendered pointless.[9]

Likewise, Adams argues that the deepest problem of evil – the problem of
how God can be good to the sufferers of 'horrendous evils' – is soluble on the
presumption of universalism but is rendered insoluble if any are unsaved.[10]

Perhaps, however, these theodicies are not, ultimately, the most powerful.
Perhaps the critic of DU thinks that the most promising line of theodicy is
something more along the lines of what Stewart Goetz outlines in *Freedom, Teleology,
and Evil*[11] – an approach to theodicy that at least at first glance might be
seen as clashing with DU. Goetz's theodicy, in the spirit of Kant, appeals to the
intrinsic value of perfect happiness being possessed by those who are worthy of
it. Goetz takes perfect happiness to be an intrinsic good that is good for its
possessor, and he holds that 'the *purpose* for which God creates a person' is to
experience this good. There is, however, in his view, an additional intrinsic
good that God seeks to actualize – namely, the good of a created person '*justly*
experiencing complete happiness'.[12]

In Goetz's view, this good is realized when a person comes to acquire perfect
happiness because, through the exercise of their libertarian freedom, they have
made what Goetz calls a 'just-good-seeking self-forming choice'. A self-forming
choice is a choice the making of which is the way an agent settles on a 'life plan';
that is, an intention about how to live life as a whole. A self-forming-choice is
'just-good-seeking' if it is directed towards becoming the kind of person who

seeks their good only in permissible ways; that is, justly rather than unjustly.[13] Goetz's idea is that while God creates persons for the end of perfect happiness, He permits moral evil as a foreseeable side-effect of creating persons with libertarian freedom – and He creates persons with libertarian freedom because this is a necessary condition for persons coming to acquire perfect happiness *because* they have made just-good-seeking life-forming choices. Persons coming to acquire perfect happiness *in this way* are intrinsically good. More precisely, it is the condition for experiencing perfect happiness *justly*. God permits moral evil, then, in order that persons have the opportunity to *justly* experience the perfect happiness for which they were made.

If we accept this theodicy as the best way of accounting at least for moral evil in a theistic universe,[14] then one might argue that DU must be rejected because, given DU, perfect happiness is extended to persons regardless of whether they deserve it on account of having made just-good-seeking life-forming choices. But if perfect happiness is extended without regard for desert, then is this account of why God allows moral evil not undermined?

We have several answers. First, the aim of making possible the distinctive intrinsic good Goetz highlights can still explain moral evil *even if* all are ultimately saved, because, even if all are saved regardless of their libertarian free choices, in a world in which libertarian freedom and hence moral evil exists, it becomes possible that *some* among the saved will experience perfect happiness on account of those choices, thereby exhibiting this good. If all were saved in a universe without libertarian freedom, it is impossible for this good to be instantiated at all. God's desire to make the instantiation of this good possible might therefore explain God's allowing moral evil even if we endorse DU. In effect, God designs the world to make this good possible, but regards the next-best alternative to be salvation achieved through the exercise of efficacious grace. Hence, when persons ultimately fail to achieve blessedness by making just-good-seeking life-forming choices 'on their own' (through libertarian free choices) God provides efficacious grace so that they make these choices (and so are sanctified) through His assistance. This, of course, is nothing other than DU1.

However, Goetz offers what amounts to a reply to this first answer. Specifically, he picks up Marilyn Adams's notion that evil calls for 'defeat' – meaning that it needs to be set into a larger 'organic unity' which makes the evil a meaningful element of a good whole.[15] The evil's being integrated into this valuable whole confers upon it a positive meaning. What Goetz argues is that moral evil can only be defeated by justice – and that justice requires that those who have *not* made just-good-seeking life-forming choices be *deprived* of perfect happiness.[16] In other words, it is not merely that justly experienced perfect happiness is an intrinsic good the possibility of which God might want to realize – it is also the case that if any come to experience perfect happiness apart from making just-good-seeking life-forming choices through libertarian freedom, moral evil remains undefeated in the world. Therefore, in creating a world in which the intrinsic good of justly experienced bliss is possible, God also creates a world in which there are moral evils which need to be defeated by withholding perfect bliss from those who have failed to make the morally best choices.

But this reply elaborates on Goetz's theodicy in a way that generates new difficulties for it, especially within an essentially orthodox Christian context. If Goetz is right that 'an experience of what is a person's greatest good must be had only by those who deserve it',[17] then Goetz must come to terms with the weight of the theological tradition, which holds that none by their own free choices, apart from divine grace, will come to deserve salvation.

Of course, Goetz's view is not that sinners deserve eternal damnation, but rather that they *do not* deserve perfect happiness. But his view goes further than that. It is not just that those who have made the wrong choices do not earn perfect happiness *in their own right* – more significantly, the positive good of eternal bliss is justly conferred only on those who do earn it in their own right by make the right kinds of choices. Combined with the idea that moral evil requires defeat and can only be defeated through justice, Goetz's view entails that God's options for 'defeating' moral evil are narrowed to a single choice, one that precludes anything like the vicarious Atonement and related theories of how God might meet the demands of justice *while* showing mercy and benevolence. Furthermore, Goetz must then construct an understanding of justice which can overcome the problems inherent in the idea that justice requires God to withhold the very thing needed to end the affront to justice. In short, once Goetz's theodicy limits the *means* of defeating moral evil in the indicated manner, His theodicy must confront all the problems with CDH discussed in Chapter 6.

Furthermore, experience with the ubiquity of human fallibility raises serious questions concerning the attainability, on Goetz's assumptions, of the good for the sake of which God created humans. Here, it is helpful to keep in mind Adams's point about the *impaired freedom* of human agents who start life helpless and ignorant in a deeply imperfect environment, saddled in adulthood with childhood coping mechanisms that more or less fully distort our adult capacity for choice. How deep the distortion is largely a matter of unchosen initial conditions. In effect, Goetz's argument rests on an optimism concerning what humans can accomplish by their own free choices – an optimism that is not only at odds with the weight of the Christian tradition, but in tension with much of our experience. If we adopt a more sober view of human potential, the implication of Goetz's insistence that perfect happiness be limited to those who deserve it is that only a very small number of humans will achieve the end for which God made them. In short, by adding to his theodicy the clause that perfect happiness must be restricted to those who deserve it in order for moral evil to be defeated, Goetz arguably implies that God's will for most humans is thwarted in the actual world. One is then led to wonder why God would allow the world to be such that the conditions under which our capacity for choice evolves are so hostile to the attainment of God's ends for the world – a new version of the problem of evil.

Goetz can, of course, avoid this last problem if, instead of holding that some are forever deprived of perfect happiness because they never come to deserve it within an allotted timeframe, he holds that persons are deprived of happiness *until* they come to deserve it – but that they are allotted an unlimited timeframe within which to come to deserve it by making the right sorts of choices. In fact, Goetz gestures towards precisely this possibility, but appears to adopt an essentially agnostic stance towards whether all would be saved under these conditions.[18] However, as we argued in Chapter 8, assuming these conditions the most reasonable doctrinal position is a species of DU, namely DU2.

In short, Goetz's theodicy is consistent with DU unless it is paired with an account of what is required for the defeat of moral evil that generates numerous problems, including a potential exacerbation of the problem of evil that the theodicy was introduced to solve. This exacerbation of the problem can be avoided by adopting presumptions about how God responds to those who remain unregenerate at the end of this earthly life – but these presumptions lead directly back to a version of DU. As such, despite initial appearances, Goetz's theodicy is *not* at odds with DU.

More broadly, we do not think the claim that DU threatens our capacity to solve the problem of evil is very compelling. First, there is a prima facie reason to suppose that DU makes the problem less severe; second, several important theodicies are *strengthened* by assuming DU; and third, of those approaches to theodicy that at first seem to conflict with DU, a deeper look at one representative theodicy suggests that this is not the case.

Thereore, it seems, we are left with little reason to suppose the good God of Christianity would fail to achieve His benevolent purposes with respect to His creatures. In the end, all will be well, and *all* will be well.

NOTES

1 Introduction

1 P. Berger, *A Rumor of Angels: Modern Society and the Rediscovery of the Supernatural* (Garden City: Doubleday, 1970), pp. 67–68.

2 For defences of this position see: I. A. Dorner, A *System of Christian Doctrine* (hereafter *SCD*), trans. A. Cave and J. S. Banks (Edinburgh: T & T Clark, 1885; repr., 2005, Eugene: Wipf and Stock),vol. 4, pp. 415–428; H. U. Von Bathasar, *Dare We Hope "That all Men be Saved"?*, trans. K. Kipp and L. Krauth (San Francisco: Ignatius Press, 1988).

3 The contrast between Schleiermacher and Hegel is helpful, especially since Schleiermacher is often classified as a 'liberal' Christian. However, as K. Barth notes, a careful reading of Schleiermacher's *On the Christian Faith* reveals that, for all of his deviations from strict Orthodoxy, Schleiermacher was a *Christian* theologian who held that the doctrine of the redemption wrought by Jesus of Nazareth is a doctrine of the *faith* pointing to a particular person who was the Son of God in a unique way. This is clearly not true of Hegel or Emerson. See K. Barth, *Church Dogmatics*, trans. G. W. Bromiley and R. J. Ehrlich (Edinburgh: T & T Clark, 1960), vol. 3, pt. 3, pp. 326–328.

4 See his *Convention Essays*, trans. A. Suelflow (St. Louis: Concordia, 1981), p. 71. William Lane Craig recently echoed Walther, claiming that DU runs contrary to Christianity's evangelical impetus. See his '"No Other Name": A Middle Knowledge Perspective on the Exclusivity of Salvation Through Christ', *Faith and Philosophy* 6 (1989): pp. 172–188, esp. p. 175.

5 There is a clear exception, even here, related to teachings about Christ's descent into hell. Though some Church Fathers held that Christ descended into hell solely to save faithful Jews who had died before Christ's birth, others held that Christ descended to save *all* those who had not had the chance to hear the gospel while alive. Even these Fathers, however, seemed to have assumed that the gospel message had reached all living humans by the time Christ died, so that after His resurrection no post-mortem conversion would be possible. On this, see John of Damascus, *On the Orthodox Faith*, [hereafter OF], trans. F. H. Chase in *Saint John of Damascus: Writings* (New York: The Fathers of the Church, 1958), bk. 3, chap. 29, p. 334.

6 On this, see G. W. Leibniz, Theodicy: *Essays on the Goodness of God, the Freedom of Man, and the Origin of Evil*, trans. E. M. Huggard (La Salle: Open Court, 1985), pp. 175–177.

7 Cf. J. L. Walls, 'Is Molinism as bad as Calvinism?', *Faith and Philosophy* 7 (1990): pp. 85–98. Walls holds to this idea while being a staunch defender of DH (but in

what seems its mildest and most philosophically plausible form). While Walls follows Molina here, the notion that God gives all grace that is *truly* sufficient for salvation was endorsed by most Eastern Fathers, whether or not they followed Origin in maintaining DU.

8   J. L. Walls, *Hell: The Logic of Damnation* (Notre Dame: University of Notre Dame Press, 1992), p. 7.

9   High Zoroastrian theology, which taught DU, maintained that the damned will be converted in hell because they are essentially good and in hell the essence of evil will be fully revealed. See R. C. Zaehner, *The Dawn and Twilight of Zoroastrianism* (London: Weidenfeld & Nicolson, 1961; repr. New York: Phoenix Press, 2002), pp. 304–305, and pp. 307–308.

10   Karl Barth, who can reasonably be taken to be a universalist, argues that without God, creatures are helpless against the forces of evil (which Barth famously dubbed 'the Nothingness'). See *Church Dogmatics*, vol. 3, pt. 3, pp. 354–355.

11   This is not to say that there are no doctrinal portions of the Bible (*Romans*, for example). What we mean is that the Bible as a *whole* is not a doctrinal treatise, but rather a sort of 'sacred history'. Of course, theologians use that sacred history as a datum for inferring things about God's nature and will. Furthermore, the sacred history includes instances of God 'speaking' to humans (e.g. through a burning bush or the Incarnate Second Person of the Trinity); but even these communications are often metaphorical or proceed through parables.

12   For a sustained argument for the need to use reason in judging revelatory claims, see S. Menssen and T. D. Sullivan, *The Agnostic Enquirer: Revelation from a Philosophical Standpoint* (Grand Rapids: Eerdmans, 2007), chap. 1.

13   Even the older Protestant Orthodoxy, which originally fashioned the doctrines of the verbal inspiration and plenary inerrancy of Scripture, held that more obscure passages must be interpreted in light of clearer ones, and that all of Scripture must be interpreted in light of its principal teaching concerning the salvation of sinners through God's grace in Christ. See H. Schmid, *The Doctrinal Theology of the Evangelical Lutheran Church*, trans. C. Hay and H. Jacobs (repr. Minneapolis: Augsburg, 1961), pp. 68–80.

14   Compare this with how nineteenth-century abolitionist theologians responded to defences of slavery based on the 'plain sense' of certain scriptural passages. They pointed to unifying themes in Scripture to argue that its holistic sense is opposed to slavery, even if particular passages might be invoked to support it. See P. P. Kuenning, *The Rise and Fall of American Lutheran Pietism: The Rejection of an Activist Heritage* (Mercer University Press, 1989), pp. 118–122.

15   T. Talbott, 'Craig on the possibility of eternal damnation', *Religious Studies* 28 (1992): pp. 495–510, esp. p. 497, in which he lays out the propositions that he later challenges.

16   W. L. Craig, 'Talbott's universalism once more', *Religious Studies* 29 (1993): pp. 497–518, esp. pp. 499–500.

17   Many suppose that for a successful defence, it is sufficient that 'P' is broadly logically possible; but this seems inadequate. Suppose 'P' is a proposition that is logically possible but is known to be false. In that case, not-P should be included within the belief set whose coherence we are attempting to establish. We have

not proven we have a coherent belief set if we show that *were* P true (which we know it is not), *we would* have a coherent belief set.

18 Craig relies on several implausible propositions in defending DH, but the pivotal one is that some persons might be characterized by 'trans-world damnation'; that is, that they would finally and irrevocably reject God if God actualized any *feasible* possible world that they are 'inhabitants' of, where a feasible possible world is one that could produce enough of the saved to 'fill' heaven ('No other name', pp. 180–184).

19 Compare this with the way some Young Earth Creationists defend their doctrine that the universe is, at most, 10,000 years old, despite massive geological and cosmological evidence to the contrary. They note that, for all we *know*, God could have created the universe less than 10,000 years ago complete with all the (false) indications that it is much older.

20 We can think of only one reason Craig would engage in such a seemingly useless exercise: because he thinks the scriptural case for DH is so powerful that anyone who accepts the authority of Scripture should embrace DH so long as doing so has not been shown to involve a contradiction. The assumption here seems to be that the only thing that can override a clear scriptural teaching is a demonstration that it is logically impossible for that teaching to be true. Unfortunately for Craig, even if we accept this strong view of Scripture's authority, DH does not fare well for reasons that will be developed in Chapter 4.

21 We have in mind here the supralapsarian doctrine that God's perfection demanded that He 'create' sinners so that the glory of His justice would be revealed in the condemnation of some and the glory of his mercy would be revealed in the salvation of others. See H. Heppe, *Reformed Dogmatics: Set Out and Illustrated from the Sources*, trans. G. T. Thompson (Grand Rapids: Baker, 1978), pp. 147–148.

22 A supporting example of this way of understanding doctrines is offered by the Christian doctrine of the Atonement. As Dorner notes, what is common to all dogmatically precise theories of the Atonement, as well as to the faith of the simple Christian believer, is simply that sinners 'owe to Christ alone the restoration of divine communion and redemption'. However, exactly how this is to be understood is not the same in every dogmatically precise theory – and there are numerous theories which have been worked out by respected theologians in the tradition. The Christian Church as a *whole* does not affirm any one of these, but rather one or another of them (or perhaps some consistent recombination of their elements). For a helpful overview of important Atonement theories, see Dorner, SCD, vol. 4, pp. 1–78.

2 Hellisms: The Species of DH

1 The clause, 'while preserved forever in being', is introduced to exclude the Doctrine of Annihilation (DA) from DH's scope.

2 See, for example, Aquinas, *Summa Theologiae* [hereafter *ST*], pt. 1–2, q. 3, art. 8.

3   On this point, see St. Augustine, *City of God* [hereafter *CG*], bk. 22, chap. 30; Schmid, *The Doctrinal Theology*, p. 661, especially the excerpt from Hollaz; Heppe, *Reformed Dogmatics*, p. 707; Dorner, *SCD*, vol. 4, pp. 430–432.

4   Cf. Augustine, *CG*, bk. 14, chaps. 3–6; Philip Melanchthon, *Loci Communes* (hereafter *LC*), 1555, trans. C. Manschreck as *On Christian Doctrine* (Grand Rapids: Baker, 1965), locus 6, pp. 75–77.

5   'Fully' here should be taken to imply that not only will those enjoying the beatific vision love God above all things (as Adam did in Augustinian theology), but also that they will love Him with an *ardour* that makes it *impossible* for them to sin (which Adam did not).

6   P. Melanchthon, *LC*, locus 6, p. 76.

7   See, for example, Augustine, *CG*, bk. 11, chap. 16, and bk. 12, chap. 8; Aquinas, *ST*, pt. 1–2, q. 82, art. 3; Melanchthon, *LC*, locus 6, pp. 75–76. We should note that when the Christian tradition speaks of 'carnal desires' it does not mean just the excessive love of sensual pleasures, but rather any excessive devotion to a created thing, the most subtle of which appears in the devotion of the Pharisee to his own self-righteousness. For particularly incisive and beautiful statements of this point see Hans Martensen's classic *Christian Ethics*, trans. C. Spence (Edinburgh: T & T Clark, 1871), pp. 102–109; and Luther's celebrated commentary on the first commandment in his *Large Catechism*.

8   Aristotle, 1165b35–1166b.

9   See Aquinas, *ST*, Suppl., q. 98; the passage from Gerhard's *Loci Theologici*, in Schmid, pp. 634–635.

10 See Augustine, *CG*, bk. 21, chap. 9; Aquinas, *ST*, *Suppl.*, q. 97; the catena of quotes from the older Lutheran divines in Schmid, *The Doctrinal Theology*, pp. 658–659, and the older Reformed divines in Heppe, *Reformed Dogmatics*, pp. 710–711.

11 When we say something is metaphysically possible we mean that it is not only non-contradictory, but also that it does not violate certain necessary truths which are not analytic (at least not in the Kantian sense); for example, every thought is an attribute of a thinker, nothing can come to be without a cause, there are no morally indifferent acts of hating God, and so on. We take such non-analytic *necessary* truths to be as necessary as analytic ones – that is, there is no possible world in which they are violated.

12 See Augustine, *CG*, bk. 13, chaps. 13–15, and Schmid, *The Doctrinal Theology*, pp. 237–238.

13 On this matter see Dorner's discussion of sin, supported by numerous biblical references, in *SCD*, vol. 2, pp. 313–324. As with all great Christian divines, Dorner emphasizes that the worst moral evil is 'spiritual arrogance, the conceit of self-righteousness, which shuts the self off from loving communion with God and neighbour.' Cf. Augustine, *CG*, bk. 14, chaps. 3–4; Maximos the Confessor, *Four Hundred Texts on Love*, trans. G. Palmer, P. Sherrard and K. Ware (London: Faber & Faber, 1981), First Century, # 46–48, p. 57.

14 See Augustine, *CG*, bk. 13, chap. 15; Schmid, *The Doctrinal Theology*, pp. 237–238. Of course the Christian tradition holds that God is somehow present to every creature, but in different ways. See Schmid, *The Doctrinal Theology*, pp. 481–486.

15   See Aquinas, *ST*, pt.1, q. 104, art. 1; Melanchthon, *LC*, locus 3, p. 41; John of Damascus, OF, bk. 1, chap. 8, pp. 176–177.

16   See Heppe, *Reformed Dogmatics*, pp. 147–149, and 166–168.

17. We say this seems to be Aquinas's view because he clearly holds that it is metaphysically possible for God to give efficacious grace, that His doing so would not violate creaturely autonomy, and that God, as Lord of all, could simply have forgiven all sinners their sin – that is, that justice does not demand that God punish any sinner, nor does it demand Christ's Atonement, even though Christ's Incarnation and Passion were the 'most fitting' way for God to deal with sin. *ST*, pt. 1, q. 82, a. 1; pt. 1–2, q. 9, a. 6 – esp. ad. 3, q. 10, a. 2, q. 112, a. 2, ad. 2; pt. 3, q. 1, a. 2. On what might be called Aquinas's soteriological 'semi-voluntarism', see Dorner, *SCD*, vol. 4, p. 18.

18. This view does not seem historically to have had many defenders in the Western Christian tradition, but one might think John of Damascus held it because he clearly thought God heaps ancillary evils on the damned for retributive reasons while implying that the damned are damned because they have, through bad choices, made themselves so morally vicious that *God cannot* save them. See *OF*, p. 210, 262 and 406. For a recent defence of this view see C. Seymour, *A Theodicy of Hell* (Dordrecht: Kluwer, 2000).

3 Universalisms: The Species of DU

1   D. Hollaz, *Examen Theologicum Acroamaticum* [hereafter *ETA*], (Stargard: 1707), in Schmid, p. 661; cf. Aquinas, *ST*, pt. 1–2, q. 2, a. 8, q. 3, a. 8, q. 4, a. 4.

2   J. A. Quenstedt, *Theologia Didactico-Polemica* [hereafter *TDP*], (Wittenberg: 1685), in Schmid, pp. 661–662.

3   See his *Leviathan*, Michael Oakeshott (ed.) (New York: Macmillan, 1962), chap. 38, esp. pp. 334–338.

4   As noted in Chapter 2, the mainstream of the Christian tradition has held that physical evils, culminating in death, come from sin, and that heaven's physical goods, above all eternal life, result from the purging of sin. This idea is found not only in Augustine, but in many Church Fathers. See J. Pelikan, *The Christian Tradition: Volume I: The Emergence of the Catholic Tradition* (Chicago: The University of Chicago Press, 1971), p. 235.

5   We use 'objective end' in the sense used by the Protestant Scholastics, according to which the 'objective end' of a being is an object the 'possession' of which (called the 'formal end') will render the being that is 'ordered' to it complete and happy. See J. G. Baier, Definition 4, *Compendium Theologiae Positivae* [hereafter *CTP*] (Jena: 1685), C. F. W. Walther (ed.) (Grand Rapids: Emmanuel Press, 2006), proleg., chap. 1, # 4, pp. 9–10. (In this and subsequent references to Baier's work, hash marks are used to indicate definitions within chapters, and letters are used to indicate lettered notes that Baier employs to further explain definitions). This terminology simply gave names to ideas long recognized in Christian Theology – see Aquinas, *ST*, pt. 1–2, q. 3, a. 8, ad. 2.

6   Something like God's sheer benevolence seems to have moved one branch of the Visistadvaita school of Ramanuja, the celebrated medieval Hindu theologian, to embrace universalism. See J. Carmen, *The Theology of Ramanuja* (New Haven: Yale University Press, 1974), pp. 223–224.

7   *ST*, pt. 1, q. 20, a. 2, Fathers of the English Dominican Province translation (Westminster: Christian Classics, 1981). Cf. John of Damascus, *OF*, bk. 4, chap. 13, pp. 354–355; and Luther's commentary on the first commandment in his *Large Catechism*.

8   See Baier, *CTP*, pt. 1, chap. 1, # 23, (e), pp. 40–41.

9   It is worth noting that Zoroastrianism, which argued for DU chiefly on God's benevolent and complacent love, also taught that sinners need a vicarious sacrifice to atone for their sins. See Zaehner, *The Dawn and Twilight*, pp. 317–318.

10   See Baier, *CTP*, pt. 3, chap. 1, # 5, chap. 5, # 9, pp. 12–14, and pp. 258–265.

11   On this point Baier says that 'the goodness or grace of God is not able to tend towards the salvation of sinful humans unless a divine saving justice is possible'; *CTP*, pt. 3, chap. 1, # 5, p. 12.

12   Anselm defends his doctrine in his celebrated treatise 'Cur Deus Homo', contained in *Saint Anselm: Basic Writings*, trans. S. N. Deane (La Salle: Open Court, 1962), pp. 177–288.

13   For a concise litany of challenges to the penal-substitutionary theory, see S. M. Heim, *Saved From Sacrifice: A Theology of the Cross* (Grand Rapids: Eerdmans, 2006), pp. 23–29.

14   See Schleiermacher, *On The Christian Faith*, trans. D. M. Baillie et al. (Edinburgh: T & T Clark, 1928), # 167, pp. 730–732.

15   Some theologians who accept an essentially Anselmian doctrine of the Atonement think divine justice *is* a manifestation of divine love. See Barth, *Church Dogmatics*, vol. 2, pt.1, trans. T. H. L Parker et al. (Edinburgh: T & T Clark, 1957), pp. 376–406.

16   See J. D. Weaver, *The Nonviolent Atonement* (Grand Rapids: Eerdmans, 2001). Certain Eastern Fathers developed a non-violent ethic based on the Gospels and on Plato's doctrine that we should pity the wicked. This may help explain why the penal-substitutionary theory never enjoyed the dominance in the Eastern Church that it enjoyed in the West. See Maximos the Confessor, *Four Hundred Texts on Love*, First Century, # 25, # 61–62, pp. 55, 59.

17   Cf. Dorner, *SCD*, vol. 4, pp. 107–116.

18   See Luther's celebrated treatise *The Freedom of a Christian*, in *Martin Luther: Three Treatises*, trans. W. H. Lambert and H. J. Grimm (Philadelphia: Fortress Press, 1970), pp. 286–289.

19   See Pelikan, *The Christian Tradition*, vol. 1, pp. 148–149.

20   See Aulen, *The Faith of the Christian Church*, trans. E. H. Wahlstrom and G. E. Arden (Philadelphia: Muhlenberg Press, 1948), pp. 223–237.

21   See Barth, *Church Dogmatics*, vol. 3, pt. 3, # 50, pp. 289–368.

22   Such Christians tend to deny that there is any wrath or retributive justice in God.

23   On these matters we share Aulen's and Barth's criticisms of purely moral theories of the Atonement, which conceive of God's love as a kind of mildness or

kindness, and thus fail to capture God's vehement opposition to sin. However, we also agree with them that the pure Anselmic theory incorrectly separates God's justice from His love, and so supposes that there is such thing as a loveless justice in God. In this way, neither purely moral nor purely Anselmic theories of the Atonement correctly understand that divine love is a holy love capable of *internal* tension. See Aulen, *The Faith of the Christian Church*, pp. 237–241.

24   See *Church Dogmatics*, vol. 2 pt.1, pp. 358–359.

25   On this idea see G. MacDonald, *George MacDonald: 365 Readings*, C. S. Lewis (ed.) (New York: Macmillan, 1947), pp. 1–5, esp. reading 7; Luther, *Table Talk*, trans. W. Hazlitt (London: Fount Classics, 1995), # 79, pp. 39–40

26   'God is the highest good (*summum bonum*), and thus He loves His own goodness itself. In man love of one's own self is vicious and damnable, because man is not the highest good, but in God he ought to seek the highest good and adhere to Him alone. God, however, loves Himself, not because He is Himself (*non tamen ut est ipse*), but because He is the highest good, for if there were a greater and more excellent (*praestantius*) good, then that and not Himself would He love (*diligeret*) ... The Father in the divine essence loves the Son, as the substantial image of Himself ... The Son loves the Father, as He was from the Father's heart before his worldly birth ... The Holy Spirit is the substantial love of the Father and the Son because He proceeds from both.' J. Gerhard, *Loci Theologici* (Jena: 1621), Preuss (Berlin: Gustov Schlawitz, 1863) (eds), locus 2, c. 7, sect. 11, p. 344.

27   This point, which is implicit in the previous quote from Gerhard, has been explicitly affirmed by many theologians in their Trinitarian doctrine. See Barth, *Church Dogmatics*, vol. 2, pt. 1, pp. 278–279.

28   This may be the philosophical idea behind the ancient Jewish notion, captured in Isa. 6:1-7, that God will not allow the sinful creature into His presence until He Himself purifies the creature.

29   On this point see A. Ritschl, 'Festival Address on the Four-Hundredth Anniversary of the Birth of Martin Luther', trans. D. W. Lotz, in *Ritschl and Luther* (Nashville: Abingdon Press, 1974), p. 192.

30   T. Talbott, *The Inescapable Love of God* (Universal Publishers, 1999), p. 167.

31   See, for example, Philip Melanchthon, *LC*, locus 3, p. 39. Cf., John of Damascus, *OF*, bk. 2, chap. 2, p. 205.

32   See Gen. 9.6, where the evil of homicide is clearly linked to the great objective worth of humans as being created in God's image.

33   See Jer. 31.20.

34   C. F. W. Walther, *Convention Essays*, p. 91.

35   Chapter 1 of Genesis repeats six times with respect to various things God created (light, water, etc.), that 'God saw' it (i.e. light, water, etc.) and 'it was good'. Then, when God finished creating, it says 'God saw all that He had made, and it was *very* good'. As Leibniz pointed out (*Discourse on Metaphysics*, # 2) the 'saw' here is important since it indicates a judgment about something that has objective worth.

36   *Loci Theologici*, locus 3, chap. 8, sect. 10, q. 1, pp. 339–340. Cf. Maximos the Confessor, *Four Hundred Texts on Love*, First Century, # 25, p. 55.

37   As quoted by A. Strong, *Systematic Theology* (F. H. Revell, 1907) p. 694.

38 J. G. Baier, *CTP*, pt. 1, chap. I, # 23, (e), pp. 40–41.
39 See Aquinas, *ST*, pt. 1, q. 21, a.1, ad. 3.
40 Cf. Leibniz, 'Ethical Definitions and Propositions', in *Leibniz Selections*, edited and translated by P. Wiener (New York: Scribner, 1951), p. 568.
41 In this regard we can point to Melanchthon, who perceived God's hatred of sin to be directed at the creature's lack of conformity with the divine nature, which is both a vitiation of the creature and an affront to God: 'The divine law, which is called *lex moralis* ... is the eternal, unchangeable wisdom and principle of righteousness in God himself ... Inasmuch as this eternal law is divine wisdom itself, first fashioned in creation, and explained in the divine word from the time of Adam to our own, it is clear that this law binds all rational creatures at all times. This law did not originate with Moses, and did not pass away with Judaism; it is and always will be; it shows us God's nature, and tells us that he wants us to be like him, and that he abhors sin.' *LC*, locus 7, pp. 84–85. In a similar vein, the Eastern Fathers often spoke of sin as essentially consisting in a falling away from the logos that God impressed on all rational creatures when He first created them, and of the Incarnation as the full and perfect impartation of the logos to human nature via Christ's humanity. This made it possible for all fallen humans to become deified. See John of Damascus, *OF*, bk. 4, chap. 13, pp. 354–355.
42 Aristotle, 1110a–24.
43 E. Stump, 'Dante's hell, Aquinas's moral theory, and the love of God', *Canadian Journal of Philosophy* 16 (1986): pp. 181–198, 194–195.
44 J. Kvanvig, *The Problem of Hell* (New York: Oxford, 1993), p 112.
45 Ibid.
46 See ibid., pp. 112–119, for his penetrating criticisms of species of DH which appeal to some divine attribute other than love as the internal impelling cause, or causes, of God's willing or permitting that some created persons be damned.

4 Universalism and the 'Plain Sense' of Scripture

1 See C. F. W. Walther, *Convention Essays*, esp. p. 74. Walther also refused to abandon his theological principles for another reason. When confronting tensions and ambiguities *within* Scripture, he chose the reading that 'gives all the glory to God' – and thought his theological principles did this. Since we think DU gives more glory to God than DH, *and* that there is tension within Scripture on this issue, we think Walther's broader approach should have led him to embrace DU rather than jettison consistency.
2 P. T. Geach, *Providence and Evil* (Cambridge: Cambridge University Press, 1977), p. 123.
3 M. J. Murray, 'Heaven and Hell', in *Reason for the Hope Within*, M. J. Murray (ed.) (Grand Rapids: Eerdmans, 1999), pp. 287–317. Quote appears on p. 289.
4 Ibid., p. 290.
5 Ibid., p. 290.
6 Ibid., p. 290, footnote 5.

7 W. L. Craig, '"No other name": A middle knowledge perspective on the exclusivity of salvation through Christ', *Faith and Philosophy* 6 (1989): pp. 297–308.

8 M. Murray, *Heaven and Hell*, p. 307.

9 Ibid.

10 Strictly speaking, this conclusion could be avoided by rejecting HI1 instead of HI2, but rejecting HI1 flies in the face of pervasive moral intuitions and so does not offer any advantages.

11 R. Parry (writing as Gregory MacDonald), *The Evangelical Universalist* (Eugene: Cascade Books, 2006), p. 152.

12 Ibid., p. 153. On this passage, see also Talbott, *The Inescapable Love of God*, pp. 92–98.

13 In addition to this problem, some scholars challenge the notion that this parable makes any claims about human fate after death. Robin Parry (writing as Gregory MacDonald) follows David Powys in arguing that Jesus' aim in the parable is simply to turn the Pharisees' own eschatology against them to expose their hypocrisy. See Parry/MacDonald, *The Evangelical Universalist*, pp. 146–147, and D. Powys's, *Hell: A Hard Look at a Hard Question* (Carlisle, UK: Paternoster Press, 1998), pp. 218–228.

14 Furthermore, it may be a mistake to assume Jesus is referring to God here. He might be exhorting his listeners to fear demonic powers (although one wonders if Jesus would attribute to them the power to destroy souls).

15 See, for example, Parry's careful universalist interpretations of Rev. 14:9-11 and 20:10-15 within the broader context of Revelations in Parry/MacDonald, *The Evangelical Universalist*, pp. 106–132.

16 J. Murray, *Epistle of Paul to the Romans*, vol. I (Grand Rapids: Eerdmans, 1960), pp. 192–193.

17 T. Talbott, *The Inescapable Love of God*, p. 63.

18 Of course, once the reader has accepted our point that the plain sense of Scripture cannot be used to support DH over DU, these interpretive disputes become very relevant.

19 Talbott makes this point elegantly in *The Inescapable Love of God*, pp. 78–79.

20 There are numerous other such conflicts. For instance, in the Calvinist/Lutheran debate concerning whether Christ died only for the elect or for all humanity, both sides marshalled scriptural texts for their views, and both sides had to interpret the texts marshalled by their opponents in ways that stretched their plain sense.

21 A. Fairbairn, *The Place of Christ in Modern Theology* (New York: Scribner, 1907), p. 507.

22 G. Aulen, *The Faith of the Christian Church*, pp. 82–83.

23 The older Protestant Orthodoxy developed a sophisticated doctrine of verbal and plenary inspiration in this way, three features of which warrant attention. First, Orthodoxy held that every scriptural passage has but one meaning: the meaning intended by the Holy Spirit (which they called the 'literal meaning'). Sometimes this intended meaning is the 'strictly' literal one, while sometimes the language is intended to be figurative. Second, in practice (if not in their explicit accounts of Scripture) the older Orthodox invoked metaphysical

doctrines to decide when a passage should be read strictly literally. Third, the older Orthodox held that every passage in scripture must be interpreted in light of the fundamental articles of the faith, such as the articles concerning Christ's Person and work, the articles concerning justification by grace through faith, and so on.

24   P. Althaus, *The Theology of Martin Luther*, trans. R. C. Schultz (Philadelphia: Fortress Press, 1966), p. 73.

25   Ibid.

26   R. Seeberg, *Text-Book of the History of Doctrine, Volume II: History of Doctrines in the Middle and Modern Ages*, trans. C. E. Hays (Philadelphia: Lutheran Publication Society, 1905), p. 300.

27   M. Luther, 'Preface to the Epistles of St. James and St. Jude', in *Luther's Works, Volume 35: Word and Sacrament 1*, edited and translated by E. T. Bachman (Philadelphia: Fortress Press, 1960), p. 396.

28   R. Muller, *Post-Reformation Reformed Dogmatics, Volume 2* (Grand Rapids, MI: Baker Publishing Group, 2003), 2nd edition, p. 208. Francis Watson develops a similar argument based on his reading of Galatians in 'Gospel and Scripture: Rethinking Canonical Unity', *Tyndale Bulletin* 52 (2001): pp. 161–182. Watson notes that if the writings of Scripture are to be a 'canon', they must 'lay claim to some degree of structure and coherence, a unifying logic inherent to the writings themselves' (p. 162), and that the only approach to scriptural unity that is true to the evangelical character of Christianity is one which reads the whole canon through the lens of the gospel – by which he means 'the message about Christ, his death and resurrection, and about what all this means in relation both to God and to ourselves' (p. 168).

29   Seeberg, *History of Doctrines*, p. 301.

30   Ibid., p. 302.

31   P. Althaus, *The Theology of Martin Luther*, pp. 80–81.

32   Ibid., p. 81.

33   Of course, the critic of Luther might argue that the only reason Luther reads Scripture in this way is because he brings his Christocentrism to it; but even if this criticism holds, it seems clear that it is more true to *Christianity* – conceived as a faith united around Christ as saviour – to favour a Christocentric reading of Scripture.

34   G. MacDonald, *Unspoken Sermons* (Sioux Falls: NuVision Publications, 2009), pp. 25–26.

35   A. Ritschl, *The Christian Doctrine of Justification and Reconciliation*, trans. by H. R. Mackintosh and A. B. Macaulay (Edinburgh: T & T Clark, 1900), pp. 1–2.

5 A Prima Facie Case for DU

1   See Schmid, *The Doctrinal Theology*, pp. 660–661.

2   The classic discussion of this is by Aquinas *ST*, suppl., q. 92, a. 1. Aquinas does not use the phrase 'light of glory', which was later adopted by Catholic and Protestant theologians as a shorthand for what Aquinas describes here.

3 While we favour a doctrine of individual essences, defending it is beyond our scope here.

4 They especially stress this in commentaries on the Genesis creation story, as well as in discussions of the Incarnation and the Atonement, hinging as these doctrines do on the idea of a common human nature.

5 See R. Cudworth, *The True Intellectual System of the Universe* (London: Richard Priestley, 1820), vol. 4, pp. 159–167.

6 See R. Price, 'A Review of the Principle Questions in Morals', in *British Moralists: 1650–1800*, D. Raphael (ed.) (Indianapolis: Hackett Publishing Company, 1991), vol. 2, pp. 147–148.

7 See R. Cudworth, A *Treatise Concerning Eternal and Immutable Morality*, S. Hutton (ed.) (Cambridge: Cambridge University Press, 1996), p. 18

8 For a penetrating account of the relation between positive and natural law, see Cudworth, A *Treatise*, pp. 18–21.

9 Luther took this as part of God's motivation for imposing ceremonial laws on the ancient Israelites. See his 'Preface to the Old Testament' in *Martin Luther's Basic Theological Writings*, T. Lull (ed.) (Minneapolis: Fortress Press, 1989), pp. 118–134.

10 See Dorner, *System of Christian Ethics*, trans. C. Mead and R. Cunningham (Edinburgh: T & T Clark, 1887), # 7, pp. 68–93; Cudworth, A *Treatise*, pp. 26–27

11 For Aquinas's way of explaining this, which proved normative for both Catholics and Protestants, see F. Coplestone, *Aquinas* (New York: Penguin, 1955), p. 220.

12 Some might question whether this is true of Luther's followers, since Luther strongly criticized Aristotle's ethics (in, for example, his *Heidelberg Disputation*, explanation of theological thesis 28, pp. 45–49 in Lull). However, Luther objected to what he controversially took as Aristotle's egoism, not to Aristotle's account of human flourishing. The Lutheran Scholastics incorporated the latter in a manner consistent with core ideas in Luther's theology. See, for instance, Baier's definition of the moral law, CTP, in Schmid, The *Doctrinal Theology*, p. 512.

13 By 'classical Catholic theologians' we mean Catholic theologians from the time of Trent until around 1900, who were in part animated by a desire to defend Rome against Protestant criticisms. By 'classical Protestant theologians' we mean thinkers of the epoch of Protestant Orthodoxy, roughly from 1560 to 1700. How far the dogmatic positions of either remain authoritative for their respective denominations is a matter of dispute.

14 See Augustine, *CG*, bk. 13.

15 See J. Pohle, *God the Author of Nature and the Supernatural* (St. Louis: Herder, 1927), p. 193; L. Ott, *Fundamentals of Catholic Dogma*, trans. P. Lynch (St. Louis: Herder, 1954), pp. 101–106

16 J. Pohle, *God the Author*, pp. 186, 228–231.

17 J. Pohle, *God the Author*, p. 228; Ott, *Fundamentals*, p. 12.

18 J. Pohle, *God the Author*, pp. 179–190.

19 See, for example, the quotation from Reush's *Annot. in Baieri Compendium* (Jena: 1757) in the Prolegomena, chap. 1, p. 11, of Walther's edition of Baier's work.

20 See the great Reformed Scholastic theologian F. Turretin, *Institutes of Elenctic Theology* [hereafter *IET*], trans. G. Giger (Phillipsburg: P & R Publishing, 1992), vol. 1, topic 5, q. 11, pp. 471–473.

21 See the passage from the Reformed theologian Hottinger, in Heppe, p. 239.

22 ST, pt. 1–2, q. 2, a. 8.

23 See Turretin, *IET*, vol. 1, topic 5, q. 11, p. 472; Hollaz, *ETA*, pt. 2, chap. 1, q. 20, prof. b, # 3.

24 Some twentieth-century theologians held that Aquinas believed humans are naturally ordered to union with God, and hence that Aquinas agreed with classical Protestantism on this matter, not classical Catholicism. See H. De Lubac's penetrating and influential *The Mystery of the Supernatural*, trans. R. Sheed (New York: Herder, 1967).

25 J. Pohle, *God the Author*, p. 276.

26 A. Ritschl, *The Christian Doctrine of Reconciliation and Justification*, pp. 331–332

27 See the passage from Hollaz in Schmid, *The Doctrinal Theology*, pp. 237–238. Not all Lutherans held this thesis; Baier, for instance, held that God withdrew Adam's concreated virtues as a punishment for sin. See *CTP*, pt. 2, chap. 2, # 10, p. 293.

28 This thesis may require further explanation. The older Lutherans, to avoid supposing God causes sin, held that the souls of all but the first humans were created, not by God *ex nihilo*, but by the souls of their parents acting on appropriately disposed matter (in the way one flame kindles another). Adam and Eve could not, after the fall, bestow on their children the virtues they had lost. Hence, all humans since the Fall are born without 'a true love and fear of God' and with attendant disordered desires. In Quenstedt's words, 'For our first parents were then considered not only as the first individuals of the human race, *but also as the true root, stock, and source of the whole human race, which in them could both stand and fall. Hence we are said to have been in the loins of our first parents.*' TDP, in Schmid, *The Doctrinal Theology*, p. 240 (emphasis ours).

29 See Schmid, pp. 237–238.

30 Some might question this, since the older Lutherans regarded inborn sin as 'sufficient' for damnation; though they also held it is not 'adequate' for damnation. Only those who freely reject the means of grace are actually damned, which infants cannot do. Hence, most Lutheran divines (including Luther) held that God saves unbaptized infants. See Dorner, SCD, vol. 3, p. 64.

31 R. Schmid, *The Doctrinal Theology*, pp. 491–499.

32 Ibid.

33 Ibid., pp. 276–284.

34 J. Pohle, *God the Author*, pp. 190–193.

35 Turretin, *IET*, vol. 1, topic 5, q. 11, p. 473.

36 Classical Catholic theologians thought this hypothetical state *might* have existed in the sense of being intrinsically possible *and* something God could have, in perfect justice, willed (hence 'extrinsically possible'). See Ott, *Fundamentals*, pp. 105–106.

37 J. Pohle, *God the Author*, p. 229.

38 For the difference between the supernatural and the preternatural, see J. Pohle, *God the Author*, pp. 180–190.

39 See Hollaz, *ETA*, pt. 2, chap. 1, q. 19, 20; Turretin, *IET*, vol. 1, topic 5, q. 12, pp. 473–477.

40 J. Pohle, *God the Author*, pp. 194–195.

41 Ott, *Fundamentals*, pp. 98–99.

42 Ibid., p. 97

43 F. Schleiermacher, *The Christian Faith*, p. 721. The classic T & T Clark translation has multiple translators. The relevant section is translated by H. R. Mackintosh.

44 T. Talbott, 'Providence, freedom, and human destiny', *Religious Studies* 26 (1990): pp. 227–245, esp. pp. 237–238.

45 See Aquinas, *ST*, pt. 1–2, q. 4, a. 8, ad. 3.

46 See Aquinas, *ST*, supp., q. 94, a. 3. Cf. *ST*, pt. 2–2, q. 25, a. 11.

47 T. Talbott, 'Providence, freedom, and human destiny', pp. 237–238. In response to Peter Geach's claim that 'someone confronted with the damned would find it impossible to wish that things so evil (the damned) could be happy' [*in Providence and Evil* (Cambridge: Cambridge University Press, 1977), p. 139], Talbott notes that this only shows that 'I could not wish to see my daughter *both* morally corrupt *and* happy,' but 'it simply does not follow that I would not wish to see her happy.' That one's own child is both miserable and morally corrupt is a double reason to be distressed. Ibid., fn. 13.

48 J. L. Walls, *Hell: The Logic of Damnation*, p. 109.

49 Walls thinks this sort of dependence would render God susceptible to becoming what he calls 'an emotional hostage', which is unfitting for God. Ibid., p. 106.

50 Ibid., p. 110.

51 On this, see J. Kronen, 'Can God feel? A critique of theological impassivism', *American Catholic Philosophical Quarterly* 71 (1997): pp. 101–111.

52 For a succinct treatment of the emotional dimension of Christian love, see F. Howard-Snyder, 'Christianity and Ethics', in *Reason for the Hope Within*, pp. 375–398 (esp. pp. 386–390). For a classic account of this matter see Jonathan Edwards, *A Treatise Concerning Religious Affections* (New York: Cosimo Classics, 2007).

53 For an articulation of this view, see R. C. Solomon, 'On emotions as judgments', *American Philosophical Quarterly* 25 (1988): pp. 183–191.

54 See G. Pitcher, 'Emotion', *Mind* 74 (1965): pp. 326–346.

55 *Schleiermacher, Christian Faith*, p. 721.

56 J. Cain, 'Is the existence of heaven compatible with the existence of hell?', *Southwest Philosophy Review* 18 (2002): pp. 153–158. Quote appears on p. 156.

57 Ibid.

58 Ibid., fn. 12, p. 158.

59 Schleiermacher, *On the Christian Faith*, p. 721.

60 This point is suggested by Talbott in 'Providence, freedom, and human destiny', pp. 237–238.

61 W. L. Craig, 'Talbott's universalism', *Religious Studies* 27 (1991): pp. 297–308. Craig responds here to an argument made by Talbott in 'Providence, freedom, and human destiny' (pp. 239–241) that is similar to Schleiermacher's. Interestingly,

Talbott's argument does not rely on ALB(4), but Craig attacks it anyway. See also the subsequent discussion in Talbott, 'Craig on the possibility of eternal damnation', *Religious Studies* 28 (1992): pp. 495–510; and Craig, 'Talbott's universalism once more', *Religious Studies* 29 (1993): pp. 497–518.

62 W. L. Craig, 'Universalism', pp. 306–307; see also his 'Universalism once more', pp. 509–510.

63 See Talbott, 'Providence, freedom, and human destiny', p. 238, and 'Eternal damnation', pp. 507–509; Craig, 'Universalism once more', pp. 508–509.

64 T. Talbott, 'Eternal damnation', pp. 508–509.

65 Craig, 'Universalism once more', p. 509.

66 *Summa Contra Gentes*, pt. 3, 26, trans. T. Gilby, *Saint Thomas Aquinas: Philosophical Texts* (New York: Oxford University Press, 1951), p. 271. Cf. *ST*, pt. 1–2, q. 3, art. 4.

67 Craig, 'Universalism', p. 306.

68 By which we mean our state is as perfect as possible for a finite human nature.

69 Talbott makes essentially this point in 'Eternal damnation', pp. 508–509, but Craig seems to miss it.

70 W. L. Craig, 'Universalism', pp. 306–307.

71 Unless, of course, God subjected them to a further deception, convincing them, falsely, that they were enjoying as full a communion with Him as human nature allows.

72 W. L. Craig, 'Universalism once more', p. 510.

73 A fact that may be lost on those who fail to acknowledge the cognitive content of emotions.

74 W. L. Craig, 'Universalism', p. 307.

75 T. Talbott, 'Eternal damnation', p. 510.

76 See S. Weil, 'Forms of the Implicit Love of God', in *Waiting for God* (New York: Harper and Row, 1951), p. 149. See also her comments on love in *Gravity and Grace* (Lincoln: University of Nebraska Press, 1997), esp. pp. 112–113.

77 M. Luther, '*The Freedom of a Christian*' in *Martin Luther: Three Treatises*, trans. W. H. Lambert and H. J. Grimm (Philadelphia: Fortress Press, 1970), p. 309.

78 W. L. Craig, 'Universalism once more', p. 510.

79 This seems to be the objection Cain intends when he says: 'It is not clear to me that one who affirms DLS (the Doctrine of Limited Salvation) claims that those who find eternal blessedness could not possibly have been even more blessed.' See Cain, 'Is the existence of heaven incompatible with the existence of hell?' p. 157.

6 Hell and Justice

1 We have in mind here the sort of pattern in which opposing parties exact retribution only to have that act perceived as a new injustice demanding retribution. See E. Wolgast, 'Getting Even', *Justice, Law, and Violence*, J. B. Brady and N. Garver (eds) (Philadelphia: Temple University Press, 1991), pp. 117–133.

2   I. A. Dorner, *SCD*, vol. 4, pp. 28–29.

3   J. A. Quenstedt, *TDP*, in Schmid, p. 657.

4   T. Talbott, *The Inescapable Love of God*, chap. 3.

5   See, for example, Schleiermacher's celebrated sermon, "The Wrath of God," in *Servant of the Word: Selected Sermons of Freidrich Scheiermacher,* trans. D. De Vries (Fortress: Philedelphia, 1987), pp. 152–165.

6   J. A. Quenstedt, TDP, in Schmid, p.120.

7   Cf. G. Aulen, *The Faith of the Christian Church*, pp. 136–142.

8   J. G. Baier, *CTP*, pt. 1, chap. 7, # 1, pp. 203–204.

9   Ibid., #4, p. 205.

10   Ibid., #5, pp. 205–206.

11   Ibid., # 8–9, pp. 206–208.

12   Ibid., #10–11, pp. 209–211.

13   Ibid., # 13, pp. 215–216.

14   Ibid.

15   Ibid., note (f).

16   Ibid.

17   Ibid., note (n).

18   Ibid., #14–15, pp. 216–217.

19   Ibid., # 15, p. 217, note (e).

20   Ibid., # 20, p. 222. In a note, Baier makes it clear that God, from *His own nature*, is unable to will damnation, since God is perfectly good. Nor did God, so to speak, will damnation in creation by looking to man taken either as *fallen or as able to fall.* However, God is not only perfectly good (benevolent), but perfectly just, and it has happened that humans sinned when they might not have. Thus, after great patience and repeated offers of unmerited grace, God heaps damnation on those who not only deserve it, but reject all the means of grace. This is really all that Baier means by speaking of the final cause of damnation as the 'manifestation of God's vindicatory justice'.

21   Ibid., # 9, # 13.

22   Aquinas, *ST*, pt. 1–2, q. 79, a. 3. S. Menssen and T. D. Sullivan have argued that, according to Aquinas, God causes hardening but does not intend it (see their 'God does not Harden Hearts', in the *Proceedings of the American Catholic Philosophical Association*, vol. 60, 7, 1993). Part of their argument hinges on the fact that Aquinas himself teaches that God does not will sin and that Aquinas can use the doctrine of Double Effect to explain how God could *causally contribute* to sin without willing it. We agree that Aquinas holds that God does not will sin, but it is hard to see how this assertion coheres with what he says about hardening, since he clearly holds that God inflicts hardening as a punishment for previous sins (ibid., ad. 1) and, in response to an objection in the immediately following article of the same question, he says that God 'orders' the hardening of the reprobate to the good end of displaying retributive justice in damning them (it is almost as if Aquinas thinks God wills the sins that result from hardening as necessary for displaying His justice). However, our case against CH2 does not hinge on whether our exegesis of Aquinas is correct, since we argue below that using

the doctrine of Double Effect, according to which God merely foresees the evil that arises from hardening, does not provide an adequate defence of CH2.

23 See Luther, *The Bondage of the Will*, trans. H. Cole (Grand Rapids: Baker, 1976), pp. 38–44, 72–74, 225–231.

24 As quoted by C. P. Krauth in *The Conservative Reformation and its Theology*, (Minneapolis: Augsburg Press, 1963), p. 375.

25 From a letter to John Lang in the year 1522, quoted by Walther, *Convention Essays*, p. 41. Cf. Luther, *The Bondage of the Will*, pp. 221–225.

26 See Augustine, *CG*, bk. 12, chap. 8. Though the doctrine that evil is a lack that has only a deficient cause, not an efficient one, is particularly associated with Augustine, other Church Fathers (including Eastern Fathers) also held it, especially when combating Manichaeism. See J. Pelikan, *The Christian Tradition*, Vol, 2: *The Spirit of Eastern Christendom* (Chicago: Chicago University Press, 1974), pp. 220–223.

27 Ott, *Fundamentals*, pp. 88–91; Schmid, *The Doctrinal Theology*, pp. 184–188; Heppe, *Reformed Dogmatics*, pp. 258–263.

28 See Aquinas, *ST*, pt. 1–2, q. 109, a. 7, a. 9. Aquinas, Luther and Calvin all teach essentially the same thing on these matters because they were all following Augustine's mature teaching. On this, see G. R. Evans, *Augustine on Evil* (Cambridge: Cambridge University Press, 1982), pp. 128–132.

29 See Hollaz, *ETA*, pt. 2, chap. 2, Q. 6–7. Hollaz's vehement insistence that God does not in any way will sin is typical of Lutheran polemics vis-à-vis the Reformed, but hard to square with Hollaz's endorsement of the doctrine that God inflicts hardening on some sinners as punishment for prior sins. See *ETA*, pt. 2, chap. 4, q. 35, (a).

30 Our theological ethics have been shaped by many theologians, but the sketch provided here is closest to Dorner's insofar as it (1) avoids both Kantian rigorism and pure consequentialism, and (2) privileges God's benevolent love without denying His complacent love for creatures and Himself.

31 See Dorner, *System of Christian Ethics*, pp. 93–96.

32 Ibid., pp. 73–93.

33 On this point we agree with Aulen's scathing criticism of the older Orthodoxy. See *The Faith of the Christian Church*, pp. 175–176.

34 See Heppe, *Reformed Dogmatics*, pp. 143–146.

35 A. Donagan, *The Theory of Morality* (Chicago: The University of Chicago Press, 1977), p. 149

36 J. A. Quenstedt, TDP, in Schmid, p.120.

37 As Aquinas noted, the evil of fault (sin) is worse than the evil of pain (non-moral evil); ST, pt. 1, q. 48, a. 6. The chief reason is that the evil of fault vitiates a person's core, making him or her an evil *person*, while the evil of pain does not.

38 Cf. M. Cronin's classic treatise on Thomistic ethics, *The Science of Ethics* (New York: Benziger Brothers, 1920), vol. 1, pp. 38–39.

39 Ibid., p. 39.

40 It not only does them no good, but clearly harms them morally. Aquinas denies this because he thinks that God only hardens those who have already sinned and thus does not leave them worse off than they were before He hardened

them (*ST*, pt. 1–2, q. 79, a. 3, ad. 1). However, this is untenable since either the sinner God hardens (a) is already in a hardened state, or (b) is not in a hardened state. Clearly (a) cannot be the case since not even God can cause something to come to be in a state it is already in (though He could cause it to continue in that state); thus we must assume (b) – but a sinner who is hardened is morally worse off than one who is not, even assuming that some sins deserve hardening (something we reject).

41   Aquinas, *ST*, supp., q. 99, a. 1, ad. 4, emphasis ours.

42   See Schmid, *The Doctrinal Theology*, pp. 348–351.

43   This comes out in the emphasis the older Lutheran divines put on the spiritual aspect of Christ's suffering, His feeling of the wrong we have done to God by our sins and of God's wrath at it. In this way they point to a notion of the Atonement that is not purely physical, not based on 'an eye for an eye' (Schimid, pp. 359–360). The spiritual aspect of Christ's suffering is intimately bound up with what the Lutherans called His active obedience – His desire to both fulfil the law and to suffer the just punishments of sin for the sake of sinners (Schmid, pp. 352–357). Finally, we should note that the Lutheran divines did not think of God the Father as some distinct deity from the Son who imposed on the Son penalties due us – for the entire Trinity, including the Son, was offended by sin and was angry with it, and the entire Trinity was active in the Atonement (though in distinct ways) – God, in other words, puts Himself in place of sinners and feels for them what they should feel on account of sin (Schmid, p. 350).

44   J. Hampton and J. G. Murphy, *Forgiveness and Mercy* (Cambridge: Cambridge University Press, 1988), pp. 122–143.

45   Cf. Aquinas, *ST*, suppl. q. 98, a. 5, a. 8.

46   J. G. Baier, *CTP*, pt. 1, chap. 6, #8, p. 187; Aquinas, *ST*, pt. 1–2, q. 4, a. 1–2.

47   *ST*, suppl., q. 98, a. 2.

48   A. Ritschl, *The Christian Doctrine*, p. 52.

49   Ibid.

50   Ibid., p. 51.

51   Hellists freely admit that the divine law is written in the hearts of all. This, however, only serves to make all without excuse, and to justify God's condemnation. The absurdity of this view comes out in J. Edwards's assertion that at their condemnation, the consciences of the damned will be fully awakened and, simultaneously, their wills brought to the consummate state of wickedness; *The Nature of True Virtue* (Ann Arbor: University of Michigan Press, 1960), pp. 72–73. This doctrine rests on a separation between head and heart that seems positively fantastical.

52   *CG*, bk. 21, chap. 23.

53   A confusion all the more astonishing in light of the number of Eastern Fathers who taught universalism.

54   J. A. Quenstedt, TDP, in Schmid, p. 351.

55   G. W. Leibniz, *Theodicy*, in Huggard, p.290.

56   *The Justice of God in the Damnation of Sinners*, in *Jonathan Edwards: Representative Selections*, C. H. Faust and T. Johnson (eds) (New York: Hill and Wang), p. 112.

57 *ST*, pt. 1–2., q. 87, a. 1, trans. by the Fathers of the English Dominican Province.

58 As Dorner noted, crude retributivism (what he calls 'compensatory retributivism') focuses on particular manifestations of sin, rather than on sin's essence. Hence, it is quantitative in its analysis rather than qualitative, and this leads its adherents to consider the degree of punishment that various sins require. By contrast, what we call vindicatory retributivism (what he calls 'absolute retributivism') focuses on the essence of sin, not particular sins, and is qualitative in its analysis. In this way, the vindicatory theory of punishment can support the need of a vicarious atonement for all sins, great and small. Dorner, *SCD*, vol. 4, pp. 28–29.

59 For a more detailed criticism of the argument for hell taken from the infinity of God, see Kvanvig, pp. 40–55.

60 R. Schmid, *The Doctrinal Theology*, pp. 256–257.

61 Aquinas, *Commentary on Aristotle's De Anima, a*, 14, c; *ST*, pt. 1, q. 5, a. 1, a. 3.

62 Quoted by F. Pieper, *Christian Dogmatics,* trans. T. Engelder (St. Louis: Concordia, 1951), vol. 2, pp. 63–64.

63 J. Gerhard, Loci *Theologici,* I, locus 2, c. 8, sect. 12, pp. 346–347; Hollaz, *ETA*, pt. 1, chap. 1, q. 44. A. Calov, *Systema Locorum Theologicorum: Tomus Secundus* (Wittenberg: 1555), 2, chap. 11, p. 565 *ff.*

64 See Baier, *CTP*, pt. 1, chap. 1, # 23, (b).

65 P. Melanchthon, *LC,* locus 7, pp. 84–85.

66 P. Melanchthon, *LC,* locus 7, p. 102; Baier, *CTP,* pt. 1, chap. 1, # 23, pp. 39–40.

67 P. Melanchthon, *LC,* locus. 7, p. 86, 99; Baier, *CTP,* pt. 3, chap. 7, # 6, p. 344.

68 J. A. Quenstedt, *TDP,* in Schmid, p. 351.

69 Hampton and Murphy, *Forgiveness and Mercy*, pp. 122–143.

70 See A. Ritschl, *A Critical History of the Christian Doctrine of Justification and Reconciliation,* trans. J. Black (Edinburgh: Edmonston and Douglas, 1872), pp. 242–243; See also Dorner, *SCD*, vol. 4, pp. 20–27.

71 Gerhard, *Loci Theologici,* in Schmid, p. 351.

72 For an excellent discussion of the inadequacies of claiming that endless punishment is infinitely severe, see Seymour, *A Theodicy of Hell*, p. 53.

73 This second response is one Seymour overlooks. It provides, we think, a better answer to the Kantian view that Seymour considers – namely, the view that an infinite succession of moments of suffering will be viewed by God, from his atemporal perspective, as a completed whole, and hence as infinite suffering.

74 See, for example, Hutter, *Loci Communes Theologici* (Wittenberg: 1619), in Schmid, p. 350.

75 On this, see R. Muller, *Dictionary of Latin and Greek Theological Terms Drawn Principally from Protestant Scholastic Theology* (Grand Rapids: Baker, 1985), pp. 272–273.

76 We should make two points here. First, the term 'objective justification' is not found in the Orthodoxy of the sixteenth and seventeenth centuries, and seems to have been invented in the nineteenth century by those who desired a return to the older Orthodoxy. This fact does not, of course, entail that the doctrine of objective justification was not taught by the older Orthodoxy. The second

point is that not all Lutheran theologians would agree that Lutheran Orthodoxy actually taught the doctrine of objective justification. Gottfried Fritschel
(1833–1900) argued strenuously that the old Norwegian Synod, along with
the Missouri Synod, had departed from Luther and the Lutheran Orthodox
in teaching the doctrine of objective justification. See his piece 'Concerning Objective and Subjective Atonement', in *Lutheran Confessional Theology in
America*, ed. Theodore Tappert (New York: Oxford University Press, 1972), pp.
141–165. We do not have space here to answer Fritschel's arguments, and will
simply point to the authority of the eminent Lutheran scholar, Gerhard Forde,
who contends that views such as Fritschel's betray the influence of pietistic 'sub-
jectivism' in opposition to orthodox 'objectivism'; *The Law-Gospel Debate: An
Interpretation of its Historical Development* (Minneapolis, 1969), p. 8.

77 J. A. Quenstedt, *TDP*, in Schmid, p. 360.

78 Quoted in Fritschel, op. cit., p. 149, ft. 9.

79 See A. Hunnius, *Epitome Credendorum* (Wittenberg: 1625), trans. P. E. Gottheil
as *A Concise and Popular View of the Doctrines of the Lutheran Church* (Nuremberg:
Sebald 1847), chap. 19, para. 522.

80 Here Charles Seymour would object to our argument, maintaining that eternal
damnation can be explained by an infinite number of finite sins committed during an endless existence in hell. We take up this objection in the next section.

81 The Lutheran Orthodox also thought that a similar problem arose in a different way. God's glory demands that the law be perfectly fulfilled, but humans, on
account of sin, fail to do this. Punishing them proportionately might repudiate
this – but it would remain true that the law had not been perfectly fulfilled. This
would continue to be a wrong that no amount of creaturely punishment could
erase. They thus posited that, in addition to atoning for our sins on the cross
(what they called Christ's 'passive obedience'), Christ also perfectly fulfilled the
law on our behalf by living a perfect life (His 'active obedience'). Insofar as Christ
was fully human, He could fulfil the positive requirements of the law on humanity's behalf – and as the infinite God, His doing so had an infinite worth that could
be attributed to humanity. See Schmid, *The Doctrinal Theology*, pp. 352–356.

82 This is a point made repeatedly in Lutheran Orthodoxy. No creature's act, not
even faith, plays any causal role, strictly speaking, in God's justification of the sinner. Indeed, faith justifies only because it is an organ or means by which we grasp
Christ's merits. See Schmid, pp. 432–440. With Scholastic precision, the Lutheran
Orthodox could assert that faith does not justify in the category of quality (in *praedicamento qualitatis*), but in the category of relation (in *praedicamento relationis*).

83 This was the position taken by Fritschel, op. cit., pp. 150–160. For a powerful critique of it, see Dorner, *SCD*, vol. 4, pp. 209–217. Dorner shows that all
those who teach that Christ's Atonement merely made God's forgiveness of
the sinner *possible* so that God is reconciled only to those who in true faith
accept God's offer of forgiveness, make the salvation of the sinner ultimately
rest on his or her *bona opera*. In this way, a door is opened in the Lutheran and
Reformed Churches for a return of the Roman Catholic doctrine of justification, although in 'Protestant garb', p. 213.

84 This point is clearly made by A. Calov in the following commentary in Rom. 5, contained in his *Biblia Illustrata*: 'We have not been redeemed and reconciled, nor have our sins been atoned for, under a condition, but we have been absolutely redeemed in the most perfect and complete manner, as far as merit and efficacy of the act are concerned; although, as regards the actual enjoyment and appropriation of salvation, faith is necessary, which is nothing else than the appropriation of the atonement, satisfaction, and reconciliation of Christ; for, in the judgment of God, if One died for all, it is the same as if all had died. 2 Cor. 5, 14. This is a golden text, which shines with the radiance of the sun even in the luminous Scriptures. Since the death which Christ died for all is a death for the purpose of reconciliation, it is the same as if all had suffered death for this purpose. It follows, then, that, without entertaining the least doubt, I can say with perfect assurance: *I am* redeemed; *I am* reconciled; salvation *has been acquired for me.*' Quoted by Walther in *The Proper Distinction Between Law and Gospel*, trans. W. H. T. Dau (St. Louis: Concordia Publishing House, 1929), p. 274.

85 It is probably because they saw this difficulty that most eighteenth and nineteenth-century Lutheran theologians, who wished to be true to their Lutheran heritage in both denying universalism and upholding the doctrine of objective justification, more and more had recourse to a strong doctrine of creaturely freedom in defending DH. Cf. Dorner, *SCD*, vol. 4, pp. 416–428.

86 See Althaus, *The Theology of Martin Luther*, pp. 144–150.

87 This seems to have been the teaching of the Arminians and the Methodists. See C. Hodge, *Systematic Theology* (Repr. Grand Rapids: Eerdmans1993), vol. 3, pp. 185–193.

88 See Isa. 53.4 sq.; Tit. 2.14; 1 Jn. 1.7; Heb. 1.3, 1 Jn. 2.2; Isa. 53.5; Gal. 3.13; Rom. 5.8-10; Heb. 2.14-15; 1 Cor. 15.14.

89 M. Adams, 'The Problem of Hell: A Problem of Evil for Christians', in *A Reasoned Faith*, ed. E. Stump (Ithaca: Cornell University Press, 1993), pp. 301–327, p. 310.

90 Ibid.

91 Seymour fully develops this defence of endless punishment in *A Theodicy of Hell* and lays it out more succinctly in 'Hell, justice, and freedom', *International Journal for Philosophy of Religion* 43 (1998): pp. 69–86.

92 'Efficacious grace' is the theological term for grace that necessarily moves the will to cling to the good (and hence to God). We discuss this at length in Chapter 7.

93 See I. Kant, *Critique of Practical Reason*, trans. L. W. Beck (New York: Macmillan, 1956), p. 129.

7 The Argument from Efficacious Grace

1 It seems 1* could not be adequately supported without recourse to a purported divine revelation.

2 While the *term* 'efficacious grace' seems to date from the seventeenth century, earlier theologians clearly held that God may and does give what was later called efficacious grace. See Evans, *Augustine on Evil*, pp. 128–136.

3   By the 'Thomistic view of freedom' we primarily refer to Aquinas's view – though, unlike some, we believe the classical Thomists (e.g. Cajetan and Banez) fundamentally agreed with their master on the points discussed in this chapter.

4   For Murray's understanding of autonomy, see M. J. Murray, 'Three versions of universalism', *Faith and Philosophy* 16 (1999): pp. 55–68. For Swinburne's cognate notion of 'efficacious freedom' see R. Swinburne, *Providence and the Problem of Evil* (Oxford: Clarendon Press, 1998), p. 11.

5   See C. Hodge, *Systematic Theology*, vol. 2, pp. 710–732.

6   On this matter see J. Pohle, *Grace, Actual and Habitual* (Toronto: W. E. Blake & Son, 1919; repr. Lexington: Filiquarian Publishing, 2010), pt. 1, chap. 3, a. 1–2, pp. 96–110.

7   See Hodge, *Systematic Theology*, vol. 2, pp. 675–710.

8   Aquinas emphasizes that, since no finite good is perfectly good, a person may elect it or not, just as they may assent or not to a merely probable argument. *ST*, pt. 1, q. 82, a. 2.

9   For Aquinas, just as the intellect is ordered to truth, so the will is ordered to goodness. Hence, just as the intellect cannot fail to believe a self-evident truth if it is presented to it, so the will cannot fail to love the *perfect* good if that good is presented to it. This good, however, is God, and so only God, if clearly perceived, necessitates the will to love [*ST* pt. 1, q. 82, a. 2]. Aquinas also holds that some goods are so necessary for flourishing (e.g. life, health, knowledge, etc.) that human nature orders us to so desire them that we can only reject them *per accidens* (e.g. if a person commits suicide it is not existence as such that they reject, but the suffering that accrues to them *per accidens*) [*ST*, pt. 1–2, q. 10, a. 1].

10   See Aquinas, *De Veritate*, trans. R. Schmidt as *Truth* (Chicago: Henry Regnery, 1954), q. 24, a. 8, pp. 167–171.

11. On the Molinist view of freedom, see D. N. Kaphagawani, *Leibniz on Freedom and Determinism in Relation to Aquinas and Molina* (Aldershot: Ashgate, 1999), pp. 32–34.

12   See J. Pohle, *Grace*, pp. 106–108.

13   Craig argues that the Molinist view of libertarian freedom cannot rule out the possibility of trans-world damnation; that is, the idea that a creature is such that it will finally reject God in every possible world in which it exists. But even if there is, for any creature C, some world W in which C freely accepts God's offer of salvation, it does not follow that C would freely do so in *every* possible world of which it is a member. It might be that every world which God could create would be one in which some persons forever reject God.

14   Thomas Talbott, 'The doctrine of everlasting punishment," *Faith and Philosophy* 7 (1990): pp. 19–42.

15   Aquinas gives a similar list of affective states that could explain a person's choice of an 'apparent' rather than 'real good' – namely, 'passion, bad habit, or disposition'. *Compendium Theologiae*, 4, 22, quoted in *An Aquinas Reader*, M. Clark (ed.) (Garden City: Doubleday & Company, 1972), p. 302.

16   See Aquinas, *Truth*, q. 24, a. 1.

17   See Aquinas, *Truth*, q. 24, a. 8–9.

18 See Aquinas, *Compendium Theologiae*, 2, 20, pp. 209–210 in Clark. Cf. Baier, *CTP*, pt. 2, chap. 20, # 27.

19 Aquinas, *Truth*, q. 24, a. 8. Cf. Baier, *CTP*, pt. 1, chap. 6, # 5, 8, p. 184, 187.

20 Aquinas, *Truth*, q. 24, a. 9, p. 172, bracketed words are ours.

21 Ibid., p. 173. Later Thomists, as well as the Reformed, taught a similar doctrine. See Hodge, *Systematic Theology*, vol. 2, pp. 685–687, 690–695

22 See Pelikan, *The Spirit of Eastern Christendom*, pp. 264–265.

23 See Mt. 5.8, 1 Cor. 13.12, Heb. 12.14, 1 Jn 3.2.

24 See Hollaz, *ETA*, pt. 1, chap. 7, q. 4, obs. 3.

25 See Pelikan, *The Spirit of Eastern Christendom*, pp. 261–270.

26 We do not mean to say that the Eastern Fathers held that God could give efficacious grace. The very concept was alien to them. What we mean is that one might answer a certain argument for the conclusion that it is not metaphysically possible for God to grant such grace by revealing His essence to a creature by making use of the doctrine of the divine energies developed by the Eastern Fathers.

27 A. M. Fairbairn, *The Place of Christ in Modern Theology* (New York: Scribner, 1907), pp. 467–468.

28 For a powerful recent defence of this view of the person see R. Chisholm, *On Metaphysics* (Minneapolis: University of Minnesota Press, 1989), pp. 25–41, 49–61.

29 See Aquinas, *Truth*, q. 24, a. 8, p. 169: 'But evil is involuntary, as Dionysius says. Consequently there cannot be any sin in the motion of the will so that it tends to evil unless there previously exists some deficiency in the apprehensive power, as a result of which evil is presented as good.'

30 See Aquinas, *ST*, pt. 1, q. 23, a. 5. The classical Thomists followed Aquinas on this; see Pohle, *Grace*, pp. 98–102.

31 Talbott, 'Towards a better understanding of universalism', in *Universal Salvation? The Current Debate*, R. A. Parry and C. H. Partridge (eds) (Carlisle: Paternoster Press, 2003), p. 5.

32 T. Talbott, 'Doctrine,' pp. 36–38

33 See Walls, *Hell: The Logic of Damnation*, chap. 5, esp. pp. 129–138.

34 Ibid., p. 129.

35 Ibid., pp. 129–131.

36 For the sake of simplicity, we will hereafter use 'ignorance' to refer to both the state of being without relevant knowledge and the state of being deceived.

37 J. L. Walls, op. cit., p. 133.

38 T. Talbott, 'Doctrine,' pp. 36–37.

39 J. L. Walls, op. cit., p. 134.

40 Ibid.

41 Ibid.

42 T. Talbott, 'Doctrine,' p. 39.

43 J. L. Walls, op. cit., p. 132.

44 Someone might note that there are those who have no concept of God, and therefore can neither experience themselves as being confronted with a choice about whether to accept God, nor understand their suffering as having any relationship to alienation from God. Their suffering would not shatter false

beliefs but would produce tragic bewilderment. Perhaps such a person – barring miraculous intervention – could remain forever ignorant despite its unremitting anguish; but in that case the ignorance would not be wilful, and God could grant the knowledge they lack without violating their freedom.

45   Talbott asks, 'Is it not precisely the function of the Holy Spirit, according to Christian theology, to release sinners from their bondage to sin?' See 'Doctrine', p. 36.

46   If, furthermore, these bad choices were made without a clear understanding of their ultimate implications, we might question whether these choices were genuinely free.

47   Walls makes this point using the philosophical terminology of first- and second-order desires. The damned are those who not only want to sin, but want to want it. Thus, Walls says, good cannot even find a 'foothold' in their souls. See Walls, op. cit., pp. 120–121.

48   M. Adams, 'The Problem of Hell: A Problem of Evil for Christians', in *A Reasoned Faith*, E. Stump (ed.) (Ithaca: Cornell University Press, 1993), p. 313.

49   Ibid.

50   Ibid., pp. 313–314.

8 Freely Chosen Universal Salvation

1   E. Stump, 'Dante's hell, Aquinas's moral theory, and the love of God', *Canadian Journal of Philosophy* 16 (1986): pp. 194–195.

2   See Schmid, *The Doctrinal Theology*, pp. 458–480.

3   See *ST*, pt. 1–2, q. 4, art. 4.

4   Consider in this regard Suarez, a Molinist on freedom, who argued in *De Anima*, 1, q. 2, that although a freedom 'of indifference' is a perfection when it comes to choosing among finite goods, the will has a telos such that anyone who sees God necessarily loves Him, and that in this case being necessitated rather than free (in the Molinist sense) is a perfection. His reasoning here is that, with finite goods, being necessitated to one choice inevitably entails the failure to recognize the real goods that characterize the alternatives. However, when it comes to the infinite good of God, the alternative to loving God has no real goods attached to it, and so a freedom of indifference exhibits an imperfection in this one case.

5   A recent defender of libertarian free will, Robert Kane, essentially admits that there is an arbitrary dimension to choices that are free in the libertarian sense. His seeks to defend the coherence and usefulness of freedom conceived as involving a random element. See R. Kane, *The Significance of Free Will* (Oxford: Oxford University Press, 1996).

6   The most important defender of this theory is Roderick Chisholm. See, for example, R. Chisholm, 'Freedom and action', in *Freedom and Determinism*, K. Lehrer (ed.) (New York: Random House, 1966), pp. 11–44.

7   Michael Murray argues that there is something morally objectionable about stripping away salvation inhibitors. See M. J. Murray, 'Three versions of

universalism', *Faith and Philosophy* 16 (1999): pp. 55–68. We directly consider Murray's arguments later in this chapter.

8 Since some will argue that communion with God is eternal in the sense of existing outside of time (rather than for an infinite duration), it would be problematic to suggest that God would sustain everyone in a temporal existence forever, since this might entail excluding everyone from communion with God. It is not similarly controversial to suggest that God would sustain those who have yet to be saved in a temporal existence. It certainly seems that God *could* do so.

9 We might believe, for example, that due to our intellectual limitations, the access we can have to the objective order of values is so restricted that we can only conclude that communion with God has an even chance of being better than alienation from God. While this view seems implausible, we assume it for argument's sake.

10 Among thinkers who argue along these lines are Murray in 'Three versions of universalism' and Walls in *Hell: The Logic of Damnation, esp.* chap. 5.

11 It might be better to say that our *autonomy* is violated, rather than our freedom. This is the approach that Michael Murray favours. See Murray, p. 64.

12 We are indebted to William Hasker for pointing out this objection.

13 This line of objection is suggested by Hermann Lotze's remarks on freedom in Chapter 7 of his *Outlines of the Philosophy of Religion*, trans. G. T. Ladd (Boston: Ginn & Company, 1886), pp. 100–106.

14 This line of concern only challenges the coherence of holding agents morally responsible for *wrongdoing*, not for behaving rightly. When they do the latter, their deliberative faculties operate unimpeded by any external force, and so it makes sense to say *they* are responsible. This absence of parity does not trouble us (and favours universalism).

15 This is essentially the thinking that led Zoroastrian theologians to embrace universalism. See R. C. Zaehner, *The Dawn and Twilight of Zoroastrianism*, p. 308.

16 His Sophisticated Universalism 2 is essentially what we call DU1.

17 M. J. Murray, 'Three versions of universalism', p. 58.

18 Ibid.

19 Ibid., p. 59.

20 Ibid., pp. 63–64.

21 That is, until one enjoys communion with God, at which point one is confirmed in blessedness. However, for reasons already discussed earlier in this chapter, confirmation in blessedness is not problematic for human freedom in the way confirmation in damnation would be.

22 M. J. Murray, op. cit., p. 64.

23 Ibid.

24 M. J. Murray, op. cit., pp. 64–65.

9 Final Concerns

1 M. Adams, 'The Problem of Hell', p. 325.

2 Ibid. Adams's point here is powerfully prefigured in Friedrich Schleiermacher's sermon, 'The Wrath of God'.

3　Consider Jonathan Edwards, among the greatest intellects in Church history and a man of deep piety and charity, who in *A Treatise on Religious Affections* worked out a sophisticated theory for recognizing the elect – and then used it to withhold communion from all members of his congregation in Northampton between 1744–1748. That so great a man as Edwards (who was no Fred Phelps) would not only develop a theory for distinguishing elect from non-elect, but would use that theory to declare his entire congregation damned (since, for a Calvinist, the non-elect cannot become elect), vividly illustrates, we think, how practically pernicious DH can be. This is not to deny the profundity of Edwards' great work. As we see it, the problem is not with what Edwards says about the traits of the converted, but with his teaching that some will never be converted.

4　J. Butler, *The Analogy of Religion*, H. Malcom (ed.) (Philadelphia: J.B. Lippincott, 1895), pt. 1, chap. 2, pp. 102–104.

5　Ibid., p. 97.

6　On this see M. Boyce, *Zoroastrians: Their Religious Beliefs and Practices* (New York: Routledge, 2001), pp. 25–27.

7　'Theology and Metaphysics', in *Albrecht Ritschl: Three Essays*, trans. P. Hefner (Philadelphia: Fortress Press, 1972), p. 161.

8　M. Adams, 'The Problem of Hell', esp. pp. 302–305.

9　J. Hick, 'An Irenaean Theodicy', in *Encountering Evil: Live Options in Theodicy*, S. T. Davis (ed.) (Louisville: Westminster John Knox Press, 2001), pp. 38–51, esp. pp. 50–51.

10　This point is developed with some care in her book *Horrendous Evils and the Goodness of God* (Ithaca: Cornell University Press, 1999). See esp. p. 41 and chap. 8.

11　Stewart Goetz, *Freedom, Teleology, and Evil* (London: T & T Clark, 2008).

12　Ibid., p. 135.

13　Ibid., pp. 128–130.

14　Strictly speaking, this is only a theodicy for moral evils – that is, an account of why God permits wickedness and sin. Further premises would be required to account for suffering and death that *results* from wickedness; and still more elaboration would be needed for this theodicy to extend to suffering and death that results from illness, famine, natural disasters, and so on.

15　M. Adams, *Horrendous Evils and the Goodness of God*, esp. p. 21.

16　S. Goetz, op. cit., p. 148.

17　Ibid.

18　Ibid.

BIBLIOGRAPHY

Adams, Marilyn McCord, 'The Problem of Hell: A Problem of Evil for Christians,' in *A Reasoned Faith*, Eleonore Stump, (ed.) Ithaca: Cornell University Press, 1993.

—— *Horrendous Evils and the Goodness of God*, Ithaca: Cornell University Press, 1999.

Althaus, Paul, *The Theology of Martin Luther*, trans. R. Schultz, Philadelphia: Fortress, 1996.

Anselm, *Cur Deus Homo*, in *Saint Anselm: Basic Writings*, trans. S.N. Dean, LaSalle: Open Court, 1962.

Aquinas, *De Veritate*, trans. as *Truth* Robert Schmidt, Chicago: Henry Regnery, 1954.

—— *Summa Theologiae*, trans. the Fathers of the English Dominican Province, Repr. Westminster: Christian Classics, 1981.

Augustine, *The City of God*, trans. G. Walsh, *et al.*, Garden City: Doubleday, 1950.

Aulen, Gustav, *The Faith of the Christian Church*, trans. E. H. Wahlstrom and G. E. Arden, Philadelphia: Muhlenberg Press, 1948.

Baier, John, *Compendium Theologiae Positivae*, Jena: 1685, ed. with notes C. F. W. Walther, Repr. Grand Rapids: Emmanuel Press, 2006.

Barth, Karl, *Church Dogmatics*, II, 1, trans. T. H. L. Parker *et al.*, Edinburgh: T & T Clark, 1957.

—— *Church Dogmatics*, III, 3, trans. C. W. Bromiley and R. J. Ehrlich, Edinburgh: T & T Clark, 1960.

Berger, Peter, *A Rumor of Angels: Modern Society and the Rediscovery of the Supernatural*, Garden City: Doubleday, 1970.

Boyce, Mary, *Zoroastrians: Their Religious Beliefs and Practices*, New York: Routledge, 2001.

Butler, Joseph, *The Analogy of Religion*, Howard Malcom (ed.), Philadelphia: J.B. Lippincott, 1895.

Cain, James, 'Is the Existence of Heaven Compatible with the Existence of Hell?,' *Southwest Philosophy Review* 18 (2002): pp. 153–158.

Calov, Abraham, *Systema Locorum Theologicorum*, Vol. 12, Wittenberg: 1655–1677.

Carmen, John, *The Theology of Ramanuja: An Essay in Interreligious Understanding*, New Haven: Yale University Press, 1974.

Chisholm, Roderick, *On Metaphysics*, Minneapolis: University of Minnesota Press, 1989.

Clark, Mary, *An Aquinas Reader: Selections from the Writings of Thomas Aquinas*, Garden City: Doubleday, 1972.

Craig, William Lane, 'No Other Name: A Middle Knowledge Perspective on the Exclusivity of Salvation Through Christ,' *Faith and Philosophy* 6 (1989): pp. 297–308.

——— 'Talbott's Universalism,' *Religious Studies* 27 (1991): pp. 297–308.

——— 'Talbott's Universalism Once More,' *Religious Studies*, 29 (1993): pp. 497–518.

Cronin, Michael, *The Science of Ethics*, New York: Benziger Brothers, 1920.

Cudworth, Ralph, *A Treatise Concerning Eternal and Immutable Morality*, S. Hutton (ed.), Cambridge: Cambridge University Press, 1996.

——— *The True Intellectual System of the Universe*, Vol. 4, London: Richard Priestly, 1820.

Dorner, Isaac, *A System of Christina Doctrine*, Vol. 4, trans. A. Cave and J. Banks, Edinburgh: T & T Clark, 1885—Repr. Eugene: Wipf & Stock.

——— *A System of Christian Ethics*, trans. C. M. Mead and R. T. Cunningham, Edinburgh: T & T Clark, 1887.

De Lubac, Henri, *The Mystery of the Supernatural*, trans. R. Sheed, New York: Herder, 1954.

Edwards, Jonathan, 'The Justice of God in the Damnation of Sinners,' in *Jonathan Edwards: Representative Selections*, C. H. Faust and T. Johnson (eds), New York: Hill and Wang, 1962.

——— *The Nature of True Virtue*, Ann Arbor: University of Michigan Press, 1960.

Evans, Gilliam, *Augustine on Evil*, Cambridge: Cambridge University Press, 1982.

Fairbairn, Andrew, *The Place of Christ in Modern Theology*, New York: Scribner's Sons, 1907.

Forde, Gerhard, *The Law-Gospel Debate: An Interpretation of its Historical Development*, Minneapolis: Fortress, 1969.

Fritschel, Gottfried, 'Concerning Objective and Subjective Atonement,' in *Lutheran Confessional Theology in America*, T. Tappert (ed.), New York: Oxford University Press, 1972.

Geach, Peter, *Providence and Evil*, Cambridge: Cambridge University Press, 1977.

Gerhard, John, *Loci Theologici*, 5 Vol., Jena: 1610–1621, Preuss (ed.), Berlin: Gustav Schlawitz, 1863.

Gilby, Thomas, *Saint Thomas Aquinas: Philosophical Texts*, New York: Oxford University Press, 1951.

Goetz, Stewart, *Freedom, Teleology, and Evil*, London: T & T Clark, 2008.

Hampton, Jean and Murphy, Jeffrey, *Forgiveness and Mercy*, Cambridge: Cambridge University Press, 1988.

Heim, S. Mark, *Saved from Sacrifice: A Theology of the Cross*, Grand Rapids: Eerdmans, 2006.

Heppe, Heinrich, *Reformed Dogmatics: Set Out and Illustrated from the Sources*, trans. C. T. Thompson, Grand Rapids: Baker, 1978.

Hick, John, 'An Irenaean Theodicy', in *Encountering Evil: Live Options in Theodicy*, S. T. Davis (ed.), Louisville: Westminster John Knox Press, 2001, pp. 38–51.

Hobbes, Thomas, *Leviathan*, M. Oakshott (ed.), New York: Macmillan, 1962.

Hodge, Charles, *Systematic Theology*, Vol. 3, Repr. Grand Rapids: Eerdmans, 1993.

Hollaz, David, *Examen Theologicum Acroamaticum*, Stargard: 1707.

Howard-Snyder, Francis, 'Christianity and Ethics,' in *Reason for the Hope Within*, M. J. Murray (ed.), Grand Rapids: Eerdmans, 1999.

Hunnius, Aegidius, *Epitome Credendorum,* Wittenberg: 1625, trans. P. E. Gottheil as *A Concise and Popular View of the Doctrines of the Lutheran Church,* Nuremberg: Sebald 1847.

Hutter, Leonard, *Loci Communes Theologici,* Wittenberg: 1619.

John of Damascus, *On the Orthodox Faith,* trans. F. H. Chase in *Saint John of Damascus: Writings,* New York: The Fathers of the Church, 1958.

Kane, Robert, *The Significance of Free Will,* Oxford: Oxford University Press, 1996.

Kant, Immanuel, *Critique of Practical Reason,* trans. L. W. Beck, New York: Macmillan, 1956.

Kaphagawani, Didier, *Leibniz on Freedom and Determinism in Relation to Aquinas and Molina,* Aldershot: Ashgate, 1999.

Krauth, Charles, *The Conservative Reformation and its Theology,* Repr. Minneapolis: Augsburg, 1963.

Kronen, John, 'Can God Feel? A Critique of Theological Impassivism,' *American Catholic Philosophical Quarterly* 71 (1997): pp. 101–111.

Kuenning, Paul, *The Rise and Fall of American Lutheran Pietism: The Rejection of an Activist Heritage,* Mercer University Press, 1989.

Leibniz, Gottfried, *Theodicy: Essays on the Goodness of God, the Freedom of Man, and the Origin of Evil,* trans. E. M. Huggard, LaSalle: Open Court, 1985.

Lewis, C.S., *George MacDonald: 365 Readings,* New York: Macmillan, 1947.

Lotze, Hermann, *Outlines of the Philosophy of Religion,* trans. G. Ladd, Boston: Ginn & Company, 1886.

Luther, Martin, *Heidelberg Disputation,* in *Martin Luther's Basic Theological Writings,* ed. Timothy Lull, Minneapolis: Fortress, 1989.

—— *The Freedom of the Christian,* trans. W. H. Lambert and H. J. Grimm, in *Martin Luther: Three Treatises,* Philadelphia: Fortress, 1970.

—— 'Preface to the Epistle's of St. James and St. Jude,' in *Luther's Works,* Vol. 35, *Word and Sacrament I,* edited and translated by E. T. Bachman, Philadelphia: Fortress Press, 1960.

——'Preface to the Old Testament,' in *Martin Luther's Basic Theological Writings,* T. Lull (ed.), Minneapolis: Fortress, 1989.

—— *The Bondage of the Will,* trans. Henry Cole, Grand Rapids: Baker, 1976

—— *Table Talk,* trans. W. Hazlitt, Repr. London: Font Classics, 1995

MacDonald, George, *Unspoken Sermons,* Sioux Falls: NuVision, 2009.

MacDonald, Gregory, *The Evangelical Universalist,* Eugene: Cascade, 2006.

Martensen, Hans, *Christian Ethics,* trans. C. Spence, Edinburgh: T & T Clark, 1871.

Maximos the Confessor, *For Hundred Texts on Love,* trans. G. H. Palmer, P. Sherrard, and K. Ware, London: Faber & Faber, 1981.

Melanchthon, Philip, *Loci Communes,* Wittenburg: 1555, trans. Clyde Manschreck as *On Christian Doctrine,* Repr. Grand Rapids: Baker, 1965.

Menssen, Sandra and Sullivan, Thomas, *The Agnostic Enquirer: Revelation from a Philosophical Standpoint,* Grand Rapids: Eerdmans, 2007.

—— 'God Does not Harden Hearts,' in *Proceedings of the American Catholic Philosophical Association,* LX, VII (1993).

Muller, Richard, *Dictionary of Latin and Greek Theological Terms, Drawn Principally from Protestant Scholasticism,* Grand Rapids: Baker, 1996.

—— *Post Reformation Reformed Dogmatics,* Vol. 2, Grand Rapids: Baker, 2003.

Murray, John, *Epistle of Paul to the Romans*, Vol. I, Grand Rapids: Eerdmans, 1960.

Murray, Micheal, 'Heaven and Hell,' in *Reason for the Hope Within*, Michael J. Murray (ed.), Grand Rapids: Eerdmans, 1999.

——— 'Three Versions of Universalism,' *Faith and Philosophy*, 16 (1999): pp. 55–68.

Ott, Ludwig, *Fundamentals of Catholic Dogma*, trans. Peter Lynch, St. Louis: Herder, 1954.

Pelikan, Jaroslav, *The Christian Tradition 1: The Emergence of the Catholic Tradition*, Chicago: The University of Chicago Press, 1971.

——— *The Christian Tradition 2: The Spirit of Eastern Christendom*, Chicago: The University of Chicago Press, 1974.

Pieper, Francis, *Christian Dogmatics*, trans. Theodore Engelder and John Mueller, Vol. II, St. Louis: Concordia, 1951.

Pohle, Joseph, *God, the Author of Nature and the Supernatural*, A. Preuss (ed.), St. Louis: Herder, 1927.

——— *Grace, Actual and Habitual*, A. Preuss (ed.), Toronto: Blake & Son, 1919—Repr. Lexington: Filiaquarian Publishing, 2010.

Powys, David, *Hell: A Hard Look at a Hard Question*, Carlisle: Paternoster, 1998.

Price, Richard, *A Review of the Principle Questions in Morals*, in *British Moralists: 1650–1800*, D. Raphael (ed.), Indianapolis: Hackett, 1991.

Quenstedt, John, *Theologia Didactico-Polemica*, Vol. 2, Wittenberg: 1685.

Ritschl, Albrecht, *A Critical History of the Christian Doctrine of Justification and Reconciliation*, trans. John Black, Edinburgh: Edmonston and Douglas, 1872.

——— *The Christian Doctrine of Justification and Reconciliation*, trans. H. R. Mackintosh, *et al.*, Edinburgh: T & T Clark, 1900.

——— 'Theology and Metaphysics,' in *Albrecht Ritschl: Three Essays*, trans. P. Hefner, Philadelphia: Fortress, 1972.

Schleiermacher, Friedrich, *On the Christian Faith*, trans. D. M. Baillie, *et al.*, Edinburgh: T & T Clark, 1928.

——— 'The Wrath of God,' in *Servant of the Word: Selected Sermons of Friedrich Schleiermacher*, trans. Dawn De Vries, Philadelphia: Fortress, 1987.

Schmid, Heinrich, *The Doctrinal Theology of the Evangelical Lutheran Church*, trans. C. Hay and H. Jacobs, Repr. Minneapolis: Augsburg, 1961.

Seeberg, Reinhold, *Text-Book of the History of Doctrine II: History of Doctrine in the Middle Ages*, trans. C. Hay, Philadelphia: Lutheran Publication Society, 1905.

Seymour, Charles, 'Hell, Justice, and Freedom,' *International Journal for Philosophy of Religion* 43 (1998): pp. 69–86.

——— *A Theodicy of Hell*, Dordrecht: Kluwer, 2000.

Solomon, Robert C., 'On Emotions as Judgments,' *American Philosophical Quarterly* 25 (1988): pp. 183–191.

Strong, Augustus, *Systematic Theology*, New York: Fleming H. Revel: 1907.

Stump, Eleonore, 'Dante's Hell, Aquinas's Moral Theory and the Love of God,' *Canadian Journal of Philosophy*, 16 (1986), pp. 181–198.

Swinburne, Richard, *Providence and the Problem of Evil*, Oxford: Clarendon Press, 1998.

Talbott, Thomas, 'Providence, Freedom, and Human Destiny,' *Religious Studies* 26 (1990): pp. 227–245.

——— 'Craig on the Possibility of Eternal Damnation,' *Religious Studies* 28 (1992): pp. 495–510.

—— *The Inescapable Love of God*, Universal Publishers, 1999.

—— 'Towards a Better Understanding of Universalism,' in *Universal Salvation?: The Current Debate*, R. A. Parry and C. H. Partridge (eds), Carlisle: Paternoster, 2005.

Turretin, Francis, *Institutio Theologiae Elenctiae*, 3 Vol. Geneva: 1679–1685, Vol. 1 trans. G. Giger, J. Dennison (ed.), Phillipsburgh: P & R Publishing, 1992.

Von Bathasar, Hans, *Dare We Hope "That All Men Be Saved"?*, trans. K. Kipp and L. Krauth, San Francisco: Ignatius, 1988.

Walls, Jerry, 'Is Molinism as Bad as Calvinism?,' in *Faith and Philosophy* 7 (1990): pp. 85–98.

—— *Hell: The Logic of Damnation*, Notre Dame: Notre Dame University Press, 1992.

Walther, Carl, *The Proper Distinction Between Law and Gospel*, trans. W. H. T. Dau, St. Louis: Concordia, 1929.

—— *Convention Essays*, trans. Aug. R. Suelflow, St. Louis: Concordia, 1981.

Watson, Francis, 'Gospel and Scripture: Rethinking Canonical Unity,' *Tyndale Bulletin* 52 (2001): pp. 161–182.

Weil, Simon, *Gravity and Grace*, Lincoln: University of Nebraska Press, 1997.

—— *Waiting for God*, New York: Harper and Row, 1951.

Weaver, J. Denny, *The Nonviolent Atonement*, Grand Rapids: Eerdmans, 2001.

Wiener, Phillip, *Leibniz Selections*, New York: Scribner's, 1951.

Wolgast, E., 'Getting Even,' in *Justice, Law, and Violence*, J. Brady and N. Garver (eds), Philadelphia: Temple University Press, 1991.

Zaehner, Robert, *The Dawn and Twilight of Zoroastrianism*, Repr. New York: Phoenix Press, 2002.

Index